ANDREA ZANZOTTO

ANDREA ZANZOTTO
The Language of Beauty's Apprentice

BEVERLY ALLEN

UNIVERSITY OF CALIFORNIA PRESS
Berkeley   Los Angeles   London

University of California Press
Berkeley and Los Angeles, California

University of California Press, Ltd.
London, England

Copyright © 1988 by The Regents of the University of California

Originally published in Italian in a modified version as *Verso la beltà: Gli esordi poetici di Andrea Zanzotto* (Venice: Corbo e Fiore Editore, 1987).

Library of Congress Cataloging in Publication Data

Allen, Beverly
    Andrea Zanzotto: the language of beauty's apprentice / Beverly Allen.
      p.   cm.
    Bibliography: p.
    Includes index.
    ISBN 0–520–05860–7 (alk. paper)
    1. Zanzotto, Andrea, 1921–   —Criticism and interpretation.
I. Title.
PQ4851.A74Z54   1988   851'.914—dc19   87–18462

Printed in the United States of America

1 2 3 4 5 6 7 8 9

for Ben

Contents

Acknowledgments	ix
A note on translation	x
Introduction	1

ONE
A FIRST ROUND KNOCKOUT 20
Zanzotto's Poetic Initiation

TWO
AFTER THE FALL 69
Early Signs of Later Structures

THREE
GATHERINGS OF POETRY AND MUSHROOMS 98
A Landscape Elegy

FOUR
ZANZOTTO'S GRAMMATICALISMO 118
Positions and Performance

FIVE
THE SEEING "io" AND THE BEAUTY OF POETIC VISION 193

Notes	265
Bibliography	281
Index	293

Acknowledgments

For the beginnings of readings in which this book originated, I fondly thank Professor Luciano Rebay of Columbia University. For his expert guidance in a continuation of the itinerary, I fondly thank Professor Nicholas J. Perella of the University of California at Berkeley. And for turning talented attention to these readings, I fondly thank Professor Allen Mandelbaum of The Graduate Center, City University of New York. My gratitude also goes to Professor Jacqueline Risset of the Magistero, Università di Roma, to Professor Keala Jewell of Dartmouth College, and to Professor Juliana Schiesari of Miami University for their helpful comments, shimmering examples of intellectual rigor and personal spontaneity, and their friendship.

Thanks to Signora Gabriella Piccinato for her friendship and for giving me a home in the Veneto. Effusive thanks to Dee Marquez for her magnificent manuscript preparation. Thanks to Stanford University for a Summer Faculty Fellowship which enabled me to revise my manuscript and for a fellowship at the Stanford Humanities Center, where the final manuscript was prepared. Thanks to the Von Hurter family, Professor Thomas Ypsilantis, and especially Everett and Berget Allen for their constant love and support, and to my son for his patience with my distractions and for the beautiful example of his own apprenticeship to adulthood. Finally, thanks most of all to Andrea and all the cherished inhabitants of Pieve di Soligo and environs (Marisa, Amneris, Nino, Giuseppe, Anna, Giovanni) for so warmly welcoming me into their landscapes, over and over again.

Chapter Four, "Zanzotto's *Grammaticalismo*: Positions and Performance" appears in a substantially similar version in the *Stanford Italian Review*, IV, 2, Fall 1984.

A note on translation

There are no ways around the difficulties that arise in translating Zanzotto. At times, his linguistic and poetic invention can feel especially designed to thwart such an endeavor. Nonetheless, to translate his poems is already to participate in his story about how being in language matters.

The translations of Zanzotto's poems offered here are intended to aid the reader in following the original Italian; they are certainly not meant to replace it. As close to being line-by-line renditions as the differing syntactic patterns of Italian and English allow, they give but a shadow of the effects of the original. I hope the shadow at least suggests the laurel tree that casts it.

Unless otherwise noted, all translations here are my own.

Introduction

Andrea Zanzotto's poetry stands out both in Italy and internationally for its rigorous intellect and its stylistic invention. This book is an introduction to that poetry based on the notion that the difficulties encountered when reading Zanzotto's well-known later works are eased by a careful look at his early books. In these, we find the groundwork for what comes after 1968, the year his work leapt into the limelight with the publication of *La beltà* [beauty]. What we see more easily in the first books than in the later ones, and what this book traces is, quite simply, a story. It is a story simultaneously of its own telling and of its teller. As such, it serves as more than an introduction to something else. It is also a parable of the possibilities of language and the self in our time.

Modern and contemporary questions regarding the constitution of the self elicit numerous ideologically determined answers. While Zanzotto's response (like that of his late friend, Pier Paolo Pasolini) skirts any particular ideology, we might think of it as a kind of linguistic materialism. As his early books make vividly clear, language for Zanzotto always circumscribes any communicable notion of the self. Paradoxically, when it is poetry, language also acts as witness for what cannot be said. In the world of perception that Zanzotto's early poetry reveals, the "self" we meet knows he is more than his linguistic "ontology" and struggles mightily with the terrible frustration this causes him. Then he rejects despair by accepting the *apparent*—and hence materially actual—linguistic determination of subjectivity because it affords him communicative possibilities.

In an age in which critical thought has often been aimed at discerning the "erotic phenomenology" that might "demystify ideology" (to use Paolo Valesio's words),[1] in which literary theory has tended to sidestep questions of value as it reveals patterns of desire, Zanzotto's insistence on language as a bottom line in the calculation of subjectivity is the basis of what I am calling his linguistic materialism. Further, his critique of individual identity as being apparently singular and unified but actually essentially dependent on a collective context (where other members of the group include not only other people

INTRODUCTION

but also language itself) attributes moral and ethical value to this materialist base. For Zanzotto, communication is more than the dynamic that allows for a notion of reciprocal subjectivity; it is also the dynamic from which all value is derived.

We should keep in mind that Zanzotto's work corresponds to a time of profound crises in Italy—the postwar years, corruption in the government and the Vatican, the Historical Compromise, and terrorism. Such Zanzottan themes as the linguistic determination of communicable and communicative subjectivity, the unconscious selectivity of memory, and the necessity for an ecological reading of history have vast social significance even though few of his poems are thematically political. Such themes testify to a consciousness of the communal that undermines and challenges the potentially oppressive authority of any discourse—even, of course, its own.

THE LATER WORKS: *La Beltà*

Since the present study covers Zanzotto's poetry prior to *La beltà*, we will begin with a brief description of that book whose appearance in 1968 was a provocative agglomeration of unlikely thematic bedfellows. Its very title evokes the nineteenth-century Italian poet, Giacomo Leopardi, whose own linguistic theory divided words into two categories: *parole* and *termini*.[2] *Parole*, or "words," are those lexical entities which, by their archaism or poetic associations or some other self-referential differentiating device, manage not only to communicate their signifieds but also to suggest ineluctable resonances—referents, say, that can only be connoted. These "words" in Leopardi have aesthetic and affective charges; they are powerful indicators of language's paradoxical ability to suggest meanings that somehow escape the very circumscription of language itself. A prime example of Leopardi's "words" is *beltà*, the archaic, Latinate, and truncated version of the standard Italian word for beauty, *bellezza*. *Bellezza*, in turn, exemplifies Leopardi's *termini* or "terms," lexical units that correspond to their denotive signifieds but suggest nothing more. For Leopardi *termini* are the "dead ends" of linguistic signification, and he holds most lexical units to be of this nature.

Zanzotto's 1968 title thus evokes the presence of Italian poetic tradition and, more specifically, the shadow of one of his own preferred poets, Leopardi. Under this shadow, *La beltà* presents a varied cast of characters—including Mao-Tse-Tung, Jacques Lacan, Nino (a peasant-poet and friend of Zanzotto from his own town of Pieve di Soligo), and the vampire encountered earlier in *Vocativo* [Vocative].

Peasant prophecies are juxtaposed with pseudo-tse-bao aphorisms that in turn encounter Lacan's mirror stage in a kind of contest for discursive stage-center.

These characters act out variant versions of linguistic arbitrariness. In each poem's scenario, multiple possibilities of meaning risk their own reduction and the consequent annihilation of existential and perceptual alternatives. Notions directly related to linguistic discourse appear as well: *petél* (dialect baby talk), the lingoes of medical chemistry and psychoanalysis, and Latin, for example. Each is marginalized by the Italian, and each represents possibilities of existence and perception which are absent from the standardized language.

Modes or tonalities of the *Beltà* poems pass from "outrange/outrage" to memory to prophecy, and the book's intense connection with its social context is evident in the—at times explicit, at times implicit—commentary these modes make on the Italian social and political realities of the sixties. These modes are present throughout Zanzotto's work and form integral parts of his polemic with an authoritative, power-serving discourse of history whenever they occur.

The metaphor of snow is perhaps the most remarkable aspect of Zanzotto's *Beltà*. From *Dietro il paesaggio* [Behind the landscape], his first book, on, the specific landscape of his hometown, Pieve di Soligo, and the neighboring regions (the pre-Alpine mountains of the Veneto, the Montello wood, the parish villages, each with its own dialect) serves as an omnipresent metaphor for complex issues of subjective ontology and linguistic arbitrariness and determinacy. With *La beltà*, however, even the reader who is used to previous Zanzottan landscapes may initially be blinded by a constant sense of the shimmering whiteness of snow. Coming just after the blue with which his previous book, *IX Ecloghe* [IX eclogues] ends, this metaphor of temporary stasis and vast promise of renewal, of possibilities of meaning (that is, if one has been following the story in the earlier books), breaks into view with renewed force.

And the force is not simply that of the metaphor. Zanzotto's second *Beltà* poem, "La perfezione della neve," is also a coming-to-light of the style that had germinated in the previous books. It begins:

>   Quante perfezioni, quante
>   quante totalità. Pungendo aggiunge.
>   E poi astrazioni astrificazioni formulazione d'astri
>   assideramento, attraverso sidera e coelos
> 5   assideramenti assimilazioni—
>   nel perfezionato procederei
>   più in là del grande abbaglio, del pieno e del vuoto,

```
        ricercherei procedimenti
        risaltando, evitando
10      dubbiose tenebrose; saprei direi.³
```

◻

```
        [How many perfections, how many
        how many totalities. It adds by stinging.
        And then abstractions astrifications asteroid formations
        starring frostbite, across sidera and coelos
5       starring frostbites assimilations—
        in the perfected I would proceed
        further beyond the great yawn, beyond the full and the
            empty,
        I would seek for procedures
        by jumping over, by avoiding
10      things dubious things shadowy; I would know I would
                                                            ⌊say.]
```

This is an example of the sweet, smart style that catapulted Zanzotto's work to fame in the fateful year of 1968. In a book whose titular banner is an archaic sort of beauty and whose goal is to push perception beyond the limits of language, subject and context or eye and sky are among the objects recognized (*ricognizioni del fundus oculi del fundus coelorum* [recognitions of the fundus oculi of the fundus coelorum]), as is the horror hidden in the present ("Napalm dietro il paesaggio" [Napalm behind the landscape]).⁴ *La beltà* is Zanzotto's clearest statement of the geometrical correspondence between the personal and the political that informs all his work.

GLI SGUARDI I FATTI E SENHAL
[Glances, Facts and Senhals]

La beltà is followed by two short books. The first of these is a single, long poem published in 1969 and occasioned by the Apollo 2 lunar landing on July 20 of that year. In Zanzotto's early volumes, the sky is a metaphor for the undefineable source of meaning. In "Gli sguardi, i fatti e senhal," the technological invasion of space (and, hence, the source of meaning) is treated via a Rorschach dynamic of perception and projection as a grave violence done to Diana, moon goddess and huntress, who speaks here of her own wounds. Thematically, this poem continues a story begun in the "Polyphemus" poem of the *IX Egloghe*, where a satellite launching serves as the occasion for another poetic conversation, with the *Odyssey* as a sub-text. Here, however, the literary atmosphere is more varied. Erostratus, Petrarch, Longinus, and Parini appear in a context that also includes the wild child, the psychoanalytic notion of foreclosure, the Eastern philosophical principle of yin and yang, and the techno-perceptive registering of decibels.

But of all the voices that speak in "Gli sguardi" only Diana's appears in quotation marks; only the voice of the goddess can claim reportable veracity, as if she had actually spoken these very words, and they had been heard, not invented, by the scribe who makes them available to us. This is an important moment in Zanzotto's vast ecology discourse: the goddess Diana tells the poet that she herself has been a wound in what otherwise would have been an unsullied "body of beauty." Yet this natural wound that here characterizes meaning differs from the wound technology has inflicted upon meaning, as we discern in this fragment of the poet-Diana dialogue set within the multi-voice conversation which is the poem itself:

```
     —Ho saputo del tuo ferimento ma tu ne sarai ne sarai
     ne sarai complice abbastanza? Ammetti che sei
70   che sei che sei tu stessa una qualche una qualche
     forma di e di e di e di // inflitta //
     nelle cose i fatti le visioni, dì di punta
     —"Ero il trauma in questo immenso corpo di bellezza
     corpo di bellezza è la selva in profumo d'autunno
75   in perdizione d'autunno
     in lieve niveo declivio niveo non più renitenza
     stelle bacche stille in cori
     viola e rosso sul lago di neve"⁵
```

◘

[—I knew about your wounding but are you really are
⌊you really
are you really its accomplice enough? Admit that you
⌊are
70   that you are that you are yourself some kind of some
⌊kind of
form of and of and of and of // inflicted //
within things facts visions, say it straight
—"I was the trauma in this immense body of beauty
the forest is a body of beauty in autumn's perfume
75   in autumn's perdition
in soft snowy slope snowy no longer reluctant

INTRODUCTION

> stars berries droplets in choruses
> violet and red on the lake of snow"]

Zanzotto's poetry in the eventful years of 1968 and 1969 show, then, two versions of problems of subjectivity and meaning, the first in a contemporary political context, the second in a contemporary technological one.

A CHE VALSE? [What was the point?]

In 1970, Zanzotto published a collection of poems he had written from 1938 to 1942, some of them contemporary with others he had selected to publish in his first book, *Dietro il paesaggio*. After the *Beltà* discursions on possibilities of meaning and the *Sguardi* dramatization of such problematics at their source, the hearkening back to his own earliest work has a mimetic quality to it. Not surprisingly, *A che valse?* bears many similarities to Zanzotto's other early work; its uniqueness lies in its relative stylistic simplicity. Simultaneously, these early poems are the strongest testimony in all of Zanzotto's *opus* to his kinship with the so-called "hermetic" poets, especially Ungaretti and Montale, a kinship many critics consider an integral element of Zanzotto's work in general. For example, "Per vuoti monti e strade come corde" [Along empty mountains and cord-like roads] contains these lines:

> Ho perduto il sole nella mia bocca
> e nel mio cuore,
> il mio desiderio è un segno
> di sangue sulla neve.[6]

◻

> [I have lost the sun in my mouth
> and in my heart,
> my desire is a sign
> of blood on the snow.]

Just as representative of these early poems published out of order in 1970, when Zanzotto's current concerns include the possibilities of meaning in contemporary contexts, is the initial line group from the book's titular poem:

INTRODUCTION

       A che valse l'attesa del gioco?
       I compagni mancavano
       o distratti seguivano dall'alto
       il volo oscuro dei pianeti.
5   La notte circola ormai
       consuma il settentrione
       ma non la tua presenza
       vasta come il candore
       di stanze senza tramonto.[7]

◻

       [What was the point of waiting for the game?
       Your playmates were missing
       or, distracted, were following
       the planets' dark flight from on high.
5   By now night circulates
       consumes the north
       but not your presence
       vast as the candor
       of sunsetless rooms.]

It is helpful to keep this particular book in mind while reading the early work discussed here with which its composition is contemporary. While the author's decision to delay publication of the *A che valse?* poems removes them somewhat from the context of his first four published books (and hence from the present study), it also serves those books as a retrospective gloss.

PASQUE [Easters]

In 1973, Zanzotto's most Lacanian book came out. The irony of the title lies in its plurality: if more than one Easter exists, then the holiday itself changes meaning. A multiplicity of easters or of meaning-producing absences is, in fact, one of the book's main themes. The other is pedagogy, but a pedagogy that extends beyond the classroom or the "Reading Center" (the title of the book's first poem) to encompass the tactics of Orpheus and Pygmalion. Pedagogy is seduction, therefore, in a chronology of celebrations that duplicate themselves and meaning.

    Pasque is Lacanian to the extent that it makes a theme of the way desire undermines subjectivity (what Lacan calls the "subversion of the subject") as well as the knowledge-seeking aspects of desire itself (what Lacan, calling on Hegel, terms the "dialectic of desire").[8] Easters are like the signifiers, the subjects, if you will, which, though devoid of content (meaning) in themselves, act like empty Easter tombs to determine the relationships between all the things that surround them. And the search for knowledge of the other involves a pedagogy not devoid of seduction.

But to insist on Zanzotto's Lacanianism is to do the Italian poet a disservice. Many notions we tend to associate primarily with the psychoanalytic theories of Lacan are discernible first in Zanzotto's poetry. They can be found, for example, in the ways poetry investigates subjectivity and desire in Zanzotto's first books. An early reader of Lacan, Zanzotto found in the French analyst notions in many ways parallel to his own. *Pasque* may, in fact, be read as a kind of epiphany of the Zanzotto-Lacan dialogue that had been going on for years before American readers took to Lacan.

There are two major easters in *Pasque*: one in the poem, "La pasqua a Pieve di Soligo" [Easter in Pieve di Soligo], and the other in "Pasqua di maggio" [Easter in May], a calendrical impossibility. Both long poems are about meaning and its vicissitudes. The "Pieve di Soligo" Easter is a homage to Blaise Cendrars' "Pâques à New York." Written in alexandrians and *rima baciata* (another Easter reference if one thinks of Judas), the village Easter is a conversation between voices distinguished from one another by the Hebrew letters which are used to mark the verses of the *Lamentations of Jeremiah* in Eastertime prayers. These letters signal an acrostic which, occurring outside its original context, has lost its initial meaning yet nonetheless still names the voices as they speak.

After a voice called HETH has evoked the shades of such martyrs as Bruno, Vanini, and Hus, another called TET responds with what we might offer here as a window-synopsis of the "meaning" theme:

> TET Ma il reale e il fantasmatico, l'autre e l'ovvio
> ∟impallidisce e vira
> di fosfeni il perverso e la regola il sempre e il mai
> ∟scema;
> lo spazio, il rastremato e sconfinato spazio di un
> ∟deficit crea
> 120 l'alibi in cui questa maramaglia e frattaglia di idee
> ∟si bea:
>
> oh ricupero in suicidio, coagulamento nell'atto-uno,
> ∟infine.

INTRODUCTION

E invece rievocazione—doping per interposta persona,
⌊esalazione di cine.
Forse l'apparato è pronto, là sul colle famoso, la flebo
col trucco, goccia a goccia nel cotto nel solfo, flebo
⌊di " ", placebo,
e io dall'alto del come-suicidio sul colle famoso guardo
⌊in tondo
e m'istituisco goccia a goccia in leader feroce del (mio)
⌊mondo.
Per questo, oggi, o maghi delle arti, dall'umana figura
nonostante i vostri editti ho tolto la censura,
per questo a ogni dichiarato spifferato spampanato
⌊discorso
130   nonostante voi, angeli del magistero, ho tolto il morso:
è roba che mai non spurga dal suo-sé e si riconvoglia
⌊nel fondo
dove sbarrato sta il significante che è leader feroce del
⌊mondo.⁹

◻

[TET   But the real and the phantasmatic, the autre
⌊and the evident pale and spiral,
the painting and my corporeal schema are crawling
⌊with phosphenes,
the perverse and the rule the always and the never
⌊diminish in phosphenes;
space, the raked-over and limitless space of a deficit
⌊creates
120   the alibi this rabble and jabble of ideas delights in:
oh recuperation in suicide, coagulament in the first
⌊act, finally.
And instead re-evocation-doping through a person
⌊interposed, cinema exhalation.
Perhaps the apparatus is ready, there on the famous
⌊hill, the phlebus
with make-up, drop by drop in the brick in the
⌊sulphur, phlebus of " ", placebo,
and I from the height of the as-if-suicide upon the
⌊famous hill look around
and institute myself drop by drop as ferocious leader
⌊of (my) world.

9

INTRODUCTION

For this, today, oh magi of the arts, I have withdrawn censorship of the human figure in spite of your edicts,

for this I have withdrawn the muzzle from every
⌊declared
130   whistled-out stripped-clean discourse in spite of you,
⌊angels of the university,

it's stuff that doesn't ever get purged from its his-
⌊himself and gets glopped together at the bottom
where barred is the signifier that is the ferocious
⌊leader of the world.]

In *Pasque*, the signified is disturbed (see especially "Turbato è il significato," p. 18). Semantically, therefore, the text is centrifugal. But its stories of easters and teachings converge toward a common theme of the possibility of meaning in spite of the problems of the signified ("—e l'insegnamento mutuo di tutto a tutto—" [and the mutual teaching of everything to everything], p. 44; "Qui tra discente e docente il divario si conclude, tra chi guidi e chi segua" [here the gap is closed between student and teacher, between the one who leads and the one who follows], p. 31). Thematically, then, the text is centripetal. Therefore, semantics and thematics pull against each other in a tension always related to the notion of a center.

The joke of *Pasque* is its inability to decide whether utterances are xenoglossic (meaningful in a foreign code) or glossolalic (unencoded, meaningless "tongues"). For pedagogical reasons, it opts for xenoglossy in order to conserve the possibility of meaning even if meaning is not immediately understood. And this option leads to a vital eroticization of pedagogy, where "insegnami" [teach me, mark me] (p. 43) is, in all senses, an invitation. This most Lacanian of all of Zanzotto's books is thus also the most Zanzottan of all possible renditions of Lacan's linguistic notions of the subject: out of the empty tomb comes a troubled sign which hints at meaning and allows us to teach (or seduce) one another and thus to come to an ontological sense of our selves through language.

IL GALATEO IN BOSCO
[The woodland book of manners]

This "woodland book of manners," published in 1978 as the first of a trilogy that also includes *Fosfeni* [Phosphenes] and *Idioma* [Idiom] seems to fulfill a prophecy found in Zanzotto's first published book, *Dietro il paesaggio* [Behind the landscape]. In the "Adunata" [Assembled] poem of that first volume we read:

> Ma, gloria avara del mondo,
> d'altre stagioni memoria deforme,
> resta la selva.[10]

> [But, greedy glory of the world,
> deformed memory of other seasons,
> the wood remains.]

The wood remains here as the repository of histories that decay and are reborn in constant simultaneity with the present. In the *Galateo*, the communicative reciprocation hinted at in the *Pasque* volume becomes more evident. Further, the notion of reciprocal communication loses its earlier tautological tinge as it expands to suggest the reciprocal creation of individual and group, the present and the past, cognition and memory, tradition and invention.

The strong metaphor here is the wood; the vehicle of the metaphor is the actual Montello wood near Zanzotto's village in the Veneto. In the Montello, known for its ossuaries (memorials to the soldiers killed there in the Italian struggles against the Austro-Hungarian empire in 1918) and its tourist-enticing sylvan charm, a casual trekker might easily turn up what Zanzotto calls a "dear old tibia" while walking along. The Montello is also the actual place where the sixteenth-century cultural theoretician, Giovanni della Casa, composed Europe's first manual of manners, the *Galateo*. Further, the Montello's Charterhouse, now gone, and the Abbey, now in ruins, were sites of much poetic activity from the sixteenth century until our own. Ossuaries and verses of other poetry mingle in Zanzotto's images of sonnet-bones, and the book's skeleton, so to speak, is a central "hyper-sonnet" in which fourteen perfect sonnets emblematize the twelve lines of a traditional sonnet, and the preface and postface, a traditional literary framing.

This woodland book of manners is also a guide to what Zanzotto calls "the incredibly thin rules that maintain symbiosis and cohabitation, and the network of the symbolic, from language to gestures and perhaps even to perception itself: poised like spiderwebs or buried, veiled like filigrees above/within that boiling of presumptions which is reality."[11] But his metaphors of humus-simultaneity or the disappearance of historical chronology within an ecological model of con-

INTRODUCTION

stant simultaneity vastly expand the Lacanian implications of the wood as the site of the "symbolique." The *Galateo in bosco* glosses the combination of the linguistic determination of subjectivity and the relation of history to life that Benjamin, for example, sets forth in his essay on translation, where he writes, "The concept of life is given its due only if everything that has a history of its own, and is not merely the setting for history, is credited with life."[12]

While any single poem from this book will only begin to suggest the sense of vitality this volume imparts, and while the selection we have made here only hints at the social implications of such a volume in the troubled year in which it appeared, the hopeful gist of the *Galateo in bosco* might be summed up in the "nonetheless" that appears in the final poem of the hyper-sonnet, "Postilla" [marginal note, gloss]. Here we find not only a clear-eyed view of language as both determinate and insufficient as far as subjectivity is concerned; we also find a praxis that puts all that in the margins, so to speak, and gets on with life:

> Somma di sommi d'irrealtà, paese
> che a zero smotta e pur genera a vista
> vermi mutanti in dèi, così che acquista
> nel suo perdersi, e inventa e inforca imprese,
>
> 5   vanno da falso a falso tue contese,
> ma in sì variata ed infinita lista
> che quanto in falso qui s'intigna e intrista
> là col vero via guizza a nozze e intese.
>
> Falso pur io, clone di tanto falso,
> 10 od aborto, e peggiore in ciò del padre,
> accalco detti in fatto ovver misfatto:
>
> così ancora di te mi sono avvalso,
> di te sonetto, righe infami e ladre—
> mandala in cui di frusto in frusto accatto.[13]

◻

> [Height of the heights of unreality, town
> that crumbles to zero and nonetheless generates to
> ˪sight
> worms changing to gods, so that you acquire
> as you lose yourself, and you invent and sit astride
> ˪undertakings,

5   your contentions pass from one falsehood to another,
    but in such a varied and infinite list
    that whatever stains and saddens itself with falsehood
                                                    ˪here
    slips off with truth to marriage and understandings
                                                    ˪there.

    A falsehood even I, clone of so much falsehood,
10 or abortion, and worse in that than my father,
    I throw sayings together in fact or rather misfact:

    so I made use of you once more,
    of you, sonnet, infamous, thieving lines—
    mandala in which I go begging from one morsel to
                                                    ˪another.]

FOSFENI

Approximately one year prior to the 1984 discovery in quantum mechanics of the so-called "truth" quark, the second of Zanzotto's trilogy books appeared. The title of *Fosfeni* implies both the plankton incandescence that shines at night on the sea and the figures we perceive when we shut our eyes. If *Il galateo in bosco* contains Zanzotto's most cohesive discourse about history, *Fosfeni* is his most cohesive discourse about perception. The book opens with a characterization of language as a cozy, even exclusive, dinner-party, but it is a dinner like the Last Supper, or like many last suppers, and so we may assume that it announces some imminent change, some radical displacement, say, of the signifier, or perhaps an emphasis on its materiality. And the book closes with a poem about the logos, where reference and essence are balanced in an ambiguous future state that confuses precedence and result. The first poem suggests a "theory of the cold" that we find again at the end, when the last poem figures the logos as shining in ice crystals, even if "logos" is only an hypothesis. Within this philosophic-linguistic frame, the book's attention repeatedly turns to notions of the possibility or impossibility of perception, whether it be of material or affective reality.

A key poem here is "Vocabilità, fotoni" [Vocabulary, photons], where we find a dramatic encounter between the "I" and Saint Lucy, who sacrificed her eyes for her faith. And a key image in this poem is the photon, the unit of light which exists simultaneously as particle and wave. By elaborating some of the notions of perception that Zan-

INTRODUCTION

zotto has already presented in his early work, notably in the *IX Ecloghe*, this poem resolves dilemmas of precedence and result that arise in the linguistic determination of subjectivity by a credo of simultaneity similar to the one regarding history in the earlier book, *Il galateo in bosco*. Here again, a blindness to the evident permits the perception of the essential (as in quark theory, it would seem):

        Dispersa entro una vocabilità dolcissima
                Eurosia, genio dei chicchi
di grandine, dispersa ivi Barbara
fotoricettiva delle radicolarità del fulmine

5   emerge ora Lùcia dal terremotato
       cristallo delle diafanità
      collinari   Diva e niña del Freddo
      forse con un certo sèguito di cupi pretuscoli
       che m'invitano a pranzo, a mensa, a caldo rancio
10   Ha in mano una scheggia di raggi
         che forano qualsiasi ubiquità
      nell'altra mano i 9 gradi sottozero
        di lieve garza-neve,
        piuma d'uccello-già-neve,
15   Non può proteggere non può guidare
      ma non sarà in secondi ordini giammai
      L'ustione le ha scorticato
       tanta parte del volto e fatto fumare via gli occhi
       —e non se ne sa più il percome il percosa—
20   Essa fu buio e viene dal buio del suo eccesso
        tutta trinata di raggi
      in nome del ΛΟΓΟΣ veniente e di tutti i freddi venturi
      ma ben schierati, schedabili in nevi,
      ma tutti pupilla e ricca lacrima d'attenzioni
25   ma in fregola di numeri e tracce
        oh come s'infittisce il dialogo a soffi a spiscii
            hints glimpses!

     Lùcia: né madre tu sei, né doni-in-tenebra o in cristallo,
      ma sei tu che aggiorni su quel che ti restava
30   alle spalle scarso dirupo d'anno,
      svenimento giù giù di collina in collina
      svenimento sù sù per le celestialità
      Entro la riaffamata tagliola del freddo
      proprio davanti a te
35   ci si dibatte

e si ha voglia di rancio
e di spicciar fuori sudar fuori dimettere zappettando,
sì, di lasciar andare tutto, le stie vuote, spalancate
È andato, niente rimpianto,
40 secchezze soltanto qua e là o brandelli,
carnicino nel selvatico dei palati—
proprio nell'occhio il secco n
          (voglia di numeri, del conto, al dopo-rancio)

(Vien drìote adès anca la Lùzhia
45 pi granda e pi scarma de la só istessa imensa bontà)

Ammetti, diva Lùcia, ai tuoi piedi—dove so io
posati, così che ne sono ben cieco di tutti
i gradi della luce—
questa sbandante per forre—dove ben tu sai—
50 umile voglia di panegirico.

                    Rimbalzo di pianto agli occhi. Blow up di
                    un solo fotone. Ω^{14}

[Dispersed within a sweetest vocability
                    Eurosia, hailstones' genie,
dispersed therein Barbara,
photoreceptor of lightning's radicularities
5   Lùcia now emerges from the earthquaked
       crystal of the hill-bound
       diaphaneities   Diva and niña of the Coldness
perhaps with a certain following of dour priestlings
       who invite me to dinner, to the mess hall, to warm
                                              ˪rations,
10   She has in hand a spawl of rays
                    that pierce any ubiquity whatsoever
       in her other hand the 9 degrees below zero
                    of light gauze-snow,
                    feather of bird-once-snow,
15   She cannot protect she cannot guide
       but will never be in second place
       The scalding has skinned
       so much of her face and smoked away her eyes
       —and we no longer know the howfor the whatfor—
20   She was darkness and comes from the darkness of her
                                              ˪excess

15

INTRODUCTION

                all laced through with rays
        in the name of the coming ΛΟΓΟΣ and all the
                                  ᴸcoldnesses to come
        but well lined up ones, catalogued in snows,
        but all of them pupil and attentions' rich tear
25   but rutting for numbers and traces
                oh how the dialogue thickens in breaths in
                                      ᴸpissings
                      hints glimpses!

      Lùcia: neither are you mother, nor gifts-in-shadow or in
                                                crystal,
      but you it is who lightens the day after what remains
30   a year's scarce ravine at your shoulders,
      the fainting down down from hill to hill
      the fainting up up toward bluenesses
      Within the rehungered coldness trap
      just there before you
35   we debate
      and we want the mess
      and to gush forth sweat forth get rid of by hoeing,
      yes, to let everything go, the hutches empty, wide
                                                    ᴸopen
      It's gone, no regrets,
40   only here and there drynesses or scraps,
      fleshling in the palate's roughness—
      precisely in the eye the dry n
                    (a yearning for numbers, for the bill,
                                    ᴸat the after-mess)

      (Now she's coming back of you like a shadow, this Lucy
45   bigger and thinner by a long shot than her own huge
                                           ᴸbountiful being)

      Admit, diva Lùcia, at your feet—where I know
      lay all the degrees of light,
      as I am surely blinded by them—
      this scattering-through-gorges—you know where they are—
50   humble yearning for panegyric.

                          A leap of crying to the eyes. Blow up of
                          a single photon. Ω]

IDIOMA

In Zanzotto's most recent book, published in 1986, we encounter a resolute rejection of whatever metaphysics might have been involved in his earlier books (especially *La beltà* and *Pasque,* the first of which he calls "gli annali della mia morte" [the chronicles of my death], p. 21, and the second, "certi sistemi del silenzio / . . . certe microvocalità stellari" [certain systems of silence / . . . certain stellar microvocalities], p. 19). This rejection is made in favor of community and life; it is a choice of participation in the communication language makes possible rather than the isolation earlier implied at certain moments in Zanzotto's discourse on the linguistic determination of subjectivity. Such a decision has vast consequences for the *io*, who states a new-found activism in the phrase, "sono partecipe, finalmente" [at last I am taking part].[15] This is without doubt Zanzotto's most directly political book. Here we encounter themes of journalism, terrorism, antimilitarism, mass media, and publicity, for example, which, while none of them are new or surprising in Zanzotto's opus, appear here in the company of a new subjective resolve.

This resolve leads to philosophical considerations, to problems of ethos and pathos, which arise when communication and community become central concerns. It also leads to notions of a particular materiality of the signifier: its dialect materiality. Most of the book's central section is written in dialect, including the "Mistieròi" [Trades] poems which had earlier been published separately. These poems should be read out loud, Zanzotto says, even by those who do not understand the dialect. Their sound matters. Their phonic materiality allows these signifiers to create a community of participants in their sound even if their referential potential has no effect. Further, if it does, if, that is, the reader understands the dialect, the "story" comes forth to support the materiality of the signifiers, for the poems tell of humble events in a village where the sense of community pervades everyday events, including the practice of trades which now are in the process of disappearing, like dialect itself.

It is not surprising that Zanzotto's most recent book gives us once again the personage of Nino, the legendary (and actual) poet-peasant of Pieve di Soligo who, still active in his nineties, has to his credit a long list of appearances in Zanzotto's poetry. *Idioma* closes with "Docile, riluttante" [Sweet, reluctant], a poem about Nino—or about dialect (although it is written in Italian)—where participation in a community of language experienced as an idiom—as an identity for both the group and the individual, that is—caressingly enfolds the

INTRODUCTION

problematic of subjectivity. Here, then, is the last part of the last poem of Zanzotto's most recent book; after this, we shall start at the "beginning":

        Nessuna tristezza per i me stessi
        che non vi ho ritrovati
        né per gli altri, i cari amici, che sempre ho ritrovati,
30   anche se talvolta più vaghi,
        più paghi
        degli ultimi arboscelli nei fondi o sui crinali—
        Nulla che parli davvero
        di cose effimere o finali
35   bensì della pertinenza,
        bensì del fatto, della mai
        mai fattuale presenza,
        che pur qui si dà giustamente straripando
        da tutti gli altrove e singolarità
40   alla nostra quasi-indolenza
        Quanto quanto qui distilla
        e si distillò quale paradiso
        perfino dolorosamente nel suo insistere muto
        ora è soltanto lieto, e non distrattamente,
45   ma i suoi valori li compie e li ritira
        e li riacconsente un posto più in là
        comodi e umili anche se dalle nostre mani
        alquanto strani e stralontani
        E nei grigiori assopiti, appena specchianti
50   con gridii di dipinte piume e sbeccuzzati silenzi
        (è) come se noi e i nostri ricordi
        ma più i nostri presenti
        si unissero senza appello, ma non sotto imperio,
        ma induzioni di ragionamenti
55   che non lo saranno mai più, per aver raggiunto
        pacatamente (e insegnandolo) gli elementi[16]

◻

        [No sadness for the myselves,
        you who I didn't find,
        nor for the others, the dear friends, who I always
                                          found,
30   even if at times they were more vague,
        more content

        than the shrubs at the bottom or on the crest of the
                                    ⌊mountains—
        Nothing that really speaks
        of things ephemeral or ultimate
35   but of pertinence,
        but of fact, of never
        ever factual presence,
        that nonetheless gives itself rightly here overflowing
        from all the elsewheres and singularities
40   into our almost-indolence
        How much how much here distills
        and distilled itself as paradise
        even painfully in its mute insistence
        now it is only happy, and not distractedly,
45   but it accomplishes and retracts its values
        and reassigns them a place further out
        they are convenient and humble even if they are
        rather strange to and very far away from our hands
        And in the drowsy greynesses, barely reflecting
50   with cries of painted feathers and debeaked silences
        (it is) as if we and our memories
        but more our present times
        were to unite uncalled, but not under empire,
        but inductions of reasonings
55   that never again will be such, since they peaceably
        arrived at (and by teaching reasoning) the elements]

ONE

A FIRST ROUND KNOCKOUT
Zanzotto's Poetic Initiation

> Viel täuschet Anfang
> Und Ende.
>> Hölderlin

Arse il motore a lungo sulla via
il suo sangue selvaggio ed atterrí
fanciulli. Or basso trema all'agonia
del fiume verso i moli ed i mari.

5 Assetato di polvere e di fiamma
aspro cavallo s'impennò nella sera;
a insegne false, a svolte di paesi
giacque e tentò le crepe dell'abisso.

Figura non creduta di stagioni
10 di creta, di neri tuoni precoci,
di tramonti penetrati per fessure
in case e stanze col vento che impaura,

aspettai solo nella lunga sosta;
finestre e piazze invisibili sostenni;
15 acuti ghiacci avvizziti di febbre
alghe e fontane con me discesero

nel fondo del mio viaggio:
e clessidre e quadranti mi esaltarono
l'abbandono del mondo nei suoi ponti
20 nei monti devastati nei lumi dei confini.

O ruote e carri alti come luna
luna argento di sotterranei ceselli
voci oscure come le mie ceneri
e strade ch'io vidi precipizi,

25 viaggiai solo in un pugno, in un seme
di morte, colpito da un dio.[1]

A FIRST ROUND KNOCKOUT

[The motor burned its savage blood
a long time on the road and terrified
the children. Now it trembles low with the river's
agony toward the piers and the seas.

5 Thirsty with dust and flame
a harsh horse reared up in the evening;
at false road signs, at turns in the towns
it crouched down and tested the crevices of the abyss.

An unbelieved shape made of seasons
10 of clay, precocious black thunderclaps,
and sunsets passed through cracks
into houses and rooms with the frightening wind,

I waited alone in the long pause;
windows I bore up, and invisible piazzas;
15 sharp ice, wilted by fevers,
algae and fountains descended with me

to the bottom of my voyage:
and water clocks and sun dials extolled to me
the world's abandonment in its bridges
20 in its devastated mountains in its border lights.

Oh wheels and carts high as the moon
moon silvered by subterranean chisels
voices as dark as my ashes
and roads I saw as precipices,

25 I traveled alone in a fist, in a seed
of death, struck by a god.]

It would be easier to begin in the middle, in a recognizable moment of trans-Alpine connections, the (in)famous poeticization of the unconscious, a dream of some originary signifier basking in unreflected glory. Or, for that matter, at the "end," the more recent forays into uncharted but old and familiar woods, the song of the giantess and the actors, the fertile sonnet-bones, the glimmer, the village. But our beginning here will be in the past, and more a beginning, perhaps, for that. Who could ever name the present (or presence) of a beginning? Yet here, in some way, we seek to name, to begin in the past, then, to set off for somewhere also already past or passing now.

But ours is a purloined beginning, one filched from the "very" beginning, doubly a past, the published *incipit* of an *opus* around which we hope to swarm for awhile. We begin to borrow, and we borrow to begin, now placing the object of this flurry in plain view: *arse*.

Past for appearing at the beginning (the first word of the first text of the first book, *Dietro il paesaggio*, 1951), past in its designatory remoteness, and past for evoking still another past from which it takes both distance and measure. Here there is no tried and true *ardere nel cuore* but only the simple, stark *arse il motore*. One brief verb is simultaneously the vestige of genteel tradition, of long-ago past when the Poet might faint in an excess of inner arson, and also the witness of a past confined more closely to the present by a bond of technological inevitability. The Poet is dead, long live the guy in the car!

The driver in this poem is one we shall perhaps feel we recognize. Sometimes we think he resembles someone from another era, an earlier time when naming was, of course, already like now, a play of hide-and-seek, when Laura gave her aura to the laurel tree. Now, there is a lack of proper names in games, but a landscape like the past one, save for a certain preposition. States of soul and geological formations, states of soul and climatic conditions: some such couplings still variously and tenuously hold. The shift from a Petrarchan context is rather more subtle than an opposition and all the more effective for its seemingly minimal disturbance of a couple of letters as *dentro* slides to *dietro*. The deserted Vauclusan fields that once were measured *a passi tardi e lenti* gave outer screening and staging for an inner burning (*com'io dentro avvampi*). But on the slippery mountain curves near Pieve di Soligo, skids are not uncommon, and the risk of landslides threatens any direct route. The roadmap, if there were one, might indicate, at least, that the *dietro* here, like the earlier *dentro*, is what is hidden. This *dietro* is perhaps a place where roaring desire or repressed yearning would arrive, a place of untraceable instincts or intuitions of the trace. It is behind the landscape, but the landscape surrounds us and so, free will notwithstanding, does the *dietro*. It is not that sector of a panorama skillfully cut from a field of vision when the observer takes some care to place himself just this side of a fortuitous *siepe*. If the landscape speaks, its speech does not tell. One might seek instead for some sign in its cracks, passes, holes, lapses or repetitions. Our driver wanders around, in the landscape only to the extent that he is on it, even skimming its ridges at times, and of it, taking essence from surroundings, but never behind it, never where he would like to arrive, never where he would like to start, never at the beginning.

And the always past beginning cedes to an always passing present; we are already in the story, caught by its scan and its rhyme:

> Arse il motore a lungo sulla via
> il suo sangue selvaggio ed atterrí
> fanciulli. Or basso trema all'agonia
> del fiume verso i moli ed i mari.

Quickly now, appears the network to be untangled, beginning (never simply) with a doubling of the screen. The landscape itself is hidden in these lines, which are already hendecasyllabic reminders not only of Vaucluse, but also of a Dantesque wood, the scene for a mid-life *smarrimento* lying in wait not far from the beginning of a context still persisting here: *selvaggio* contains *selva*; *atterrí* is more earthy, more soil-filled than a pavid *spaventò* would have been. And suddenly the car or, rather, the bus, as Zanzotto himself would have it,[2] like the lexicon, comes down to earth (*Or basso*) and trembles (in a kind of metonymy not unfamiliar in these mountains: that which formerly frightened is now shaking with fear; an affective contagion here effected by a minute step into the present). The vehicle crouches low and waits (*trema*, still, in extensions of its virtuality; *trema*, a defective anagram of *terra*) to be washed away, still lower, by waters rushing to communicate with the sea at distant points which themselves echo communicability and place the scene by differentiation at some inland site: *i moli*.

But the image does not dissolve into these outlets.

5
> Assetato di polvere e di fiamma
> aspro cavallo s'impennò nella sera;
> a insegne false, a svolte di paesi
> giacque e tentò le crepe dell'abisso.

The image re-enters the past just when (*e poco dopo un gran destrier n'appare*) a marvelous, heroic steed rears up as in a fable, risking the treachery of false signs, leaving the towns (which might offer directions), inching forward in great peril, at great risk (the abyss, the void).

This little scene, a fairy-tale drama of terrible wonder, was in fact part of what had already passed: the missing center of the past that passed as a beginning, the empty time between period and capital, between *Arse . . . ed atterrí* and *Or basso trema*. The scene gives us an illuminated-manuscript accident report with only slight insinuations of liability in its *insegne false*.

10
> Figura non creduta di stagioni
> di creta, di neri tuoni precoci,

di tramonti penetrati per fessure
in case e stanze col vento che impaura,

aspettai solo nella lunga sosta;
finestre e piazze invisibili sostenni;
15   acuti ghiacci avvizziti di febbre
alghe e fontane con me discesero

nel fondo del mio viaggio:
e clessidre e quadranti mi esaltarono
l'abbandono del mondo nei suoi ponti
20   nei monti devastati nei lumi dei confini.

There is an expansion of rhythm or breath (two sentences in the first stanza, one in the second; but the third, the *figura* stanza, overflows), now, for the strange (*non creduta*) appearance of the guy, the driver, the storyteller, *solo*, not as sign, emblem, representative, or messenger (neither Beatrice nor Clizia here), but in the reductive simplicity of *figura*. No *uomo di fumo* appears either, but a figure composed from the landscape, from seasons of clay both earth and body, signs of storms, and a twilight glimpse of an interior which may still echo with cries of "*Zvanì* . . .": sketches for a portrait if the subject would be still.

And, for two moments (*aspettai, sostenni*) he is, as the unexpected *sosta* sets the stage for an hallucinatory city-scape sustained by our driver (for lack of any *sostegno* he himself could lean on). If such squares and windows as these mountain-bound ones are the workings of an overexcited mind, mental feverishness passes before utterance to an exterior provenance, where it melts as *acuti ghiacci avvizziti di febbre*: is mountain synesthesia the product of an exalted imagination?

But the motion begins again; it continues. Not only glaciers, but water plants and fountains join our driver as this confusion of landscapes accompanies his Carrollian slide even further down the slope, *nel fondo*. There, at the bottom of his voyage (where there is finally a colon: and therefore, no finality) is exaltation, there where the world has been not regained but abandoned, to the glee of an array of relic timepieces (the outmoded technology of water and sun, nature-powered markers of old time somehow qualitatively different, the past, history, now being made his story). The sites of this abandonment surround and show a gap. They are bridges, appositively designated as the *monti devastati*, as the *lumi dei confini*: exaltation exists in the depths where presence is abandoned not in words but border lights (but really in words of border lights), the edge of *dietro*.

A FIRST ROUND KNOCKOUT

A shrill whine remains to give an edge to other, deep, vowels, as each word, when *mondo* is left behind, terminates in the *-i* of the masculine plural; vocalization closes on its own highest range.

Suddenly, there is a cry: the oldest cry of Poetry, language rounding in search of some assurance that it is being received, defining by beseeching the point at which it would arrive.

> O ruote e carri alti come luna
> luna argento di sotterranei ceselli
> voci oscure come le mie ceneri
> e strade ch'io vidi precipizi,

The cry hearkens back to the present as it appeared earlier: *O*, though well announced just now in *abbandono, mondo, ponti, monti* and *confini*, echoes most precisely the present told earlier, *Or basso trema*. The vocative evokes a past present and now a presence of old-time vehicles attaining unlikely celestial heights, heights like the moon, reflective orb, here mirroring itself first, secretly, in the shape of the *ruote*, and then, openly, in a Narcissus-pond repetition, *luna / luna*. The reflection seeks deep (*Or basso*, even now), drawing its silver shine from sites even lower (from workshops of *sotterranei ceselli*) than where our driver has found exaltation and the *terminus* of his trip.

Underground hammers, wheels, carts, and the moon all speak indistinctly, in whispers. Our driver hears them as if from his very ashes, from a future place of his own non-presence, from a place *dietro* whatever he can "be" at present. Are these some immigrant voices come from a helpful nostalgia for the gods, filtered through Italo-Austrian passes to buzz in the ears of this (exalted) traveler? Are the voices obscure like his ashes and like the roads he mistook for precipices, or is this an invocation of both voices and mistaken roads? Not one of these, but only both are possible; voices, like roads, resist location here.

And now, the message carried by the invocation is no more than a simple call for an ear, an eye, to receive not a request, not a promise, nothing but his story:

> 25   viaggiai solo in un pugno, in un seme
> di morte, colpito da un dio.

The story of a trip, *solo*, leads not to an opening but to a constriction, a forceful refusal of opening; it brings not a handshake but a fist closing within and around the driver. And the fist is substituted by a final oxymoron: seeds promise life but not here. Closure all round, rounding off both the *O* and the *Or*, the call, now, a beginning (*seme*) of an ending (*morte*), or some confusion of these. But what of the low exaltation?

But this is the low exaltation, a mountain metonymy as *in un pugno* slides to *colpito da un dio*. Our driver has been laid low by the swipe of some vaguely defined, certainly not capitalized deity and has found in this downward circuit something uplifting, something to call out about, something to write home about or to a friend ("Mein Teurer! . . . kann ich Wohlsagen' das mich Apollo geschlagen . . . Dein H.").

This one verb (*viaggiai*), past echo of past beginning (*arse*), is the summary, the *toto*, the bottom line (almost) of his story, an accident-prone travelogue noting seasonal consistencies and geographic inconsistencies, a slide down the mountain to exaltation, to some kind of divine fist-in-the-face at an imaginary moment (a beginning) of death's germination. This small-case god is a knockout; a life-and-death blow testifies to his (past) presence just as our driver's story ends, just at the edge of the story, just at the edge of *dietro*.

This roller-coaster reading with feet flying un-noted is offered *in limine* here as a signal of what lies both ahead of and behind this study. Behind lie readings of Zanzotto's texts, readings leaky at first, but gradually filling to a level permitting a certain degree of paraphrase. Ahead lies an attempt to trace Zanzotto's major themes and techniques at some emblematic moments in his early work through close readings. I began here with a reading intended to demonstrate the high degree of thematic motivation that occurs in Zanzotto's work. In this single poem may be found not only the Petrarchan referent which runs throughout *Dietro il paesaggio*, but also a statement of distance taken by the poetic voice here in relation to that referent (for example, the differences between a Petrarchan *ardere nel cuore* and a Zanzottan *arse il motore*, between *dentro* and *dietro*, between a Vauclusan landscape that may mirror subjective states and a Pievan one that may determine them). At least two other famous landscapes may be contrasted to the one presented here: Zanzotto writes not of a Leopardian landscape that remains partly hidden to accommodate the viewer's desire for an illusion of infinity, but of a landscape which itself, in its entirety, is hiding something; and an unspoken reference to Dante's woodland bewilderment is difficult to avoid in the presence of the stately hendecasyllable and the early appearance of an adjective echoing the *Commedia*'s *selva*.

In addition to these self-imposed measurements taken against early masters of Italian poetry by one both daring and humble (as De

Sanctis would imply any person must be who chooses to write Italian poetry after the fourteenth century),[3] a touch of the fiabesque is found, evoking magical Ariostan steeds in a preview of one of the significant movements throughout Zanzotto's work, the hallucinatory or dream-like vision of potential terror often coupled with images or small twists of lexicon or even suffix that minimalize the elements of the vision and reduce epic horror to fairy-tale fantasy. This movement toward the minimal is an important part of Zanzotto's polemic against what he considers the oppression of history, or what might also be called the narrative tyranny of any epic. In *Dietro il paesaggio* are found some beginnings of these themes, which will be more fully developed later on, especially in *IX Ecloghe* (1962).

Also in the first poem is our first view of the personified *io*. In keeping with an insistence on the minimal, the *io* appears not as a vague subjectivity or a precise symbol but as an individual voice, the voice of one who both takes consistency from and lives at the mercy of his surroundings after technology—or the promise of the modern world—has failed him. Exaltation for this individual is a lowly affair, fraught with feverish hallucination rather than noble ascendancy. It involves a personalization of the massive forces of history into a single story that he can call his, with fond nostalgia for some ideal past where time was measured by natural means rather than according to the exploits of humans.

Finally, the use of the vocative to address what we might call "found objects" emphasizes the degree to which the author is convinced that poetry now is distant from Poetry when it could invoke the gods (this was the topic of conversation at my first meeting with Zanzotto in 1976). The final stroke, what we are calling the knockout, is a misquote of Hölderlin's well-known letter to Casimir Ulrich Böhlendorff, where the German poet says that he has been struck by Apollo, in other words, that he has been given the gift, or the curse, of Poetry.[4]

Zanzotto's reference to Hölderlin is perhaps the most prophetic in the entire text, for if Petrarch is here the emblem of a theme upon which Zanzotto writes rich variations, Hölderlin is emblematic of some of the strongest stylistic convictions obtaining throughout Zanzotto's work. We may mention here in passing that the poems of Hölderlin's madness, with their schizophrenic voices and broken syntax, may be seen as models for Zanzotto's later valorization of dialogue, of silence or empty space, and even of apparent nonsense when risking meaning nothing can lead to new meaning. In a book itself emblematic because of its quality as a beginning, and in one which so intentionally evokes the shades of so much of Italian poetic history, it is worth noting that the only epigraph, occurring directly at the center of the book, is from Hölderlin: "Ihr teuern Ufer, die mich erzogen einst" [You noble shores, which once raised me].[5]

By beginning at the "beginning" and with a reading, we hope to demonstrate not only how much of what is to come is signalled from the start, but also the extent to which a reading even of one of the earliest texts of this writer, whose later work is often considered extremely difficult, may come as a shock. This may be especially true for someone tempted by the fallaciously revelative seductions of translation-as-reading-aid, a common enough temptation, perhaps, in our century and in this country.[6] Here, in aftershock, we shall present some readings of Zanzotto's texts in attempts at paraphrase rather than translation; but first, briefly, we offer some thoughts about reading Zanzotto's poetry.

It would be fortunate if the surprise in an encounter with Zanzotto's texts could be attributed simply to an unexpected stumble over a modern-day incarnation of talents that had set the standards at the start of Italian literature. But initial readings, and especially initial readings of these texts, performed by the creature known as a "non-native speaker," may stumble more into a fright of incomprehension than onto any unexpected inventiveness. It is this stumbling block that makes Zanzotto's texts so wonderfully apt as tools in a reading lesson that has been pressing in on literary studies for some time now and that I would like to record here.

The lesson starts off simply: an attitude passing for passivity is what now might most gently help a reader in relation to Zanzotto's—or any other highly motivated—texts. This would not be passivity, however, as much as a quiet receptivity even when the "item" to be received is unknown, unexpected, even unimaginable. Critical discourse begins with reading; and the most engaging of such discourse is that which holds closely the text being read. Willingness to read and to read and to read is the beginning of this engagement.

But a reading is not necessarily an understanding. Perhaps the reader's stand is neither under nor over but somewhere just beside the text, in a proximity distant enough to prevent reading "into" the text. An advance upon a text by a reading full of dread at not getting the meaning risks missing it completely, even if remnants of some familiar diachronic or synchronic intertextuality are salvaged for discernment and faltering discourse. So, in some way which each reading would define differently, by observing the text as it happens, by acknowledging its autonomy in the face of a sensibility that may or may not understand it, but that will not attempt to appropriate it, settling instead for nearness to it, a field may be prepared for the reception, if not the immediate profit-oriented assimilation, of even that which holds "meaning" hidden for awhile.

This reading initially eschews peripheral contributions. Because it does not attempt to read into the text, it can most happily bring to the text as "preparation" only an awareness of mutating context (literary tradition being one of the vast possibilities of context). Paradoxically, only when it occurs outside as well as within the traditional realms of expectation of "meaning," "content," "signified," can the reading begin to receive the myriad little messages operating at such minute levels as to risk either being overlooked as insignificant or despaired of as confounding. The reading is traumatized, first, in a displacement—of the eye, if you will—from the "outside" to the "inside" of each word, from its everyday existence as signifying entity to the revolutionary potential, the fissions and fusions of signification, which might arise from an awareness of its composition or its decomposition.

These musings on a possible contemporary *lectura lectionis* (but also an ancient one, as Plato's Cratylus might maintain) come out of a contact with even Zanzotto's very first book and so may serve here as a starting point for methodology: the beginnings in this case being no more than a set of readings which, initially baffled, turn constantly toward what is not understood in a movement at times centripetal, gathering into themselves other texts and contexts which are somehow attracted by the text as a magnet or mirror at the core, and at times centrifugal, flying out in many directions to signification discovered in unexpected sectors of a widening whirl, orbits held distantly fast by the text at the core.

Giuseppe Ungaretti recognized some of the traumatization caused by reading (or by lack of reading) in his "Piccolo discorso sopra *Dietro il paesaggio* di Andrea Zanzotto," presented at a conference in San Pellegrino three years after that book's publication and four years after Ungaretti, along with Montale, Quasimodo, Sinisgalli, and Sereni had conferred the Premio San Babila-Inediti upon the unknown verse writer from Pieve. In his "little discourse," the modern master calls for new efforts at providing a critical context for reading:

> La critica ha difatti prestato poca attenzione al suo libro *Dietro il paesaggio*, e se è in commercio sino dal 1951, credo che per il pubblico sia ancora a tutt'oggi ignoto, come non mai apparso. Forse la critica oggi trascura un po' troppo quella parte delle sue funzioni che consiste nel suggerire al lettore modi di lettura, con citazioni, con prove eventuali di derivazioni, con conseguente isolamento e dimostrazione della novità recata

dall'esaminato. La critica soffrí generalmente di distrazione all'apparire del libro di Zanzotto.[7]

▫

[In fact, little critical attention has been paid to his first book, *Dietro il paesaggio,* and although it has been available since 1951, I think that even today it is as unknown to the public as if it had never appeared. Criticism today perhaps neglects a little too much that part of its task which consists in suggesting, with quotations, possible sources, and the consequent isolation and demonstration of the newness contained in the text under consideration, ways of reading to the reader. Criticism generally suffered from distraction when Zanzotto's book appeared.]

Distrazione: "not getting it," missing the point because a point was expected where instead there lay constellation upon constellation of "points": face-saving inattention in the face of traumatized reading, the *novità* of something looking like poetry that begins with its own eternal disclaimer: *dietro* is unattainable, and poetic "meaning" is always *dietro*. (Pity, then, the poor Apollo, god of poetry—evoked as if in *recusatio* simply as *dio* by our driver—when poetry's finest prize is also Daphne's fate, the eternal concealment—or changed nature—of all the poet did desire: the laurel, like poetry itself and Zanzotto's landscape, holds desire's end, from the very beginning, always *dietro*. But in the shade of the laurel one may perhaps still imagine Daphne's beauty.)

Later, the landscape of this first book, its stases and meltings, comforts and threats, and our driver's missed arrivals, his arrivals at misses, will wend their way, strangely familiar, in many guises and mutations through the books to come, and will signal this one, *après-coup*, as a kind of symbolic Ur-text for a chapter of poetic history written on fly-away paper, unbindable with old glue and thread. An Ur-text, but extant, a container of signals, of stop's and go's, a universe of seedlings reaching toward themes and styles still new while carrying a pale flag of hermeticism as it hesitates on the fringes of the big parade. History and time, presence and the present, desire for and fear of the other, these themes gradually come out of a "word work" that takes all technicalities into a realm of productiveness, scorning the gratuitous gesture and holding in a pattern of game-like grace where even the slightest motion (change, distinction, difference) strives for consciousness of its significative virtue. *Dietro il paesaggio* hovers in the hazy, fecund ambiguity of beginnings, behind all that comes after.

But before we return to it, and since Ungaretti's spirit has already been evoked, let us pause for a moment to consider some aspects of the relation between Zanzotto's early text and those of his early reviewer. The intertextuality that exists between Zanzotto's first book and the so-called hermetic poets in general has been noted by Amedeo Giacomini: he mentions such figures as *l'angelo* [the angel], *la chimera* [the chimera], *i rischi appassiti* [wilted risks], *le larve beate* [blissful spectres], *le logge vibrate* [vibrating loggias], *la terra estinta* [the extinguished earth], *i fiumi traboccanti dal deserto* [the desert's overflowing rivers], *la morte vagabonda* [vagrant death], *le forme sensitive* [sentient shapes], all of which are found in *Dietro il paesaggio,* as typical of hermetic taste and thus emblematic of the influence of the hermetic poets on Zanzotto's work in the early fifties.[8] This evidence is convincing but perhaps does not portray the complete picture. Such a list of figures may also show Zanzotto's taste for the baroque, for superficial juxtapositions which contradict banal reality, for personifications of abstractions indicating perhaps not only the discrete or even unconscious presence of recent master models and contemporary readings but also a more old-fashioned complaisance in the audacity of the image. This is not a gratuitous audacity, but rather a tearing of lexical continuity which operates traumatically at the level of the signifier and secondarily takes its being at the level of the signified. Or, further, if one is willing to consider a figure like *la terra estinta* as being something more than solely the property of the post-Onofri "generation," can one not find in it some Petrarchan contamination, so to speak, or an Italianization of T. S. Eliot in a hands-across-the-waters gesture to *The Wasteland*?

There is something about the procedure here in *Dietro,* however, that bespeaks a deep reading of the Ungaretti of *Sentimento del tempo,* especially, and of the early Montale: a question of space, or, if one resuscitates the text to verbal utterance, of breath.[9] In all these texts, the traditional hendecasyllabic landscape persists in pre- and postwar subdivisions side by side with septenarii, echoes of long-established patterns and grateful acknowledgment of debts to forefathers. Three fleeting examples:

> In questa notte che è preda del vento
> ho presagio della luna
>
> Luna allusiva, vai turbando incauta
> Nel bel sonno, la terra

Ti guardiamo noi, della razza
di chi rimane a terra

◻

[In this night which is prey to the wind
I have a premonition of the moon

Allusive moon, incautious you go, disturbing
the earth in its beautiful sleep

We gaze at you, we of the race
of those who remain earthbound]

(The first is from Zanzotto's "Balsamo, bufera," in *Dietro il paesaggio*; the second, from Ungaretti's "Quale grido," in *Sentimento del tempo*; and the third, from Montale's "Falsetto," in *Ossi di seppia*.)

As concerns versification, Zanzotto's constancy is one of simplicity here: the short sentence, the fragmentary syntax, a unified rhythmic alternation that bends from time to time in homage to the octave.[10] But it is tempting for one who has visited Zanzotto in his mountains to find remnants here of *villotte* and other old Venetian dialect rhythms underlying the lexicon of a modern-day rapport with otherness. Tempting, too, is the desire not only to recognize familiar ties to modern Italian tradition but also to hear a distant rhythm of an utterance more intimate, more regional than the standard, to hear remnants of a repressed speech figuring skeletally at the depths of highly polished textuality.

Zanzotto himself recognizes the texts of Ungaretti and Montale as among the most important for him at an early stage.[11] And one may certainly dwell on an intertextuality of similarities. We would like to slip away from these for a moment, however, to rest briefly on an intertextuality of contrasts which may help to situate Zanzotto's iconoclastic production in a chronology of its recent Italian context.

If we take a sweeping glance at twentieth-century Italian poetry, we may see Zanzotto "emerging," or hatching, as it were, from the hermetic tradition. But after we account for a heritage common to both the hermetics and Zanzotto, such as debts to Petrarch, Dante, or Mallarmé, we find that perhaps the strongest tie between Zanzotto and the hermetics is, paradoxically, the differing but shared attention they all give to a kind of otherness, to something whose existence is signalled by its very absence, something which resists presence and being known. The common concern with otherness is paradoxical, though, for while it provides a point of similarity between Zanzotto and several of his most well-known immediate predecessors, it also demonstrates an—or perhaps the—essential difference between himself and those poets.

Systems of thought—or themes—which give a great deal of importance to the idea of an otherness are structurally central to the work of Ungaretti and Montale, for example. In each, these systems are arrived at individually, even (but for the eventual fact of publication) privately, and they find indirect expression in texts which make of the reading process a kind of decoding activity.

For Ungaretti, the otherness which is decipherable through a reading of his metaphors as a lexical system is a kind of Bergsonian nostalgia for origins; in a world where the constant passage of time makes for qualitative differences between what one was and what one becomes, the otherness yearned for is a static, pristine, original essence which has long ago been lost and is constantly being lost even further. This intra-referent metaphorico-lexical system may be found in the six cantos of "La morte meditata," in *Sentimento del tempo*, for example. When one reads these poems closely, metaphor by metaphor, and finds all other instances of each metaphor in Ungaretti's earlier texts, the "sealed" meanings of this set of poems open directly onto the notion of progressive rather than repetitive time and the psychological and metaphysical toll it takes as each generation succeeds the preceding one.[12]

In Montale, the potential presence of an otherness is found in the vast and intricate system of *senhals* which at times delineate a Nestorian deity, a messenger figure which could appear at any moment, bringing an inkling of different, hopeful life to otherwise existential man. In this context, we might think especially of Montale's early books, *Ossi di seppia* and *Le occasioni*.

Ungaretti's version of Bergsonian philosophy and Montale's use of the Nestorian heresy, especially when elaborated to the degree of poetic motivation found in their texts, remain two profoundly individualistic attempts to deal with the modern malaise of uncertainty in terms of an awareness of otherness. Where otherness is concerned, however, Zanzotto is perhaps both more elaborate and more direct than these poets, for he addresses himself to the idea of otherness in many guises: first in Petrarchan garb, later in a well-developed polemic with history, later still in some of the terms established by Freud and Saussure, and more recently, in an incorporation of all of these in a linguistic-psychoanalytic simultaneity drawing from all sources, from all roots (as in *Il galateo in bosco*, 1978).

But at the center of Zanzotto's poetics sit two fundamental tenets of modern thought: from Freud, the discovery of the unconscious, and from Saussure, the positing of the signifier-signified composition of the linguistic sign. Central also is the equating of the unconscious and the processes of language that links Zanzotto's work to that of the French psychoanalyst, Jacques Lacan. It is within the realm of this correspondence of the unconscious and language that Zanzotto's texts lie; his lines slip on the precipices of "meaning" so that the notion of "meaning" is radically altered. His poems reach for snowy dark realms, ultimately unsayable and unknowable, forever other, regions swarming with lost sacred mysteries and forgotten origins. Zanzotto's is an endeavor progressively risking the self-destruction of meaninglessness, a technique of scalpel rather than pen, a contemporary exacerbation of what has perhaps always symptomatically distinguished poetry from prose.

Given these contexts, the enigmatic title of Zanzotto's first book begins to expand in several signifying circles. As first word in the title of what we are calling an extant Ur-text, *dietro* signals an early and lasting desire for contact with or recognized existence in rapport with what lies behind the evident. And . . . *il paesaggio*, as if in compassion for unassuageable desire, signals a companion and guide, a figure not unknown in Italian literature, one who has been there already, as it also signals the critical decision taken by our author to make his literary debut under the aegis of the author of the *Canzoniere*: poetry as the utterance of desire and, finally, of absence. (To Zanzotto, Petrarch is a metaphor for poetry itself; Petrarch "has" his beloved Laura only to the degree that she is present in the *lauro* of the crown his verse will bring him: slight variations on the theme of Apollo, lover and then, alas, poet, as the bereft god scratches out his own small consolation in whatever shade the pen might leave.[13])

By choosing Petrarch as his first "compass," Zanzotto takes an early stand (which will later be modified) first, on the side of standard Italian (with a skeletal presence of Latin, here especially in the syntax) as opposed to dialect and, second, on the side of poetry as opposed, in a "visceral polemic," to history.[14] In this polemic, Petrarch is of pivotal importance as the discoverer and symbol of the "lymph of poetry," as Zanzotto calls it, in a circuit of onomatopoeia which arises from the world in order to take itself away from the world and create for itself a new, other space. Thus, for Zanzotto, Petrarch discovers style as a parthenogenesis of a world different from the world of history. "His story," being minimal, single, unique, and internal, contradicts as it mimics the "great," coercive movements of narrative imperative in history; the driver's mountain accident is poetic but not historic. The emblematic anti-historicism which Zanzotto attributes to Petrarch and to style (and so to poetry in general) functions thematically from the outset in Zanzotto's work, as we have seen; it becomes the central concern of his fourth book, *IX Ecloghe*, where it adopts another emblem bearer, the Virgil of the *Bucolics*, as we shall see further on.

At the beginning, *Dietro il paesaggio* presents familiar elements of the Pieve di Soligo landscape—the mountain passes, the rivers that flow alternately above and below ground (providing Zanzotto with yet another metaphor for poetry), the fields, animals, seasons, festivals, and especially the place-names. These landscape elements, like those in Petrarch, are metaphors for subjective affective states, but they also maintain an awareness, even at the vehicular level of the metaphors, of all that is hidden by those very elements. The concatenation of associations signals the unconscious, the signified, all that which is covered—and suggested—by the apparent. Poetry under the sign of Petrarch and the emblematic landscape itself become metaphors for a different world, or better, a world of difference; Zanzotto has called it "un mondo autre."[15] It is a world of otherness, an alternative world in which the brutal relations of history no longer prevail, where a utopia in embryo is configured.

atollo (Dizionario Zingarelli): . . . prob. dal singalese *ätul* 'dentro' a.m. Isola corallina elevata fino a 4 m. formata da un anello nel cui centro sta una laguna comunicante col mare.

atoll (OED): . . . prob. Malayalam *adal* 'closing, uniting.' A coral island consisting of a ring-shaped reef enclosing a lagoon. Darwin's theory, now generally accepted, is that a lagoon occupied the place of a submerged island.

atollo (Zanzotto): a single word appearing at the center of a white page prior to poetic texts in *Dietro il paesaggio*; title of first section of that book; title of a poem appearing at the center of that section, in a counting that reveals the introductory nature, like that of Dante's first Canto, of "Arse il motore"). Also the geological formation of the Bikini islands, where atomic bombs were tested in the early 1950s.

The mountain landscape appears like a (missing) jewel in the tropical (non-) island setting which emblazons the first part of the first book. Missed beginnings, the beginnings of a miss. But superimposing the mountain scene on the atoll makes our driver's fall no less steep: the mountain landscape holds no apex at the center here but instead marks circumference, signalling otherness behind while frustrating level footholds. The implications are Darwinian: something is sinking, submerged, missing. Something has disappeared at the center (of the mountains, of the atoll, of the reading). Reading upon the mountains, upon the atoll; the traveler's disorientation when, upon arriving at an unknown place, he finds it lacks the hoped-for amenity of a *centro di lettura*.

Stepwise we proceed for now, uncentered except by a metaphorically insistent lack (of what? so a double lack, and mystery for our sleuthing). The *motore* burning in the first poem leaves a trail in its coda, the second, "Primavera di Santa Augusta" [Spring in Santa Augusta]. In this town not far from Pieve, a springtime otherness (*tu*) keeps silent, holding back presence, too, of this other, *tu*, and the book's second machine rests immobile in its plurality, not even trembling, as the day draws to a close.

```
              Alla pioggia dei monti, dei castelli,
              le bandiere cadono in sfacelo;
              leggero come scheletro
              m'avventuro in questo giorno
    5         che selvoso si versa sul mondo.

              Dietro cieche evasioni di ghiacci
              e i filtri densi delle paludi,
              nell'azzurro defunto delle valanghe
              arrestate dal tuo silenzio
   10         arrestate agl'inizi del mio terrore,
              vacillano le scale dell'inverno;
              per un'altra fronte della pioggia
              primavera dolce
              tuona sui monti

   15         La tua vicenda avvampa
              ancora, discendi in tumulto
              dalle madide chiome dei paesi
              coi torrenti del cielo e delle strade,
              e snudi abissi sotto le mura
   20         e sotto i treni
              immoti davanti alla sera.

              Le voci della vera
              età chiara ti fanno
              ma gli occhi restano spenti
   25         su questa terra che di te s'estenua
              e dal tuo volto vinto da morte
              il mio conosco.[16]
```

[In the mountain rain, in the castles' rain,
flags fall undone;
light as a skeleton
I venture into this day
that pours itself woodsy upon the world.

Behind the ice's blind escapes
and the dense philtres of the swamps,
in the avalanches' dead azure
arrested by your silence
arrested at the beginnings of my terror,
the steps of winter vacillate;
on another of the rain's fronts
sweet spring thunders over the mountains

Your event still
burns, in tumult you descend
from the damp tresses of the towns
with the torrents of the sky and the streets
and expose abysses beneath city walls
beneath trains
immobile as evening falls.

The voices of the true
age make you clear
but its eyes remain extinguished
over this land exhausted by you
and from your face bested by death
I know my own.]

The driver ventures out into a rain of used-up past (castles, banners now frayed). He is a skeletal presence (death signs—*leggero come scheletro*—give him weight here, as *un seme di morte* did in the first poem) in a time that takes its essence from the landscape (*giorno . . . selvoso*). The steps of winter hide in precarious balance behind glaciers that evade the downward pull as long as *tu* is silent (*arrestate dal tuo silenzio*). As long as *tu* is silent, nothing will change, nothing will come undone, and the terror of the *io* will stop where it began: at its intuition, that is, or perhaps at its seasonal expectation that *tu* might speak. Were *tu* to do so, it would bring spring, thus ending the winter's tale that here is no tale (no past) but rather a description of present virtuality, perfect for never having begun its incompletion. In this poem's landscape, *valanghe*, when *arrestate*, create that which does not exist, the *azzurro defunto*, another death seed. These arrested avalanches thus show present and presence frozen in blind evasion, temporarily avoiding what might be, what will be—the passage of time, the utterance of the other.

For now, all remains in the now, and the present accommodates by moving ahead to what, in effect, happens next. The terror itself is present, in the present, and therefore terrifying, for here there is neither historical account nor future scenario to offer the convenience of a narrative assurance that the presence of the *tu* is caged in some frozen place away from this present. Terror is served up here with sweet spring, *primavera dolce*, like Botticelli's beflowered harbinger of new life, of sweet change now suddenly shortchanged of some sweetness by the bellowing verb that follows. This spring is no silent season: *tuona sui monti*. And the Botticellian maiden is swept into a Valkyrian rush down the precipices. This sweetness sweeps all before it in a powerful descent. The macro- of our driver's earlier micro-slide-down-the-mountain, it blazes its way in wetness (which is no longer the old rain) to the revelatory moment when it exposes voids (*snudi abissi*) under protective barriers (*sotto le mura*) and under vehicles suddenly incapable of escaping the present and going somewhere else (*e sotto i treni / immoti davanti alla sera*).

No time has passed; time has no past here. The present remains while *tu*, this sweet *primavera*, thunders, breaks its silence, dissolves what once was hard and fast into torrents of fluidity as it uncovers the abysses beneath the most fastly held assurances of both stability and mobility. The *tu* speaks, and the landscape (which is also *io*) is changed.

Speaking also, but in chorus, are the voices of the "true age." Whatever this might be is circumscribed only by the implication (*ma*) that it is not the present one but rather another time that calls this present reenactment of events *chiara*. In this winter place passing now, through exhaustion, into spring (*su questa terra che di te s'estenua*), the lights have gone out in eyes dead to sight, in a blindness which discerns only one face, or two. And the ambiguous advent of spring which promises new life here shows an aspect of death. The springtime seed may be a *seme di morte*, a kind of slightly divine punch in the driver's face. This springtime is *tu*, the other, the voice that makes *io* a listener, the place from which *io* is made both double and alone; and this springtime other, *tu*, has a face already molded in a death mask, frozen, static, fixed.

But, in a final seasonal draught of ambiguity, *vinto da morte* could be read with *il mio* as a moment of recognition echoing an earlier signal of death in the poem (*leggero come scheletro*) and now seeming more like a death sentence than a lament, a sentence seen only too late, at the exhausted end of winter, of syntax, of poem.

And the presence of death hangs between one face and the other and over the final moment in this present tense account of terrifying and sweet change: *conosco*. The *tu* speaks; the *io* recognizes *il mio [volto]* in a movement where something dies. When the *tu* speaks, the *io* finds itself simultaneously in the loneliness of its individuality and the communion of a message, but never more in the unspeakable bliss of its origins, in the bliss that speaking breaks; and the child *io* was before *io* was *io* ceases to exist.

At this, then, another lost beginning, we feel on our skin an uncanny tropical breeze, one most inappropriate to the pre-Alpine summits near Pieve di Soligo. This is the breeze around the atoll, coming from nowhere, as our probings get us nowhere in our search for a place for this emblem. Atoll: that which no longer has a center. Mountain: that which rises at the center. Negatives to be developed in reverse. Everything (nothing) hinges on the (lack of) center. (Is the atoll perhaps another set of parentheses? How much can be swallowed up by curves closing upon sometimes missing content? Do these purportedly staunch signifiers of asides, whispers, hints, and insinuations really contain that which is central to meaning but hidden? Or are they an empty womb?) A paradox of mountain and atoll: our driver descended to exaltation; now, to reach a trace of writing holding forth in the void of an empty center, we must climb a summit.

> Il faut aller plus loin.
> Formuler la critique est déjà décliner.
> Le fait de "parler" d'une morale du sommet relève lui-même d'une morale du déclin.
>
> Bataille, *Sur Nietzsche*

Not quite half way through the "Atollo" section of *Dietro il paesaggio* lies a text with a doubly prophetic title. "Elegia pasquale" [Easter elegy] is an anti-triumphal textualization of an uncannily ahistorical moment. Here are plotted several movements which, after showing us its latitude and longitude, will continue far beyond this landscape (*Pasque* the book was published over twenty years later). This Easter elegy is not a lament for a sacrificial victim but an elegy by that victim for Easter itself, for what Easter once (or never) was, for a crown and a wound found only at a summit.

A FIRST ROUND KNOCKOUT

Pasqua ventosa che sali ai crocifissi
con tutto il tuo pallore disperato,
dov'è il crudo preludio del sole?
e la rosa la vaga profezia?
5   Dagli orti di marmo
ecco l'agnello flagellato
a brucare scarsa primavera
e illumina i mali dei morti
pasqua ventosa che i mali fa piú acuti

10 E se è vero che oppresso mi composero
a questo tempo vuoto
per l'esaltazione del domani,
ho tanto desiderato
questa ghirlanda di vento e di sale
15 queste pendici che lenirono
il mio corpo ferita di cristallo;
ho consumato purissimo pane

Discrete febbri screpolano la luce
di tutte le pendici della pasqua,
20 svenano il vino gelido dell'odio;
è mia questa inquieta
gerusalemme di residue nevi,
il belletto s'accumula nelle
stanze nelle gabbie spalancate

25 dove grandi uccelli covarono
colori d'uova e di rosei regali,
e il cielo e il mondo è l'indegno sacrario
dei propri lievi silenzi.

Crocifissa ai raggi ultimi è l'ombra
30 le bocche non sono che sangue
i cuori non sono che neve
le mani sono immagini
inferme della sera
che miti vittime cela nel seno.[17]

[Windy Easter, you who ascend to the crucifixes
with all your desperate pallor,
where is the sun's crude prelude?
and the rose the vague prophecy?
5   From marble gardens

behold here the flagellated lamb
come to graze scarce spring
and the windy Easter that makes them sharper
illuminates the ills of the dead

10   And if it is true that they composed me oppressed
in this empty time
for the exaltation of tomorrow,
I have so much desired
this garland of wind and salt
15   these slopes that calmed
my crystal-wound body
I have consumed purest bread

Subtle fevers chap the light
of all of Easter's slopes,
20   they open the veins of hatred's frigid wine;
this unquiet Jerusalem
of residual snows is mine,
make-up accumulates in the
rooms in the sprung-open cages
25   where huge birds brooded
colors of eggs and rosy gifts,
and the sky and the world are the unworthy shrine
of their own light silences.

At the last rays the shadow is a crucifix
30   mouths are nothing but blood
hearts are nothing but snow
hands are infirm
images of the evening
that hides meek victims in its breast.]

   In France, to explain to children the Lenten silence of the church bells, a saying has it that before Easter all the bells travel to Rome to return amidst great clangings only on the day that marks resurrection. A different Easter migration from France may be hinted at here, and it will show up again years later in homage to Blaise Cendrars' *Paques à New York* in *Pasque*.[18] For now, not New York skyscrapers but Pievan mountains surround the scene, and the first Easter toll of the hendecasyllable is extended one syllable beyond its final accent to verge on an alexandrine, ringing against the slopes in a suggestion of importation reminiscent of an age-old trek. French rhythms have been brought over the Alps since the thirteenth century in transformational adoptions aimed at making the old new: what rhythmic implication could be more fitting to this Easter theme? The possible suggestion of francophonic meter here stretches twice across the line, addressing a pale, personified Easter as it ascends to the crucifixes. Not until the third-line question will the hendecasyllable ring clear with its *parola piana* accent falling on the tenth beat, a familiar presence in search of harsh sunlight.

"Elegia pasquale," along with "Montana" and "Atollo," which we shall touch on later, contains most succinctly the problematics of Zanzotto's early themes. This Easter egg with voided core conditions readings of all the texts that surround it, just as the event of Easter conditions western readings of time and eternity. There will be many easters in Pieve di Soligo, for Easter, in this *paesaggio*, is the emblem par excellence of the only time in which a present exists: the moment when the past is destroyed and the future does not yet hold is an act of presence (marked by absence, by an empty tomb) which takes determining power over time. This Easter present, this presence of the present, is an enigmatic moment for our driver. It is an empty time, a void, yet the only time he can "know"; it is the only time that speaks to him of his existence because it is the only time that lets him speak. Easter, for Zanzotto, begins as and remains an image of the ambiguous miracle of the empty present (an empty tomb marks new time, divides the old past from the new future) and consequently of presence defined by absence (Christ is not in the world; therefore, he is always in the world). By extension, Easter "time" is also like the dividing line between signifier and signified, a signal of difference based on an enigmatic concept of unity (λόγος 'ερχδμενος).

Alongside this temporalization, aspects of Easter can be seen which remain most strongly in our driver's heritage and which are totally in keeping with the trajectories of his most impressive movements. His attempted ascents and sudden descents, the endless ups and downs of his adventures on the slopes, are mirrored in two images of opposed directionality: the hilltop cross and the implied empty tomb are now superimposed in our reading upon the Pieve mountain and the ocean atoll.

The best crucifixions do not happen in flat places. The erection of important crosses traditionally occurs at a summit. The text here remarks this coincidence in its first verb which, we note, is in the present tense, as is the entire narration to follow. A present Easter still tinged with winter, a *pasqua ventosa*, here ascends to the crosses (and so we read of an Easter in its early stages rather than at the moment of its resolution), an Easter still pale from a winter lack of sun that perhaps continues here. The vocative personifies, calls forth a person to pale at the ascent. The harsh sun does not go, lantern-like, ahead here (the *preludio* is missing); one wonders where shadows might fall. Is this a dawn which will be completed today, in a *sera* of closure? Then the fourth line is as vague as its "contents." Without a comma between, *la vaga profezia* may be in apposition to *la rosa*, so that the rose would have been hoped for here; or this could be a run-on articulation slipping from divisible clarities to a stuttering of adjectives in which the prophecy would be both *rosa* and *vaga*.

A minimal *agnus dei*, one already beaten, scarcely presented as if in his prime, appears from marble gardens (*orti di marmo*) in lines six and following: this lamb is a veteran, one might imagine, of hard institutions meant to last forever but bearing no real fruit. Here he grazes in a less than bountiful meadow. Is this the sacrificial lamb of antiquity and the early church? Is this the done-in heritage of an evaporating hope for salvation, for some way out of what it seems that fate, or history, decrees? This miserable beast has already been had, and it now finds what might once have been the sacred promise of renewal reduced to a *scarsa primavera*.

Then, in a moment of suspended logic (what is the subject of *illumina*, this poor lamb or an Easter still to come?) which serves as a kind of syntactic metonymic link between *l'agnello flagellato* and the *pasqua ventosa* of the stanza's final line, we are presented with the enigmatic image, *i mali dei morti*. If this is a suggestion of something other than a hellish situation such as that described by Dante in *Inferno* V, 121–123 (Francesca's *nessun maggior dolore*), we may perhaps find some referent from the context. In a "scarce spring," a "pallid" Easter suggests faded hope, the faded hope, perhaps, of the present. A few verses ahead, we find three succinct lines of time: an oppressive past, an empty present, and an exalted future. These temporal surroundings are close upon the *mali* which, appearing twice, offers a doubling of sufferings only made worse by "Easter." Without losing ourselves to speculation, we may suggest that these sufferings be read as *dead* sufferings, past and progressively more accutely past; history, the narration of the past, the present hope of speaking the past, is perhaps painfully far from any "truth" of those beings for whom what we call "history" was the present, far from any clarifying revelation that Easter, traditionally, might have promised.

The next stanza, shorter by one line, condenses the problem of the *io* in time. The longest line, the first, gives a resumé of historical supposition as it centers on the *io*:

10   E se è vero che oppresso mi composero

A FIRST ROUND KNOCKOUT

They, whoever they are, may have determined a lack of freedom felt by the *io*. But the key here, as we see by going on and finding it missing, is *composero*, as much for its remote past tense as for its lexical charge. The past is the place of uncertain subjective beginnings (*se è vero*), of individual oppression (*oppresso*) and of subjective determination—even if only after death—emanating from an indeterminate other (*mi composero*). This unspoken *loro* is perhaps a kind of pluralized, distanced version of the *tu* we saw in the spring season closer to Pieve ("Primavera di Santa Augusta"); in any case, we shall find it again at the book's end. For now, suffice it to note that, if past others have determined the oppression of the *io*, they have also made its existence possible, for they have composed it, like a text. This Easter present thus historicizes the intersubjective dynamics we saw earlier, when the *io* recognized its own identity by means of its relation with the other. This historicization occurs not only because of the verb's aorist tension but also because the agent is external. History, that is, here removes causal responsibility from first persons.

From the longest line to the shortest in this stanza:

11   a questo tempo vuoto

Here, brevity would mirror a void. The present is empty, like an Easter tomb. But, like an Easter tomb, after all the oppressive composition of history, it may be an emptiness full of significance, a void holding a promise of change, a seductive cavity of now-where.

12   per l'esaltazione di domani

At this point, the identity of *io* and Christ (and hence also the lamb) is becoming more evident. The past of oppression may have climaxed in a crucifixion; the present void may be not only the implied empty tomb, but empty time between the old writing of the past and a new destiny of salvageable humanity. In any case, in the set of differences given here, the future is presented as an exaltation, a high point, a summit (where earlier there was a descent) of virtuality. Mountain and atoll, both hold exaltation in store. In the three lines which give, in rapid-fire succession, the *mise-en-abyme* image of the entire poem, and perhaps of all the "Atollo" section of *Dietro il paesaggio*, it seems significant that, of the three tenses described, only the past one is literally verbalized. *Composero* is the switch controlling all that follows. It suggests that the building blocks of history, or an otherness manifest in history's words, may determine the structure, or our perception of the structure, of both present emptiness and future elevations.

The past returns in line thirteen, but nearer than before, as the *io* describes subjective desire in an utterance which, by omission of it, almost causes to ring in our ears a familiar old *ma pur*, "Ma pur sì aspre vie né sì selvagge. . . . " The *io* takes exception in a minimal challenge to the tyranny of time; in spite of the oppression of the past, the void of the present and the exaltation of the future, the *io*, rather recently, has desired. This desire associates itself not only with Petrarch, and consequently with poetry, but also with the present. It is the first *passato prossimo* we have seen, acting almost more on the side of the present (*prossimo*, proximation, nearness) than on that of the past. (We may recall in this context that Benveniste has clearly shown the dependence of all perfect verbal forms on their simple counterparts.[19]) Desire is cloaked in a time just escaping into the already. It arrives in the presence of *questa ghirlanda*, an unexpected halo not of laurel but of wind and salt. These essences are chosen, one might suspect, because of the windy, ascendant Easter they echo (*questa ghirlanda di vento e di sale : Pasqua ventosa che sali*) in a slip at the level of the signifier, in an alliteration (*sale / sali*) that rises to the occasion.

An opposition follows; the presence implied in *questa* passes to *queste* in a move from garland to landscape, a widening of the gyre to the slopes that encourage the slips, and here, in a body that is *paesaggio*, calm another body, which is *io*, in a cradling embrace. There is a minimal broken bridge here, the missing comma, and *il mio corpo* is a crystal wound in the verse that holds a *ferita* taut at its center. After a slight pause, an hendecasyllable speaks of a moment which, like the desire, is not long ago, a moment more of the present than of history when the *io*, as if in ritual communion, takes in something superlatively pure, some bread, like the "original" sacrificial lamb, colored snow-white. This participation in a substitute sacrificial rite is contemporaneous with the desire four lines earlier: sacrifice and desire occur in one moment, loss and hope of achievement are simultaneous: the atoll, the mountain.

But subtle fevers of spring break in on this whiteness, cracking the very light of all Easter's slopes. Mountain synesthesia transforms landscape and body by confusing the attributes of each from here to the poem's sunset. In this, the longest stanza, the fevers "open the veins of hatred's frigid vines." The negative passion is released by this springtime undoing just when (in a semicolon signal of simultaneity) the *io*, having consumed the purest bread, now appropriates this landscape as its own Jerusalem—the topography (and the physiology) of Easter.

The *discrete febbri* of this stanza's first line may signal fevers in the *io* as well as in the landscape (always closely associated with the *io*) as this hallucinatory stanza, echo of early feverish visions, abuts onto a *stanza* suddenly social, peopled by birds, or people-birds, in a disdainment of the natural residues of seasonal passage. What might have been (and what might be misread as) *la belletta* is passed over in favor of a gender slip onto the superfice of vanity, *il belletto*.[20] Makeup accumulates surreally here in rooms becoming birdcages sprung open. Perhaps these signs of homey life hinge here, as in *composero*, on the remote past, *covarono*.

In yet another contrast of past preparation and present realization, where forms usually taken for granted are perceived instead as results of former oppression, this long-ago brooding process quickly undergoes a metamorphosis as *colori d'uova* brings the images of *covarono* abruptly back to a present Easter (to Easter presents, in fact) where things are rosier, where sky and earth stub their toes on one another as they vie indecisively for subject status of the enigmatic present of the verb *to be*. The unit of land- and sky-scape which is the totality of what may be beheld in this surreal confusion is now declared an unworthy shrine of its own light silences. Silence belongs elsewhere and should be honored outside of presence. The implication is, perhaps, that presence is related more to speech than to silence. Still, in this besmirched but sacred landscape, which the *io* takes as its own, as a body now belonging to itself, the *silenzio* is all that is *proprio*. Subjective status blends with surroundings, melts, muted, in a silence that, though appropriate, is misplaced. Is this a reminder of subjective fear that the other might speak in springtime, returning now to strike dumb or to hold silent a voice which anyway does not find its place, though it recognizes its body everywhere?

The last stanza is a room where the light once subjectively sought (*dov'è il crudo preludio del sole?*), later crystallized as subjective body (*il mio corpo ferita di cristallo*), and traceable from then on only in *residue nevi* or, perhaps, *colori d'uova*, is at last shut out, ray by final ray, in a present shadow:

29   Crocifissa ai raggi ultimi è l'ombra

It is a shadow in the present: è; it is the image of a summit sacrifice at the end of a unit of time. But, as time runs out, the present itself is sacrificed, given up, to persist in shadowy form, as a signal of something else. Like a beginning, the present is intangible and exists only to delineate, to give shape to "weres" and "will bes." In this crucifix shadow, in this darkness streaming from the summit, human features and organs are assimilated into a great crucifixion synesthesia which dilutes by metonymic degrees; *sangue* leads to *cuori, cuori* return to the landscape with *neve, mani* nestle slyly within *immagini* which are images of the landscape time, *sera*. This is a time of ending, but it is still the present, a sickly, dimming present which encloses its unprotesting victims in a final synesthetic cradling, a *seno*. The void of the present, a present taking presence only as *ombra*, a shadow figure in the place of an empty tomb, a signal of otherness in an empty time. This is the lament of the *io* for the Easter that barely lays claim to a dividing-line presence only to lose it immediately in all directions to the surrounding landscape of melting snows and unworthy silences. Here has been sung the lament for a present which could change the world, a song that departs with a final image—of an image.

Immagini of *mani* insists on visual trickery: not hands, but their images. Our imagination. And we have in fact been reading, throughout this crucifixion poem, not of crosses (*croci*) but of their images (*crocifissi*). The difference between *cross* or *croce* and *crucifix* or *crocifisso*, as English and Italian dictionaries concur, is that *cross* / *croce* is the sign for the object itself, while *crucifix* / *crocifisso* is the sign for the image of the object. The elegy here is not for some "real" Easter but for an "image" of Easter, for a sign, that is, or a word, that could indicate or even somehow contain presence *in absentia*. It is an elegy for a signifier that would abolish the bar between itself and its signified, for a presence that would abolish present, past, and future, for a word that would make itself. *Crocifisso*, the central image here, is an image of an image. It is presence twice removed, absent twice: not here, but there; not there, but behind. It is a shadow at the summit, the atoll on the mountain. From here, as our fallen but exalted driver has demonstrated, there's nowhere to go but (up and) down.

The entire first section of *Dietro il paesaggio*, in fact, is a series of these ascents and descents. The "Atollo" is characterized, in contrast to the two sections which follow it, by its narrations of subjective (mis)adventures in landscapes which verge on the hallucinatory, in mountainous regions which are suddenly, by a twist of metaphor, transformed to tropical realms. From the accidentally initiated divine knockout, from our passive driver's initiation into the exaltation of poetry, meaning refuses to be relegated to one realm alone. The process of poetic signification here not only takes as its province the traditional functions of linguistic signs (and, notably in this book, rhetorical devices), but also exposes the beginnings of the almost surrealistic textual tinkerings that open chasms of new signifying possibilities and will later become Zanzotto's stylistic trademark. We have attempted to show some of these devices, "slips," as we have called them, in the three poems we have presented here. *Dietro* as a "slip" from a Petrarchan *dentro*, for example, gives an idea of Zanzotto's literary referentiality and predilections. Then, the possible referential ambiguity in a passage like *e dal tuo volto vinto da morte / il mio conosco* demonstrates how ambiguity can add rather than confuse meaning. Finally, the expanding possibilities of signification and referentiality caused by a gender substitution, as when *il belletto* appears in a landscape context where one might more readily expect *la belletta*, slides the entire image into a realm of fantasy and surreal juxtapositions.

We might pause at this point to consider, on a cue from Marziano Guglielminetti, the remarkable economics of rhetoric in these early texts.[21] Even in the three single poems read here, we may already note the presence of such devices as anaphora, anadiplosis, the vocative, and the polysyndeton characteristic of some hypotactic procedures. Such potentially coercive stylistics have had perhaps no primary importance in poetic texts since the early part of the century, if then. Yet they are dug up from the past and replanted in *Dietro il paesaggio* with no excuses. Apposition is used in "Arse il motore," for example, to elaborate the *figura* image prior to its resolution as *io* in *aspettai*; the reader "waits" for the verb in a process of stylistic suspension mirroring the referent of the verb itself. Another mirroring similar to that created by this apposition is found at a more literal level in "Primavera di Santa Augusta" where, as we noted earlier, the moon reflects itself by immediate repetition over the line's *terminus*: *luna / luna*, an anadiplosis suggestive of the referent upon which it insists, of the very essence, in fact, of the object. In the first poem, the use of the vocative provides a vivid moment of encounter between an ancient rhetorico-poetic device and a modern, surreal sensitivity. *O ruote e carri alti come luna* is a vocative, not an apostrophe; the addressees of such a cry must be present, and so we find a call to carts and wheels, objects that, in spite of an assumed inability to hear or respond, at least fill a requirement of "being there" according to the poem's narrative fiction.

In more than one case, then, even in a relatively small sampling of texts from this beginning book, we discern a typically Zanzottan procedure. At the same moment that he recuperates a traditional rhetorical device from pre-experimental usage for his own post-hermetic poetic utterance, he undermines and minimalizes the traditional impact of that device by a kind of reverse telescoping. He swings it, so to speak, into a twentieth-century environment notably lacking (in an absence that might prove helpful, as Hölderlin suggested some time ago) in gods. A similar encounter of rhetorical device and Zanzottan minimalization of concept occurs even with the opening apostrophe of "Elegia pasquale" where Easter is personified, characterized as pale and desperate, and addressed directly in a question that ends abruptly, leaving no room for response but rather providing a dramatic introduction to the narrative that follows. It is this coincidence, which occurs many times throughout *Dietro il paesaggio*, this encounter of device chock-full of traditional motivation and lexicon charged with no respect for that fullness, that leads us to suggest a modified version of a statement made by Guglielminetti with regard to this book: He says, " . . . dovrebbe subito risultare evidente che Zanzotto nel decennio '40-'50 non ha sottratto il linguaggio poetico ai limiti assegnatigli dai manuali di retorica. . . ."[22] If Zanzotto's first published texts made use of some devices which are described in manuals of rhetoric, it is less with the result of confining his poetic discourse to manual-set limits than rendering those very manuals, if not obsolete, at least in need of new editions in the face of his subversive, minimalizing processes of signification through stylistics.

For all its demonstration of unique applications of stylistic or rhetorical devices, for all its sounding of the Italian literary past in order to form a contemporary poetic lexicon, and for all its indications of images which will continue to be significant in later books. *Dietro il paesaggio* also has a story to tell. Not surprisingly, this story (which, as we have seen, makes no claims to being history) is constantly revolving around or within landscapes as well as "persons"—first, second, and third persons, in fact. We will consider the pronouns later. For now, a look at the landscapes.

From the occurrence of place-names in the titles of poems here, from titles which, though not actual place-names, indicate places, and from the two brief, unassuming notes furnished by the author at the end of the book, our reading is encouraged to chart a kind of topographical sequence. But "Primavera di Santa Augusta," "L'Acqua di Dolle" [The water of Dolle], "Declivio su Lorna" [Lorna's slope], and "Lorna" lose little of their vague place-name allure in Zanzotto's nonspecific note, "Santa Augusta, Dolle, Lorna, San Fedele: nomi di località" [place-names]. These actual places in the vicinity of Pieve di Soligo are left as nominal indications that take on additional significance in the texts as points of reference, surroundings or *loci* for the personal pronouns. Their actuality as place-names, that is, contributes to an illusion that referents of those pronouns might be located.

Other titles of poems, such as "Via di miseri" [Road of the wretches], "Montana" [Mountain], "Atollo" [Atoll], "Le case che camminano sulle acque" [The houses that walk on water], "Grido sul lago" [Cry on the lake], "Nel mio paese" [In my town], "Al di là"

[Over there], "Là cercando" [Seeking there], "Là sul ponte" [There on the bridge], "In basso" [Down below], "Al bivio" [At the crossroads], "Dietro il paesaggio," and "Nella valle" [In the valley] contribute further to the ambiguity of the topography the titular place-names paradoxically spur our reading to chart. To situate or confuse things even more, seasons are also signalled in titles: "Primavera di Santa Augusta," "Elegia Pasquale," "Equinozale" [Equinoctial]. Furthermore, times of day and night and weather conditions also appear as title-clues in a textual landscape that grows more external and, by traditional allusion, more internal as it becomes more detailed: "Indizi e luna" [Signs and moon], "Là sovente nell'alba" [There, often, at dawn], "Balsamo, bufera" [Balm, storm], "Notte di guerra, a tramontana" [Night of war, in the north], "Quanta notte" [So much night], and "L'amore infermo del giorno" [The infirm love of the day]. With their teasing hints at possible locations, relative positions, and times, then, the titular landscapes create the situation, in both senses of the word, of the pronouns.

The clearest signposts of the story's "progression," however, if we may call it that for now, are perhaps the section titles. "Atollo," with all its contradictory juxtaposition to the mountain landscapes woven into so many of the texts of that section, is followed by a section the title of which, and the central placement of which in the book's tripartite division, utilizes the literary lexicon we mentioned in an allusion to Dante. "Sponda al sole" suggests an arrival, after "Atollo," at some place holding, if not the promise of redemption as in the *Purgatorio,* at least the suggestion of some more peaceful alternative to the hallucinatory, disorienting landscapes of the opening section. Finally, the enigma of the book's title is echoed as if in sonata-form resolution as the title of its final section, where the return of *Dietro il paesaggio* may tempt a reading to go "there" first, to see how it ends, or where it all arrives.

"Dietro il paesaggio" repeats rather than resolves the initial enigma, however, the enigma resembling that of Apollo, that of poetry and, in a closely related way, also that of painting. In Western art, Italian painters were the first to attempt the representation of landscapes. In many of these representations, Lorenzetti's, for example, there is an eerie absence of persons. Yet, soon after the beginnings of landscape painting, landscapes, even those at times hallucinatory and unrealistic, like Leonardo's, fade into the background, ceding *primo piano* status to human figures considered more suitable for central representation by a philosophy calling itself humanistic. Zanzotto obfuscates this historical perspective. He puts the landscape in the foreground and depicts his personages in the shifting guise of pronouns at times expressing the desire to go behind or beyond what, in past times, seemed already to be always behind or beyond. In this way, identities of landscape and human figures are blurred: if the landscape is in the foreground, is the *io*, for example, already behind it? The notion of perspective has been challenged, and, as we mentioned earlier, the situation (*situs*) of the landscape and the situation of the pronouns are the same.

To return to the story, a kind of circular movement becomes discernible within the three part structure of *Dietro il paesaggio*. If "Atollo" is an account of the *io*'s poetic knockout in a landscape offering no assurances—an account, in other words, of the *io*'s sudden thrust into a world of unordinary meanings—it is not simply the declaration of a writer's encounter with the traditional muse. It is, rather, the onset of a contradictory awareness of both the vast possibilities of signification and the drastic impossibility of signification. It is the entry into a world where everything has meaning and where any attempt to "mean" something may risk falling into nonsense. "Atollo" is a story of distress and disorientation, of disappointed expectations, unexpected exaltation, and fears of successful communication, as we have seen emblematically in "Arse il motore," "Primavera di Santa Augusta," and "Elegia Pasquale."

When the "Sponda al sole" is reached, however, an abrupt change occurs. Here, first of all, is the epigraph from Hölderlin: "Ihr teuern Ufer, die mich erzogen einst" [Dear riverbanks that once reared me and taught me],[23] an evocation not only of a landscape and hence a location, but also of a childhood place of security and nurturing, a place of the *io*'s past. The first text here, in fact, is "Nel mio paese" [In my town], an account of the return of the *io* to a place of origins so free of conflict that, in a stylistic mimetization of the manifest "content," rhyme appears not only literally but also as a metaphor of elemental concord:

> Del mio ritorno scintillano i vetri
> ed i pomi di casa mia,
> le colline sono per prime
> al traguardo madido dei cieli,
> tutta l'acqua d'oro è nel secchio
> tutta la sabbia nel cortile
> e fanno rime con le colline.[24]

15

> 　　　　[The windows and doorknobs of my house
> 　　　　sparkle at my return,
> 　　　　the hills are the first to arrive
> 15　　　at the skies' damp winning-post,
> 　　　　all the golden water is in the bucket
> 　　　　all the sand in the courtyard
> 　　　　and everything rhymes with the hills.]

Here everything is in its place in a shining, full scene, a kind of glowing renovation of Pascolian domesticity. In the opening lines of this poem, we see that the *io* has effectuated this return by giving itself over to primary processes, in this case those of dreams, which are not personal but universal:

> 　　　　Leggeri ormai sono i sogni,
> 　　　　da tutti amato
> 　　　　con essi io sto nel mio paese,
> 　　　　mi sento goloso di zucchero;[25]

> 　　　　[By now my dreams are light;
> 　　　　beloved by everyone,
> 　　　　I remain with them in my town,
> 　　　　I feel a craving for sugar;]

The landscapes in this section of the book, while evoking childhood desires of the *io*, also present an image of the other, the *tu*, in a state of innocence which, in turn, elicits childlike innocence from the landscape itself. This unusual mirroring, with its Petrarchan interplay of state of mind and state of surroundings, is yet another step toward the identity of pronoun and landscape which characterizes the entire book and, as we have seen, is not limited to the first person we met in "Arse il motore" or "Elegia pasquale," but also includes *tu*, as in "Primavera di Santa Augusta," and others elsewhere as well. We see another instance of this identification in "Al di là" [Over there], which begins,

> 　　　　Al di là tu falci e componi
> 　　　　le gentili somiglianze dei fiori
> 　　　　al di là non è sazia
> 　　　　mai la tua fame di bambina
> 5　　　ed hai la mela e il ghiaccio vegetale,
> 　　　　là ti punge al polso la tua bussola

A FIRST ROUND KNOCKOUT

>   per indicarti la stella
>   ch'è il tuo vero gemello;[26]

and continues several lines on,

>   È per te che la gioia dei paesi
> 20 liberamente va imitando
>   i tuoi semplici atti;
>   e per te questa terra non è
>   che un mite minuto satellite
>   che ben sa dove si dirige.[27]

◻

>   [Over there you mow and compose
>   the amiable likenesses of flowers
>   over there your little-girl hunger
>   is never satisfied
>   and you have the apple and the vegetable frost,
>   there your compass pricks at your wrist
>   to show you the star
>   that is your true twin;
>
>   . . .
>
>   It's for you that the joy of villages
> 20 freely imitates
>   your simple acts;
>   and for you this earth is nothing more
>   than a meek minute satellite
>   which knows very well where it's headed.]

Traditional notions of cause and effect are confused here. When the *io* finds himself in the company of dreams in his place of origin, that place creates a childlike sense of well-being for him. In an opposite but complementary movement, however, when the *tu* is imagined as *bambina*, the place of childhood imitates her simplicity. This ambidirectional oneiric causality is part of the story of how protagonists and settings, by gradually losing their separate distinctive identities and even functions (here in a dream-like confusion of realistic expectations), eventually place nothing less than their own assumptions of separate existence into question. Examples of this accumulate throughout the book, as we shall see.

   The dream-return to the supposedly concordant landscapes of childhood is not without its sinister moments, however, moments that threaten like approaching storms in Pascoli. The light that causes windows to sparkle at the *io*'s return in "Nel mio paese," for example, becomes a "blond rain" and takes on a sharpness appropriate to harvest time in "Là cercando." There, in the place vaguely designated as "là," death suddenly appears in the pathetic image of a buried child, while the landscape itself is painted as both fecund and threatening, like a promise one hopes will never be kept. In this mixing, the fruits of the landscape are made joyful by the child's buried body; the landscape is a tomb, a *melange* of the human and the vegetal. The border between these realms is obscured, and *tu* is *erba*:

```
       Là cercando
       si nutrivano di bionde piogge
       volpi, e splendevano
       d'astuzia nel profondo
5      dei cimiteri e delle vigne
       oltre il cielo stagione senza senso.
       Luci armate di falce discendevano
       per la miope foresta delle erbe,
       la falce si appiattava
10     nell'erba che tu
       da tanti anni eri divenuta,
       le uve e le mele si allietavano
       del ricciolo di un bimbo sepolto
       e il lago era il colore mai toccato
15     il colore non usato
       mai né da piogge né da falci.[28]
```

◻

```
       [Seeking there
       foxes fed themselves on blond rains
       and gleamed
       with cunning in the depth
5      of the cemeteries and the vineyards
       beyond the meaningless-season sky
       Scythe-armed lights descended
       through the nearsighted forest of grass,
       the scythe was lurking
10     in the grass that you
       for so many years had become,
       the grapes and the apples grew happy
       on the curls of a buried child
       and the lake was the never-touched color
```

| 15 | the color never used
either by rains or by scythes.] |

Both the feminine *tu* who had already "turned to grass" (vv. 10–11) and the dead child, others with whom the *io* identifies its own past, are depicted in a contaminatory metonymy of human and plant forms, in yet another blurring of the distinction between persons and landscape.

Coupled with this iconoclastically integrated appearance of *mors in arcadia*, and in a kind of consolatory compensation for the distancing from childhood innocence experienced even in this "Sponda al sole" [Riverbank in the sunlight], are moments promising integration for the *io* through an implied erotism. The erotism takes form, as does every other movement in the story, in the landscape. In "L'Acqua di Dolle," for example, the womanly and suggestive mountain shapes near Pieve, in a reversal of the *io*'s usual patterns of regression, provide a shadowy alternative to the innocent sunshine of childhood as they gush forth the water which holds celebration and contact with the other in store (we may recall once again the spring floods that *tu* can unleash in "Primavera di Santa Augusta"). Simultaneously (and in another echo of the "Primavera" poem), the solitude that the *io* desires both to keep and to lose is threatened. We cite in full this text as a prelude to the moment when the *io* will come to find a different rapport with the past.

>   Ora viene a consolarmi
>   con una lunga visita
>   l'acqua di Dolle
>   che portò dieci colline al paese
> 5   sfuggì tra le api e i lor castelli di acume
>   toccò le forme sensitive
>   di un'isola di pura sabbia,
>   ora viene quest'acqua ch'io sospiro
>   perché traspare dalle tue
> 10 membra gemelle;
>   perché a lungo
>   indugiò nello scrigno d'ombra
>   dove il fico s'affaccia guardiano
>   e il sole non fa piú musco né felce,
> 15 dove sono già aperte
>   le scene da festa del cielo.
>   Acqua ignara della creta
>   che già fuoresce dai suoi viluppi,

fiera del rosso momentaneo
20 dei fiori celebrati da quest'ora,
tu vai dovunque lambendo e tentando
le piú ritrose solitudini:
lasciatemela mia,
per la mia lampadina di chiocciola
25 per l'orto di che il nano è mezzadro,
lei dal fittissimo alfabeto
lei che ha i messaggi
di nobili invasioni
degli astri che ritornano dalle alpi
30 ormai pingui d'argento,
lei che va promettendo
una notte fresca come un domani.[29]

◘

[Now to console me
with a long visit
comes the water of Dolle
that brought ten hills to the village
5 escaped among the bees and their castles of keenness
touched the sensitive shapes
of an island of pure sand,
now comes this water I long for
because it shines forth from your twin limbs;
10 because for a long time
it lingered in the shadow's coffer
where the fig tree appears as guardian
and the sun no longer makes moss or fern,
where the sky's festive scenes
15 have already opened.
Water ignorant of the clay
that already overflows its entanglements,
proud of the transient red
of the flowers this hour celebrates,
20 you go everywhere skimming and probing
the shyest solitudes:
let my water stay with me,
for my little snail's lamp
for the garden whose sharecropper is the dwarf,
25 this water, she of densest alphabet
she who has messages
of noble invasions

of the stars returning from the Alps
rich by now with silver,
30   she who keeps promising
a night as fresh as a tomorrow.]

The *io* asks the others to leave him his share of water (*lasciatemela mia*). Then, in "solitude," the *io* will still have the company of the minimal guiding light for the snail-like pace with which he can reduce big stories—history, in fact (*i messaggi / di nobili invasioni*)—to dwarf-like stature. The watery erotic sweep into the realm of the other (formally mirrored here by sentence length and the shunning, rare in this book, of stanzaic divisions) carries, as always, the risk of change. When confronted by this risk, the *io* begs to be left in a watery place where there is room only for *lei*, an indicator, like *là*, of somewhere or someone else, outside the circle of direct communication (*lei dal fittissimo alfabeto / lei che ha i messaggi / di nobili invasioni / . . . lei che va promettendo / una notte fresca come un domani*). This watery landscape seems to contain many possibilities of signification (*fittissimo alfabeto*), of a reductive writing making fairy-tale messages of Alpine or astral movements and Austrian invasions. Such controllable (writable) reductivity appears as one with an onrush of "invading" erotic presence; it both suggests a reassuring stasis and an emanation of floodings from the other. In any case, the *io*, in his little place, will not be swept away. The longed-for night may well be one of passion and present loss of self in the presence of the other. It is also *fresca*; it looks toward the future.

Yet this night is central to the section bearing the sun in its title, "Sponda al sole," where the sun-related images may provide a key to the mutable temporal situation of the *io*. In Zanzotto's landscapes, the sun is of pivotal importance; not only does it provide the light which renders the landscape visible, but it also allows for the play and variation which change the appearance of the landscape.

There are several large groups of images which relate either metaphorically or metonymically to the image of the sun. Mirror images may be considered among those metonymically related. In a poetic discourse where the identity of *io* and *tu* are ambiguous and in both complementary and contradictory rapport with each other, it is not surprising to find mirror images. Some are literal as in "Indizi e luna," where we read, *La verde sera al suo specchio s'adorna* [the green evening adorns herself at her mirror]; or as in "Là sovente nell'alba," where we find *Tra i monti specchi eccelsi del primordio* [among the mountains, lofty mirrors of the primordial]; or, further, in "Elianto"

[Helianthus], with, *camminò negli specchi e nei boschi* [it walked in the mirrors and the woods]. Others are figurative, such as images of the moon, snow as a reflecting agent, or twins (as in "Arse il motore," "Indizi e luna," "Là sovente nell'alba," "Via di miseri," "Elegia pasquale," "Serica" [Silky], "Balsamo, bufera," "Montana," "Notte di guerra, a tramontana," "Quanta notte," "Reliquia" [Relic], "Oro effimero e vetro" [Ephemeral gold and glass], "Al di là," "L'Acqua di Dolle," "Lorna," "L'Amore infermo del giorno," "Là sul ponte," "Equinozale," "La fredda tromba" [The cold trumpet], "Perché siamo" [That we may be], "Al bivio," "Immacolata" [The immaculate one]). We should also recall, as an integral part of this series of mirror-type images, the intricate superimposition of mountain and atoll effected in the book's first section, for that superimposition is an example par excellence of the reversal and reproduction which occur simultaneously in a mirror image.

While the play of identity and difference suggested by such mirror images has more specific reference to Lacanian thought in Zanzotto's later *Vocativo* than it does in *Dietro il paesaggio*, we nonetheless notice that, even in Zanzotto's early work, mirror images occur as figures of the *io*'s relation with the other. Sometimes, as we have seen, that other is designated directly as *tu* and, at other times, it is designated less directly as a landscape or some aspect of a landscape (or all of these). This imagery thus recurrently emphasizes a dynamic of identity and difference at work between the subject and the other which resembles the dynamic Lacan calls the mirror stage. We may, with chronology of thought in mind, think of these notions as being as much Zanzottan as Lacanian. In any case, they demonstrate a kinship of convictions arrived at, by Zanzotto, via a poetic investigation of the workings of language and, by Lacan, a psychoanalytic one. Poetry easily appears, then, as an analysis of the psyche of language. And *Dietro il paesaggio*, as we shall see when considering some of Zanzotto's later books, especially *Vocativo*, is a detailed "preparation" of some now familiar post-Freudian terrain.

To return to the "Sponda al sole," however, we may note that the sun images that occur throughout *Dietro il paesaggio*, and that, as we mentioned, render the landscape visible to varying degrees, seem also to be closely connected to change. In Zanzotto's light imagery, the presence of the sun creates the possibility of shadow and hence of variation, subtlety, differences in perspective, and the passage of time. These images are opposed, therefore, to the mirroring images that suggest repetition and loss of self-other differentiation through identification, for the literal sun images allow the self to cast a shadow and thus to gain visual reassurance of its own presence while marking the present time with a comfortingly visible trace. In "Quanta notte," we find one of the most direct examples of this procedure at the end of the second stanza: *e il sole mi ha ricordato / mi ha distinto / da me stesso e dal mondo* [and the sun remembered me / distinguished me / from myself and the world].[30] The opposition of sun images to mirror images is not a neat one, however, for one of the most often used mirror images (as we saw in "Arse il motore," for example) is that of the moon, whose light, of course, is nothing more than what it reflects from the sun. This connection between seemingly opposed imagery of similarity and difference adds to the ambiguity of yet another supposed distinction, like that of person and landscape, or of *io* and *tu*.

Differences in landscape are often suggested by the simple device of a single adjective describing the sun. In "Montana," we read of *un sole acquatico* [a watery sun], for example; *un sole estraneo* [an alien sun] sets the stage in "Reliquia"; "Nel mio paese" contains *il sole limpido* [the limpid sun]. In this sunny realm, but without attempting to analyze all the occurrences of shadow imagery and the differentiating possibilities it holds, (we may recall our reading of "Elegia pasquale" as an example), we might pause for a moment at the moment of no shadow, at noonday. For if it is the sun that offers possibilities of shadow, of assurance of presence, of variation in Zanzotto's landscapes, that same sun at noon robs for an instant all it previously gave and subsequently will give again. Like an Easter, which by its emptiness defines a present and separates past history from future hope, the noonday sun, by casting no shadows, creates a moment of presence which, unlike past or future, neither promises nor leaves a trace. At noontime there is too much light, and the life-giving force becomes a threat to differentiation, like the speech of the other in "Primavera di Santa Augusta." This threatening aspect of the midday sun connects Zanzotto's early midday images to his more directly erotic images of landscape and water, which, as we have seen, are also threats to subjective differentiation. Images of midday are not always erotic, however, in Zanzotto's work; they occur in decidedly nonerotic contexts in *Vocativo*, for example, as Nicolas Perella has remarked.[31]

In our glance at Zanzotto's sun, we shall turn back for a moment to the first, "Atollo," section, to present in its entirety the namesake poem of that part of *Dietro il paesaggio*. In this text, a lazy sun has devoured differences which might offer tenuous shelter for more differences in turn, so dear to the *io* and so necessary both to its sense of its own past, a minimal past outside history, and to an utterance which is originally the mother tongue. These differences, the *fragili Italie*, may be considered linguistic in nature. Among other remnants of childhood, they may be, in fact, the language of that time of life, the dialects protected now only by childhood-related imagination, castles of sand—in verses which stand, moreover, as a fragile monument at times to both Montale—*già stringe il muro e il cortile* rings with "Meriggiare pallido e assorto" from *Ossi di seppia*—and Ungaretti—*le clausole / della mia memoria infelice* brings to mind "La morte meditata" in *Sentimento del tempo*. (In recalling, also, Ungaretti's favorable review of Zanzotto's first book, we may imagine that its "Ungarettian" aspects did not escape the reviewer's attention.) Here is the text:

>   Un sole che con oziosi giri
>   sedusse e divorò l'ombra del mondo
>   e crebbe sui giorni e sui mesi
>   già stringe il muro ed il cortile
> 5   scruta le differenze d'ago
>   della sabbia dei piccoli castelli
>   e brilla da mille bandiere
>   da scudi e da porte
>   dagli angoli dei morti.
> 10   Tra quei precari monumenti,
>   io là vi collocai, fragili Italie
>   i cui minuti segmenti
>   avido sale stinse,
>   la brace là s'indovina
> 15   dell'insetto e del libro,
>   là tra giochi vuoti e pericoli
>   al silenzio si appoggiano le clausole
>   della mia memoria infelice
>   e monti decrepiti affidano
> 20   alla sabbia insensibili sfaceli,
>   la sabbia senza parsimonia
>   colma i volti e i sorrisi
>   spegne l'oro dei suoni.
>
>   Già il sole penetra per le
> 25   cieche gallerie delle finestre
>   sugge e scinde gli ultimi
>   legami della mia sostanza.³²

▫

>   [A sun that in lazy circlings
>   seduced and devoured the world's shadow
>   and grew over days and over months
>   already presses in on the wall and the courtyard

5	scrutinizes the needle-like differences
	of the sand of the small castles
	and shines from a thousand flags
	from shields and doors
	from the corners of the dead.
10	Among those precarious monuments
	there I placed you, fragile Italies,
	whose minute segments
	greedy salt discolored,
	there are foretold
15	the insect's ember, and the book's,
	there among empty games and dangers
	the clauses of my unhappy memory
	lean on silence
	and decrepit mountains entrust
20	imperceptible dissolutions to the sand,
	the unsparing sand
	fills faces and smiles
	extinguishes the gold of sounds.
	Already the sun penetrates
25	the blind window-tunnels
	it sucks and splits the last
	ties of my substance.]

If we return to the middle section of Zanzotto's book, "Sponda al sole," we find the noontide once again, this time in "Con dolce curiosità" [With sweet curiosity], which in the book follows directly the "Acqua di Dolle" we read earlier. This "sweet curiosity" poem describes a small mill near Pieve in an image evoking both the passing of time with the repetitive turning of its wheel and time which is past with its outmoded technology. The *io* here is not free from one of the well-established clichés of modern Italian literature, however, as this *occhialuto uomo* evinces a kind of acceptance of his somehow changed position in relation to the landscape.[33] The final two stanzas show how he will now try to use the light, how time has placed him in a new relation to it:

	Forse è tempo di metter gli occhiali
	per diventar familiari
	con le distanze e i puntigli del vetro,
	forse chi computa
35	ha già un errore in eccesso

per il meriggio celeste fiammifero
per la mano golosa che tocca
i larghi petali del miele

Ecco l'acqua risolta nei suoi sorsi
40 e il mulino
nelle sue molle d'orologio
e gli uomini della calura
nei lor modesti vizi d'orecchio e di gola;
di me si giova la luce per vedere
45 il fico va sillabando dolcezza
il carbone sotterra allarga
le sue piume di struzzo;
conduciamo la ghiaia a bere
a piccoli sorsi,
50 dissetiamoci alla notte,
inventiamo una fanciulla
educabile al vento alla frescura,
dissetiamoci all'ombra di giglio della sua mente.[34]

◘

[Perhaps it's time to put on our spectacles
in order to become familiar
with the distances and ostentations of glass,
perhaps he who reckons
35 already makes one mistake too many
for the blue matchstick noon
for the tasting hand that touches
honey's wide petals.

Here is the water settled in its drops
40 and the mill
in its watchsprings
and the heat-dried men
in their modest vices of ear and throat;
the light uses me to see,
45 the fig tree keeps whispering sweetness,
the underground coal fans out
its ostrich feathers;
we lead the gravel to drink
sip by sip,
50 we quench our thirst with the night,
we invent a girl
who can learn the wind the coolness,

we quench our thirst with the lily-shadow
of her mind.]

As the "Sponda al sole" section begins to draw to a close with this text, a kind of peaceful internalization of light has been experienced by the *io*: *di me si giova la luce per vedere*. Fantasy, invention, imagination may come into play along with this eyeglassed observation. *Noi*, a confraternity perhaps or in any case a socializing pluralization of *io*, will invent a non-menacing other, a *fanciulla*-object for a sylvan version of Pygmalion's project. From Apollo to Pygmalion: the dream of capture gives way to one of invention. In this purgatory-like context, however, we may read the *io*'s self-identification with others (*noi*) and the imagination as elements in a peaceful resolution, as an arrival at some alternative to the hallucinatory ups and downs of the "Atollo" mountain landscape.

In the final section of *Dietro il paesaggio*, we arrive at a series of landscapes that differ markedly from the earlier ones. Something changes in the *io*. To prepare for our own "arrival" in "Dietro il paesaggio," however, we should mention that the two poems which close "Sponda al sole," "Declivio su Lorna" and "Lorna," the former in free verse and the latter in the measured pace of unrhymed quatrains, are among the most thematically encyclopedic of the middle section. In these texts, the mountain, Lorna, is indistinguishable from a woman ("Lorna" may echo "Laura" in the rarefied air; we should forego no possibilities of referentiality): the landscape is the other, sometimes present as *tu*, sometimes elsewhere as *lei*. *Tu*, however, is reserved for Lorna in "Declivio su Lorna" while, in "Lorna," Lorna's pronoun is most likely *lei*, and *tu* serves as an index of the populated landscape—the valley, the town, the marketplace. The other is thus indicated as the ensemble of people in the landscape, and the landscape thereby becomes an imminent object of joyful, if not always simple, love in the poem's final lines.

In addition, both of these poems contain a metaphor that works as a leitmotif throughout Zanzotto's work: birds as the last repositories of disappearing dialect speech. Not far from these birds are images, also constant, of traps, snares, and other entanglements placed by man to disturb traumatically the natural order of small-scale forest life. Water also appears, but here in "Declivio su Lorna" its potentially erotic charge is deactivated in a regressive movement toward a childhood of timid beginnings. Similarly, in the same text, the sun is an *innocuo lume* surrounding innocent childhood games.

The *io* finds peaceful rapport with the landscape's (and the woman's) otherness by retreating into it or behind it (*sul colle meno visibile* in "Declivio su Lorna"), back to a time when it held more promise than threat, more cherries, chrysanthemums, and harvest times than accidents, springtime floods, and hallucinatory holidays. Here is the text of "Declivio su Lorna":

> Mese di pochi giorni,
> o tu dalla docile polpa,
> chiaro collo curioso
> seno caldo che nutre,
> 5 dolce uva nella gola,
> teneri uccelli che si districano
> dai vischi della lontananza
> e che indugiano audacemente
> tra gli equilibri delle dita
> 10 a illustrare le loro piume
> e le loro gioie minute,
> uccelli disingannati,
> maiuscoli pavoni delle siepi,
> aiole come mazzi improvvisati,
> 15 laghi dallo stupore di goccia:
> ogni albero ha dietro di sé
> l'ombra sua bene abbigliata,
> paradisi di crisantemi
> si addensano in climi azzurri.
>
> 20 Ho raccolto la foglia di colore
> e la ciliegia dimenticata
> sul colle meno visible;
> infanzia raccolta acino ad acino,
> infanzia sapido racimolo,
> 25 la formica ha consumato il gusto
> mutato della ciliegia,
> l'acqua movenza timida
> inizia radici.
>
> Tra le folle ricciute delle vendemmie
> 30 la frescura guasta ed apre
> l'innocuo lume del sole
> alle rapine svagate dei bimbi.[35]

> [Month of few days,
> oh you of the docile flesh,
> clear curious neck

             warm nurturing breast,
5   sweet grape in the throat,
             tender birds who untangle themselves
             from the snares of distance
             and audaciously linger
             among finger balancings
10   to elucidate their feathers
             and their minute joys,
             disenchanted birds,
             enormous peacocks of the hedges,
             flowerbeds like improvised bouquets,
15   lakes made from droplet's stupor:
             each tree has behind it
             its well-adorned shadow,
             chrysanthemum paradises
             thicken in blue climes.

20   I have gathered the colored leaf
             and the forgotten cherry
             upon the least visible hill;
             infancy gathered grape by grape,
             infancy savory cluster,
25   the ant has consumed the changed
             taste of the cherry,
             the water, timid gesture,
             starts up roots.

             Among the curly-haired crowds of the grape harvests
30   the coolness breaks and opens
             the sun's harmless light
             to the carefree robberies of children.]

We should remark in passing how the second stanza turns on the sound *-ci-*: *ciliegia* continues, through alliteration and assonance, two lines later in the iterated *acino,* which in turn resounds in the following line as *racimolo,* passes once more through *ciliegia* two lines later, and finally ends with a beginning in *radici*. This is an example of the way in which Zanzotto allows sounds to lead towards signification: the *-ci-* sound, once begun, makes a round from "cherry" to "roots" in a series of images of infancy. The phonetic structural basis for this stanza exemplifies a favorite technique of the author, one which will often recur, especially in more highly condensed versions suggesting shared but false etymologies.

In "Lorna," the final poem of the middle section, the sun no longer has a center, and questioning the secrets of hidden or salvaged things (*il perché dei monti rimasti addietro*) is now in vain. Some harshness has either disappeared or been ignored (or repressed) in this voluptuous and all-encompassing Lorna-land. Here, in an image of netted birds which will come to mind again in *Filò*, the sweetness of being misunderstood becomes clearer when one remembers that, in this context, those who fail to understand are the captors; the captives retain their unique identity at least on a linguistic level in spite of their lack of freedom. (In one of the many contexts in which a reading of this poem may occur, it would take but a short step from this image to arrive at a parable of the linguistic and political situation of preunification Italy in the nineteenth century, or to Zanzotto's sense of his own linguistic situation in the twentieth.)

Here is an autumn sun, but even this (by association ripe, or wise) sun may not know Lorna the way the *io* does, in sweetly erotic stanzas uncannily opposed to the sun-drenched erotism of something like D'Annunzio's famous dithyrambs. "Lorna" gives us a moment of immersion of *io* in the otherness of the landscape or the other person, the joy of finding company in this moment, and a kind of *piccole cose* familiarity. This is a new version of poetic exaltation: *ogni giovane mosto arde e s'esalta*. At this high point, there is also a new light of accord: *ogni fuoco è giardino ogni strumento / s'accorda al nuovo tocco del sole*. A new aspect of Zanzotto's poetics will follow.

> Una luce senza centro spazia
> già la terra attutisce labbra rosse
> e bambini, negli eremi fragili
> dell'aria si raccolgono api e stelle;
>
> 5   e già vano è chiedere alle alluvioni
> il perché dei monti rimasti addietro
> il perché delle zinnie che si dissetano
> al gelo dei chiostri di Lorna.
>
> Tra gli esempi compiuti delle notti
> 10 e le rugiade ordinate e le foglie
> trapassate un instabile miele
> definisce il suo zodiaco d'oro.
>
> Ma non c'è voce d'uccello preso
> nei lacci esigui delle cacce
> 15 nei riflessi allegri delle nevi
> che dolce non trovi esser fraintesa,

A FIRST ROUND KNOCKOUT

        ogni giovane mosto arde e s'esalta
        liberato dalle prigioni,
        ogni fuoco e giardino ogni strumento
20   s'accorda al nuovo tocco del sole.

        Sole piú piccolo piú umile
        perché ti lodarono da tutte le parti:
        che sapesti di lei, della sua voce,
        della sua bocca segreto di menta?

25   Uccelli che parlate il mio dialetto
        là dal prato che balza ad inebriarmi,
        là dietro il focolare e tra la siepe,
        che sapeste delle sue fresche ciglia?

        Che del fiume, se si perdette
30   e divenne celeste per giungere a vederla
        là dove indugi fruttiferi del vento
        danno equilibri di vele alle colline?

        Canestri colmi di pioggia di valle,
        settimana ingombrata dalle spine
35   e dalle zinnie, dovunque tu ospiti
        miti mercati nelle tue radure

        e nelle tue piccole sere
        compero e vendo e sorrido talvolta
        agl'inviti della prima brina
40   e bevo al di là delle labbra

        e so cosí spontaneamente
        tante gioie e tanto sento
        legate insieme dita e mani
        ombra e respiro da far dire

45   precoce e propria l'ora dell'amarti.[36]

◻

        [A centerless light already
        roams the earth soothes red lips
        and children, in the air's fragile retreats
        bees and stars assemble;

5   and it is already useless to ask of the floods
        the why of the mountains that stayed behind
        the why of the zinnias that quench their thirst
        with the frost of Lorna's cloisters.

A FIRST ROUND KNOCKOUT

        Among the completed examples of nights
10   and the tidy dews and the dead
        leaves an unstable honey
        defines its golden zodiac.

        But there is no bird's voice caught
        in the thin traps of the hunters
15   in the gay reflections of the snows
        that doesn't find it sweet to be misunderstood,

        each young wine must burns and exalts itself
        freed from the prisons,
        each fire is a garden each instrument
20   tunes itself to the sun's new touch.

        Sun smaller humbler
        because they praised you from all around:
        what knew you of her, of her voice,
        of her secret mint mouth?

25   Birds who speak my dialect
        on the other side of the field that jumps up to
                                    inebriate me,
        there behind the fireplace and among the shrubs,
        what knew you of her cool eyelid?

30   What of the river, if it lost itself
        and turned blue to gain a glimpse of her
        there where the wind's fruitful lingerings
        bring balancings of sails to the hills?

        Baskets full of valley rain,
35   week laden with thorns
        and zinnias, wherever you host
        meek markets in your plains

        and in your small evenings
        I buy and sell and sometimes smile
40   at the invitations of the first frost
        and drink further than my lips

        and know so spontaneously
        so many joys and feel so very joined
        fingers and hands shadow and breath
45   that now it may be said

        the hour to love you is near and appropriate.]

TWO

AFTER THE FALL
Early Signs of Later Structures

> sei più in là
> ti vedo nel fondo della mia serachiusascura
> ti identifico tra i non i sic i sigh
> ti disidentifico
> solo no solo sì solo
> piena di punte immite frigida
> ti fai più in là
> Zanzotto, "Oltranza oltraggio"
[Outrange, Outrage], *La beltà*

◘

> [you're further away
> I see you in the depths of my
> ₍enclosobscurevening
> I identify you among the nos the sics the sighs
> I disidentify you
> alone no alone yes alone
> full of pitiless bumps, frigid,
> you move further away]

As we continue our initial endeavors to show the beginnings, in *Dietro il paesaggio*, of structures that persist in later works of Zanzotto and to establish ways of reading which will be sensitive to the varied appearances of those structures, we shall now track the *io* into the landscapes of *Dietro il paesaggio* proper. In the final section of Zanzotto's first book, we shall note innovations in style as well as in the nature of the *io*'s "descent." As we shall see, the subjective trajectory begins to take on quite clearly certain aspects of regression. But our immediate attention, in this section, is drawn to a remarkable change in style, as if a season had turned. Here, suddenly, in this punctuated chronicle of the *io*'s progressive loss of childhood and memory appears a relatively extreme parataxis as if in syntactic echo of the thematic stark winter landscapes it is used to describe. This parataxis is most surprising in "L'amore infermo del giorno" [The day's infirm love], which opens the section "Dietro il paesaggio," since it stands in striking contrast to the voluptuous long sentences and indulgent use of vocatives of the final two poems of the preceding section. Here is the complete text:

> L'amore infermo del giorno
> i monti fa deserti
> e inaccessibili ormai.
> I cimiteri oscuri diluvi
> 5   hanno accolto l'odore delle macerie,
> le innumerevoli gale
> della pioggia si assottigliano
> e vanno ai cieli di carta
> delle girandole e delle tende.
> 10   A lungo ésita il verde
> nelle soste dei prati
> e tra i suoi fregi fiordalisi,
> l'ombra è caduta nelle piazze
> si è fatta freddi umidi cervi.
> 15   In città deboli di muffa
> nate sotto i venti
> nelle vetrine e nei gioielli
> fanciulle non vedute
> schiudono il loro sopore
> 20   di semplice crisantemo.
> Stanca allenta le dita
> cerule e svela i puri
> lineamenti la neve
> dietro balconi e corti.
> 25   Dal suo vaso odoroso
> il vespero ricciuto di germogli
> indugia sopra il lento
> discendere del mondo.[1]

◻

> [The day's infirm love
> makes mountains deserts
> and inaccessible by now.
> The cemeteries, dark floodings,
> 5   have welcomed the odor of the wreckages,
> The rain's countless galas
> thin out
> and go to skies of paper,
> pinwheels and tents.

10	The green hesitates long
	in the pauses of the fields
	and in its own fleur-de-lys friezes,
	the shadow has fallen in the piazzas
	and has turned into cold damp deer.
15	In mould-weakened cities
	born beneath the winds,
	in windows and in jewels
	unseen girls
	open their simple
20	chrysanthemum torpor.
	Tired, the snow loosens
	its cerulean fingers and reveals
	its pure lineaments
	behind balconies and courtyards.
25	From its fragrant vase
	the vespers hour curly with buds
	lingers over the slow
	descending of the world.]

While it does not go so far as to eliminate all conjunctions, the syntax here contains no dependent clauses and is, in general, much less hypotactic than in many of the preceding texts (we may note especially the contrast between this syntax and that of "Elegia pasquale," "Balsamo, bufera," "Atollo," and "Le case che camminano sulle acque," for example). The impression of paradigmatic brevity lent by the parataxis here is reinforced by the recurrent appearance of seven- and eight-syllable lines. These establish an undercurrent of rhythmic regularity which in turn reinforces the syntactic order. These compositional calculations support the descriptive presentation of several quite separate landscape views, a presentation whose very orderliness is nonetheless undercut by the affective allusions it contains.

This allusive language provides one of Zanzotto's most "Florentine" moments, in fact. His candidacy as a hermetic poet might here be established were it not for the remarkable absence of *io*. The same *io* which, at the end of the "Lorna," says *e so cosí spontaneamente / tante gioie e tanto sento / legate insieme dita e mani / ombra e respiro da far dire // precoce e propria l'ora dell'amarti* [and [I] know so spontaneously / so many joys and feel so very joined / fingers and hands shadow and breath / that now it may be said // the hour to love you is near and appropriate], now renounces both the *tu* and itself in a text lacking personal pronouns. The first person, in whose presence we have remained until now, is not entirely absent, however. Context implicates the *io* as narrator here, in a position just outside the landscapes it describes, one to each sentence. Some of these seem more like metaphysical paintings (the third sentence is perhaps especially reminiscent of De Chirico) than like the pullulating, promising river- and mountain-scapes of earlier poems (which we associated, at some points, with Leonardo's backgrounds).

One of the scenes described in "L'amore inferno del giorno" is, in fact, unseen—*fanciulle non vedute*. These are perhaps nothing like the mythical Pygmalion-girl whose existence implies desire on the part of the one who creates or imagines her. These unseen girls are the objects of an agent of observation who himself is removed. And the discourse of this poem seems to be neither history nor the story we have referred to as "his," until, perhaps, the final lines, where a familiar descending motion recurs. But where one might expect a sunset, a contamination of descent causes the world to go down instead. It is this very metonymy of descent which brings these slide-projector articulations of landscapes within the realm announced by the story of "Arse il motore." The world's descent here may be read as a kind of universalization, analogous to the switch from *io* to *noi*, of the driver's early slide to exaltation. Whatever the outcome, whoever the participants, the direction is the same.

The theme of descent in the third section of the book differs from the earlier one, however, in a marked fashion. Before, descent was involuntary and led to exaltation, to ambiguous juxtapositions of the high and the lowly, to poetry. Now, in the poems that follow, one might speak of a willful descent to origins, to childhood. This "descent," or conscious attempt at regression, becomes evident especially after the first four poems of the "Dietro il paesaggio" section, each of which describes a landscape in terms at times static and hallucinatory (and often reminiscent of the work of a later collaborator of Zanzotto, Federico Fellini[2]).

For example, the *io* returns in "Salva" [Safe] to discover landscapes in tombs in another version of descent, this time to points—*tombe*—implying death and stasis, in verses 14–21.

> Antichi raggi affascinano
> 15 le forme più ardue
> e la mia meraviglia scopre
> che le tombe sono
> paesi di calce
> che escono dal sole già disseccato

20   e che i serpenti hanno in becco
            un acuto fermaglio.³

◻

            [Ancient rays charm
15   the most arduous forms
            and my wonderment discovers
            that tombs are
            villages of lime
            bursting from the already desiccated sun
20   and that snakes have sharp
            buckles in their beaks.]

In this evocation of stasis and things held fast, even the serpents, whom one might expect to provide suggestions of certain sinuous kinds of motion, appear not in virtue of their motor capacities but as holders, so to speak, of a clasping instrument, *fermaglio*.

The next poem, "La fredda tromba," ends with the *io* speaking of *la mutata mia memoria* [my changed memory],⁴ and "In basso," which follows next, contains these lines.

5   Tanto godé chi visse
            che la ricca memoria marcisce
            e di bellezza l'anima è stanca.⁵

◻

            [He who lived had so much joy
            that memory's wealth stagnates
            and the soul tires of beauty;]

As memory fails or mutates, cheating the *io* of its possession of the past, the subjective desire to rediscover that past seems only to increase. An apogee of regressive desire is reached, finally, in the poem "Perché siamo." This is a kind of ode to the essential mother (the mother of the child's linguistic identity, that is) in an evocation of intimacy which reinforces the dearness of dialect, the true mother tongue, for the *io*. With his recollections of a childhood passed in the bliss of maternal love, the *io* implies that the early, originary, initial moments of his being are related not only to the dialect he learned as his mother tongue, but specifically and exclusively to the female parent. In the beginning, for the *io*, there was no father: in Freudian terms, no super-ego; in juridicial terms, no law; in linguistic terms, no logos; in Zanzottan terms, no Italian, language of law and logos, of external authority, but only dialect, direct connection, mother's milk, and mother tongue.

In the vocative which fills the final three stanzas of the poem, we find an identification of *io* and mother in the water images, now appearing as metaphors of health rather than erotism. Finally, the mother is the escort, the guide, the only human companion for the *io*'s dream of the world and his glance toward a season of endings:

> O mamma, piccolo è il tuo tempo,
> tu mi vi porti perch'io mi consoli
> 30 e là v'è l'erba di novembre,
> là v'è la franca salute dell'acqua
> sani come acqua vi siamo noi,
> sana azzurra sostanza
> vi degradano tutte le sieste
> 35 cui mi confondo e che sempre più vanno
> comunicando con la notte
>
> Né attingere al pozzo né alle alpi
> né ricordare come tu non ricordi:
> ma il sol che splende come cosa nostra,
> 40 ma sete e fame all'ora giusta
> e tu mamma che tutto
> sai di me, che tutto hai tra le mani.
>
> Con la scorta di te e dell'erba
> e di quella lampada precaria
> 45 di cui distinguo la fine,
> sogno talvolta del mondo e guardo
> dall'alto l'inverno del nord.⁶

◘

> [Oh mama, your time is small,
> you take me there so that I may console myself
> 30 and there there is November grass,
> there there is the water's frank greeting,
> there we are as healthy as the water is;
> healthy blue substance
> there diminish all the siestas
> 35 I merge with and which
> are growing ever closer to the night
>
> Neither drawing from the well nor from the Alps
> nor remembering as you do not remember:

```
            but the sun that shines like something of ours,
40          but thirst and hunger at the right hour
            and you mama who knows
            everything about me, who has everything in her hands.

            With you as my escort, and the grass
            and that unstable lamp
45          whose end I can feel,
            I sometimes dream of the world and gaze
            from far on high at the northern winter.]
```

Luigi Milone has suggested most astutely a double regression in *Dietro il paesaggio*. First, there is the desire to return to the initial space of dialect:

> Il *dialetto* non è soltanto l'immediato, naturale sostituto della *lingua standard*: rappresenta anche una sicurezza (legata all'infanzia, all'ambiente ecc.) di tipo realistico (in senso psichico). Abolire il dialetto vorrà dire allora non soltanto rinunciare al più usuale mezzo di comunicazione, ma anche e soprattutto creare un vuoto traumatico, una vasta lacuna che per ora (con gli strumenti cioè in possesso di Zanzotto all'altezza di *Dietro il paesaggio*) è incolmabile.[7]

> [Dialect is not just the immediate, natural substitute for the *standard language*. It also represents a kind of security (bound to infancy, to one's surroundings, etc.) which is realistic in a psychic sense. To abolish dialect, then, would mean not only to give up the most common means of communication but also, and above all, to create a traumatic void, a vast lacuna which for the time being (with the means Zanzotto has in hand, that is, at the height of *Dietro il paesaggio*) is impossible to fill.]

Second is the literary conditioning of Zanzotto's texts, which may be seen as a literary sort of regression. This, we pointed out in our reading of "Arse il motore," is a defensive attempt to counter the threat of a traumatic disappearance of dialect by creating a super-literary lexicon or referentiality. Such a lexicon thus enables the dialect speaker to identify with and, in dismembered bits, to master the most aulic corpus embodying that threat: literary Italian. In Milone's words,

> È possibile solo aggirare la depressione prodotta nella sfera comunicativa costruendo *in laboratorio*—al di sopra e non all'interno di questo vuoto—un linguaggio sostanzialmente alienato.
>
> In altre parole, l'unica operazione possibile è l'acquisizione di un linguaggio che presenti il massimo grado di letterarietà, che sia costruito cioè esclusivamente a partire dai testi più illustri e autorevoli della storia letteraria.[8]

[The only way to get around the depression produced in the communicative sphere is by constructing *in laboratorio*—above, that is, and not within, this void—an essentially alienated language.

In other words, the only possible operation is the acquisition of a language that presents the maximal level of literariness, one constructed exclusively, that is, from the most illustrious and authoritative texts of literary history.]

What we earlier called a literary sort of regression loses its regressive qualities, however, when the standard, literary language it intends in some way to subvert is considered analogous to paternal authority. In this perspective, the patchwork use of aulic verses becomes symptomatic of a defensive subjective identification with the very paternal authority that formerly appeared as a threat to individual (dialect) being. The lines cited by Milone at one point as an example of the decontextualization of illustrious texts in Zanzotto's work evoke, in fact, two of the "fathers," as they are often called, of Italian literature. These lines occur in "Dietro il paesaggio," the penultimate text of Zanzotto's book:

20   Per le estreme vie della terra caduta
     assistito da giorni tardi e scarsi
     discendo nel sole di brividi
     che spira da tramontana.[9]

◻

20   [On the farthest paths of the fallen earth
     attended by days late and lean
     I descend in the shuddering sun
     that blows past the mountains from the north.]

Milone notes that "l'endecasillabo *assistito da giorni tardi e scarsi* è il prodotto di un contesto dantesco—*Noi andavam con passi lenti e scarsi* (*Purg.* XX, 16)—e di un contesto petrarchesco—*vo mesurando a passi tardi e lenti* (*Rerum vulgaria fragmenta*, XXXV, 2)."[10]

The historical irony, of course, in Zanzotto's evocation of Dante's or Petrarch's hendecasyllables as implicit symbols of the rule of standard Italian (and of the rule it stands for to Zanzotto, especially the rule of public language over the warm, cozy language of dialect) is that, in the contexts in which the *Commedia* and the *Canzoniere* were composed, they themselves represented the warm familiarity of the spoken language, the vulgate, as opposed to the official Latin that, in the thirteenth and fourteenth centuries, served as the rule for literary discourse. Both then and now, however, the opposition is not so much one of dialect versus Italian, or of Italian versus Latin. The common element in both oppositions is the confrontation of spoken (and unofficial) language (compounded in its importance for Zanzotto, who speaks dialect as his original, mother tongue) with written (and official) language for Zanzotto as the language of the media and coercion. Dante and Petrarch transgressed the rule of the official language by writing a spoken language. Zanzotto transgresses the rule of official language by minimalizing it—by rendering it minimal, by rending it into pieces, by rendering those pieces in a patchwork where the original is always in evidence but out of context. The times, it would seem, determine the means. It is by writing in standard Italian, and by subverting through minimalization (or decontextualization, if you prefer, or miniaturization) the highest moments of standard Italian in its most glorious literary form, that Zanzotto brings an accusation against the language of the rule right to the heart of that language itself.

Both he as a writer and we as readers are implicated in our complicity with the rule he indicts. He is writing, after all, for the non-dialect speaker with whom he identifies as a matter of course by his use of standard Italian. In this way, when he talks of dialect, that dialect remains all the while, for us, over there, *al di là*, behind the very signs of his message to us. At the same time that he points to dialect as the original language, however, he hides it from us, or shows us that we are excluded from its space. Here there are no convivial crumbs of accessible wisdom, but the formal, inculpating positionings which leave the reader, in the very course of reading, outside the realms to which the *io* in the text longs to return. Thus we, as readers, are in relation to that originary space of dialect as the *io* is, except for the most significant fact that he "remembers" that space while we do not.

This is part of the fascination of the text: the implication that the *io* knows what is *dietro* draws us to trust, to hope that the screen of the landscape (of the *io*, of the language) will be penetrated. But, like words, *io* and the landscape (undifferentiated, finally) are fooling us. As we see from the book's penultimate poem, a vision of what lies *dietro* is possible for the *io* (and consequently for the reader of the *io*'s story) because of its specific and somewhat privileged location. But, as we see from the book's final poem, such a vision is obtained not by actually going "behind" either landscape or language or *io* as misleadingly distinct from *tu*, but by hazarding to negotiate the edge of a narrow precipice separating one side of meaning, of language, of identity, from the other. In Italian, this very precipice is, first of all, a *presepe* [crib, manger].

AFTER THE FALL

The penultimate poem of *Dietro il paesaggio* is the namesake text of the book:

        Nei luoghi chiusi dei monti
        mi hanno raggiunto
        mi hanno chiamato
        toccandomi ai piedi.

5   Sulle orme incerte delle fontane
        ho seguito da vicino
        e senza distrarmi
        le tenebre tenere del polo
        ho veduto da vicino
10   le spoglie luminose
        gli ornamenti perfettissimi
        dei paesi dell'Austria.

        Hanno fatto l'aria tutta fresca
        di ciliegi e di meli nudi
15   hanno lasciato soltanto
        che un piccolo albero crescesse
        sulla soglia della sua tristezza
        hanno lasciato fuggire in un riverbero
        un tiepido coniglio di pelo.

20   Per le estreme vie della terra caduta
        assistito da giorni tardi e scarsi
        discendo nel sole di brividi
        che spira da tramontana.[11]

◻

        [In the mountains' closed places
        they caught up with me
        they called me
        by touching my feet.

5   Upon the fountains' uncertain tracks
        I followed closely
        and without distraction
        the tender polar shadows
        I saw from up close
10   the luminous spoils
        the most perfect ornaments
        of the villages of Austria.

	They made the air all cool
	with naked cherry and apple trees
15	they let only
	a small tree grow
	on the threshold of its sadness
	they let a warm furry rabbit
	escape in a dazzle.
20	On the farthest paths of the fallen earth
	attended by days late and lean
	I descend in the shuddering sun
	that blows past the mountains from the north.]

Instead of the opposition and interaction of, for example, *io* and *tu*, or of *io* and landscape, this text presents the double agency of *loro*, on the one hand, and *io* on the other. Previous contexts have familiarized us with the ambiguous identity of *io* so that at this point we may accept its appearance as the voice of self-referent individualization not always distinguishable from its surroundings or from others of its kind except grammatically, as first person singular. But *loro* may now engage our curiosity as the indication of a heterogeny not susceptible to the ambiguity of opposed—or mirrored—identity, as is the *io/tu* rapport. *Loro* is a pluralization of otherness but, unlike *voi*, it is not an index of presence. *Loro* is linguistically, therefore, a plurality of otherness which is elsewhere. These two characteristics, its plurality and its (lack of) location, make *loro* unsuitable as a measure against which the *io* may attempt to recognize itself; it lacks the very characteristics which render both landscape and *tu* apt for this purpose.

These negative considerations lead us back to the question of *loro*. "Who are 'they'?" is often asked of casual speech, and the "they" in this text may appear as, among other things, a cliché providing ironic commentary on the claim to specificity of grammatically determined "persons" in general. At this point, however, we may recall the book's central epigraph which, being from Hölderlin, might suggest, to a reading willing to test all possible referentiality, a presence of Hölderlin not limited to the lines quoted.

As we begin our consideration of the presence of Hölderlin in Zanzotto's texts, we might note that Zanzotto's own readings of Hölderlin are conducted in German with the aid of Italian translations. In the 1940s, the two translations available to Zanzotto, both of which he utilized, were those of Lorenzo Bianchi and Vincenzo Errante.[12] This inter-lingual reading process in which the original is always somehow inaccessible, or only indirectly "reachable," places Zanzotto in a position with regard to Hölderlin's German analogous to our own symbolic position with regard to Zanzotto's dialect, except that no dialect text presents itself as yet for our deciphering.

For example, the opening lines of the German poet's well-known "Patmos," describing a homeland from which Genius will carry him, depict not only a landscape similar in certain respects to some we have seen in *Dietro il paesaggio* but also, in terms consistent with Hölderlin's own metaphysics, a situation reminiscent of one described more than once by the *io* in Zanzotto's work:

> Voll Güt'ist; keiner aber fasset
> Allein Gott.
> Wo aber Gefahr ist, wächst
> Das Rettende auch.
> Im Finstern wohnen
> Die Adler, und furchtlos gehn
> Die Söhne der Alpen über den Abgrund weg
> Auf leichtgebaueten Brüken.
> Drum, da gehäuft sind rings, um Klarheit,
> Die Gipfel der Zeit,
> Und die Liebsten nahe wohnen, ermattend auf
> Getrenntesten Bergen,
> So gieb unschuldig Wasser,
> O Fittige gieb uns, treuesten Sinns
> Hinüberzugehn und wiederzukehren.[13]

◻

> [Most kind is; but no one by himself
> Can grasp God.
> But where danger threatens
> That which saves from it also grows.
> In gloomy places dwell
> The eagles, and fearless over
> The chasm walk the sons of the Alps
> On bridges lightly built.
> Therefore, since round about are heaped, around clearness,
> The summits of Time,
> And the most loved live near, growing faint
> On mountains most separate,
> Give us innocent water,
> O pinions give us, with minds most faithful
> To cross over and to return.]

Many literal similarities with Zanzotto's *paesaggi* are evident in this text: the "located" threat, mountains specified as the Alps, chasms, bridges, summits, water. Even more strikingly similar to what we have already seen in Zanzotto, however, is the way Hölderlin situates in these mountain surroundings the unsituatable entity or force that he calls "God." The peaks here are hiding a vision that "no one by himself / Can grasp." The German poet's vocative is a cry for the equipment which would make it possible for himself and others "To cross over and to return."

What Hölderlin sees ideally as a collective concern ("no one by himself / Can"), the *io* in Zanzotto's text tends to experience alone, perhaps finding in any *tu* that might share the quest for whatever lies *dietro* too much similarity with both himself and the otherness that he seeks to allow for participation in the quest itself. The *io* in Zanzotto's text seems, in this respect, not quite sure of himself, not sure that his "self" is his alone, not sure where *io* stops and *tu* begins, nor to what extent *io* remains separate from the situations (landscapes) in which he finds himself or from the other (*tu*) he may tangibly desire.

Another instance of trans-Alpine analogy between a text of Hölderlin and one—or several—of Zanzotto may be found in Hölderlin's "The Poet's Vocation," where we note another version of Apollo's fateful blow:

Und dennoch, o ihr Himmlischen all, und all
    Ihr Quellen und ihr Ufer und Hain'und Höhn,
        Wo wunderbar zuerst, als du die
            Loken ergriffen, und unvergeßlich

Der unverhoffte Genius über uns
    Der schöpferische, göttliche kam, daß stumm
        Der Sinn uns ward und, wie vom
            Strale gerührt das Gebein erbebte,

Ihr ruhelosen Thaten in weiter Welt!
    Ihr Schiksaalstag', ihr reißenden, wenn der Gott
        Stillsinnend lenkt, wohin zorntrunken
            Ihn die gigantischen Rosse bringen.[14]

[And yet, you heavenly powers, you all, and all
    You fountains, all you banks and you groves and peaks
        Where marvellous at first when by the
            Forelock you seized us, and unforeseen the

Divine, creative Genius came over us,
  Dumbfounding mind and sense, unforgettably,
    And left us as though struck by lightning
      Down to our bones that were still aquiver,

You restless deeds at large in a boundless world!
  You fateful days, you sweeping ones, when the God
    Drives calmly pondering where, drunk with
      Rage, the gigantic horses take him.]

Such descriptions and narrations of allusive or metaphoric settings and events are abundant in Hölderlin's texts, and the analogy with those of Zanzotto is recurrently striking. One may note, for example, similarities between Zanzottan texts already considered and aspects of other texts of Hölderlin such as "At One Time I Questioned the Muse" ("Einst hab ich die Muse gefragt"), "Return to the Homeland" ("Rükkehr in die Heimath"), "Bread and Wine" ("Brod und Wein").

There may also be a clue in Hölderlin to the identity of the *loro* in "Dietro il paesaggio." If, in fact, this *loro* might be related to the "gods" found in Hölderlin, then Zanzotto's *loro* might be read as a pluralization of the *dio* who dealt the stunning blow in "Arse il motore." Here, in the plural, however, the identity of the *dio* is not restricted to being a donor of the gift, or curse, of poetry. This identity is amplified, instead, in *loro*, in a suggestion of pervasiveness similar to that of Hölderlin's pantheism, to include the entire landscape as both setting and agent of a revelatory experience. In other words, the first stanza of "Dietro il paesaggio" may be seen to recount, with some variations of plot, the events narrated in "Arse il motore." This time, however, there is not a knockout, but a touch, and not one god, but many "agents," *loro*.

Returning now to "Dietro il paesaggio," if we analyze how this Zanzottan *loro* acts, we find that certain stylistic considerations are revealing. In Zanzotto's first line group, for example, the anaphora *mi hanno raggiunto/mi hanno chiamato* (framed on top by a prepositional phrase and below by a gerundial phrase acting syntactically as an ablative of means) is centrally positioned and thus of emphasized significance. By the second stanza, the earlier anaphora may be retrospectively identified as a paradigm for the anaphora which now occurs, *ho seguito da vicino . . . ho veduto da vicino*. The *io* voice picks up the anaphoristic pattern begun by the *loro* voice. An association between what the *io* did and what the *loro* did is thus established by rhetorical means.

Reinforcing this association is the prepositional phrase of location, *Sulle orme incerte delle fontane,* which introduces the second line group. Its syntactic similarity to the poem's initial line (the *Nei luoghi chiusi dei monti* which partially frames the first anaphora) provides yet another level of anaphora and encourages our reading, perhaps, to anticipate a further *mi hanno* . . . where, instead, a first person singular arrives, as we have seen. The rhetorical and syntactic context of this pronominal switch may even suggest an association of apposition between the first verbal anaphora, *mi hanno raggiunto/mi hanno chiamato,* and the second, *ho seguito da vicino . . . ho veduto da vicino.*

The anaphoristic paradigm continues in the third line group with a return to *loro (Hanno fatto . . . hanno lasciato . . . hanno lasciato fuggire)* but without an introductory prepositional phrase. The fourth line group, however, begins with just such a phrase establishing the location of the final verb which acts as a kind of present tense resolution or result of the structures that have preceded it: *discendo.*

This rhetorico-syntactic analysis outlines the technical means used to imply similarity between the two agents, *loro* and *io.* But what does such similarity contribute to the semantics of the text? What, in fact, does the similarity of position "mean"? Here we may find a clue in Hölderlin's "Rousseau":

> Dem Sehnenden war
> Der Wink genug, und Winke sind
> Von Alters her die Sprache der Gotter.[15]

> [For the yearning man
> The hint sufficed, because in hints from
> Time immemorial the gods have spoken.]

If we find in the nonspecific *loro* something like Hölderlin's gods (and Zanzotto has spoken of these in a similar context[16]), we may see *loro* as being the senders and *io* the receiver of a series of hints such as those of which the German poet speaks. We know from other *Dietro il paesaggio* poems (*Ho tanto desiderato,* for example, in "Elegia pasquale") that the *io* is, in Hölderlin's terms, a "yearning man." The trajectory upon which his desire has taken him is traced in the second line group here, where, not surprisingly, it appears in terms of landscape and location. With traditional associations going back to Horace's "O fons bandusiae," the *orme incerte delle fontane* may be an indication of the *io*'s not always confident relation to notions of poetic inspiration. The *tenebre tenere del polo* which *io* has pursued intently may then be all that shadows have come to signify in the course of the book, with the added specification that these are *polar* shadows, differentiations and signs of existence produced at some extreme or even original place from which those differentiations and signs of existence can be measured. In contrast to the extremity suggested by *polo*, however, is the adjective *tenere* with which, in a sleight-of-letter by now familiar to his readers, Zanzotto modifies *tenebre*: the tenderness arises from the shadows as if tenderness and shadows were consubstantial (for indeed, literally, in this text they are).

The final image in the second line group of "Dietro il paesaggio" is one of light:

>   le spoglie luminose
>   gli ornamenti perfettissimi
>   dei paesi dell'Austria.

The *io* has followed close upon tender polar shadows and has seen—close by—the shining spoils. These *spoglie*, "spoils," are also, of course, *spoglie*, "leaves," minimal units of a landscape. We thus find that what might be glimpsed while following the *orme incerte delle fontane* or from a polar vantage point or from the mountaintops near Austria, what, in other words, might be found behind the landscape, is yet another landscape, but one perceived in its smallest parts. Furthermore, these *spoglie* are described appositively as the most perfect ornaments of the *paesi dell'Austria*, a place which in other contexts has been associated with history (in "L'Acqua di Dolle," for example, as we noted earlier).

Austria, as a nation, is part of the discourse of history. But here, in an anti-nationalistic reduction, the *io* sees not Austria *tout court*, but *i paesi dell'Austria*, Austria's small components, its regions, like leaves in a landscape. These *paesi* appear here in a minimalization of a traditionally grand nationalistic concept, a minimalization which, in Zanzotto's system, carries the higher value of lowliness and suggests, like the precarious sandcastle fragility of the *Italie* in "Atollo," a level of life close to origins, an intimate life, a life, according to associations we have noted (in "Atollo," "Declivio su Lorna," and "Lorna"), of dialect. *Austria* alone would stand in opposition to *Italia* and imply complicity in history's discourse. But *i paesi dell'Austria* are merely one version of *paesi* in general; the thread of small-scale values in Zanzotto's landscape runs across historical and regional boundaries and delineates a space for poetry.

The return of *loro* as the anaphora continues in the third line group underscores the pronominal interchange we mentioned above between third person plural and first person singular. The narration continues without interruption. The verbal phrases occur in their established places in the paradigm, but now the agent is *loro* once again. This line group recounts what *loro* has done to the landscape. It is a winter scene (*l'aria tutta fresca, i meli nudi*) where trees now bare but promising the fruits dear to the *io*'s childhood (as in "Declivio su Lorna") appear, where one new tree begins to grow, and where one young rabbit scurries away. Perhaps here, at last, are the hints or signs sent by *loro* to *io* with the landscape as intermediary or medium. ("For the yearning man / The hint sufficed, because in hints from / Time immemorial the gods have spoken.") These inscriptions on the landscape are signs of promise: the bare trees will bear fruit; the small tree is growing; the warm young rabbit will survive the winter and bring springtime (and perhaps Easter) renewal. The readability of these signs is effectuated partly by the pronominal interchange established in the anaphora. That interchange would seem to suggest that, even though *loro* is the agent, *io* is "in" the line group (and landscape) too, even somehow "in" the sign system. Such rhetorically implicit imminence is reinforced thematically by the identity of *io* and landscape at work throughout the book. The gods (or, in any case, some plural alterity) have found him in the landscape (*Nei luoghi chiusi dei monti*), he has risked his footing for a vision (*Sulle orme incerte delle fontane*), and they, finally, have given him readable signs from *dietro*, signs which, partaking of the nature of the landscape as both the *io* and *loro* do, imply that the "content" of whatever message there may be is inseparable both from its sender and its receiver.

As we mentioned above, the result and resumé of all that has gone before occurs in the brief line group which closes the poem. Here, the *io* continues upon his extreme or final course (*Per le estreme vie*). This course traverses a world that has seen its sunset yet persists after its fall. In "L'amore infermo del giorno," we saw *il lento / discendere del mondo;* here the world's descent is complete, *della terra caduta*. The *io* has renounced the accoutrements so dear to him in "L'Acqua di Dolle" and is now accompanied only by the winter days—and, of course, Dante and Petrarch and perhaps others as well in the decontextualized hendecasyllable's "Poetic" cadence.

Finally, there is the one verb, in present tense, to which the rhetoric of the text has led the *io: discendo*. And a movement that began with the *io*'s passivity in *colpito da un dio* in the first poem is completed with the *io*'s active descent in "Dietro il paesaggio." That this is a descent to poetry (as was the initial fall) is signalled here by more than the hendecasyllable. *Discendo nel sole*, for example, recalls the sun, source of differentiating shadow and hence of sign production, of "meaning," as we have noted. The sun, moreover, is also associated with Apollo who, besides being the strong-fisted god of poetry, is also god of light. But this is an oxymoronic *sole di brividi,* one that brings the unexpected, a chill. Where does it come from?

In a resolution of the suggested difficulty or ambiguous possibility of experiencing poetic "inspiration" we saw earlier (*Sulle orme incerte delle fontane*), the *brividi* modify a *sole* that synesthetically breathes or even blows as if it were wind. The sun (like poetry, a source of differentiation and signification) becomes like wind in order to "inspire," to breathe or blow by means of a verb which, at least since love inspired Dante to write his *dolce stil novo,* has been the very breath of poetry: *spira.* The *io*'s descent is thus hallucinatory only in realistic terms; it holds a reason of its own when taken, in a *summum* of imagery established throughout the book, as the subjective movement into new meanings made possible when one goes "behind" the everyday surface of language into the realm of risky significatory procedures which is poetry. The *sole di brividi* into which the *io* descends, moreover (poetry being for him a matter not lofty, but lowly), blows *da tramontana.* This north wind bears implications of influence from across the Alps, once again, and the spirit of Hölderlin perhaps still lingers in yet another reference to the possibilities of a poetic use of language. In a reading sensitized to ways in which what is present in the text may carry signals of signs not actually present, our eyes may note that *tramontana* is orthographically close to *tramontano* [beyond the mountains] and only one syllable removed from *tramonto* [sunset], yet another ramification of the themes of sun and descent. All these suggestions of spelling-change variants may be seen to contribute peripherally to the signifying process here, as does the prefix *tra-* itself. The sun thus blows between the mountains as well as from the north, from beyond them, in a moment of descent and "ending" accompanying the *discendo* of the *io.* Here, at the end of "Dietro il paesaggio," is the "end" of the landscape in a melange where *io,* poetry, and setting abandon realistic pretense in favor of amalgamated processes of signification: poetry, as an otherness which seemed to be *dietro,* has wafted through spaces in a *superfice,* the landscape's mountain passes, and the *io* is now immersed, at some lowly place, in its light.

After "Dietro il paesaggio," a text as tightly and intricately constructed as lace, there yet remains one final poem in the volume. "Nella valle" stands at the "very" end of *Dietro il paesaggio* as a statement of the aftereffects of the *io*'s descent, as a description of *io*'s modified view of—once again—the landscape:

AFTER THE FALL

      Oltre la mia porta le ultime colline
      dell'anno e della guerra
      s'alzano al vento di san Silvestro
      un uomo che non subisce
5   le leggi della notte
      e che ha il mignolo d'oro
      s'annuncia sulle strade
      presagendo i suoi doni,
      io vado ai ponti del presepe.
10   E l'ambra sottilmente
      è cresciuta dovunque
      è cresciuta la gioia
      di chi non sa parlare
      che per conoscere
15   il proprio oscuro matrimonio
      con il cielo e le selve;
      le mense ed i giardini
      traboccanno di riccioli d'indivia
      di lumache dolcissime
20   di zuccheri preziosi,
      una stella dai suoi paesi
      di solitario cristallo
      ha osato sporgersi piú acuta,
      l'insetto sale al puro volto affranto
25   e diviene farfalla
      e delude la fredda polvere
      fuochi sicuri scarabei
      si accampano con le alpi nuove
      e col cielo formato dal domani

30   Nella valle scricchiolano porte
      e botole, nella valle
      mi hanno preparato il caro pasto
      hanno rifatto il mio letto
      di cruda indivia e di vischio.[17]

◻

      [Beyond my door the last hills
      of the year and of the war
      rise in the Saint Sylvester wind,
      a man who is not subject
5   to the laws of the night
      and who has a golden finger ring

AFTER THE FALL

```
              appears in the streets
              portending his gifts,
              I go to the bridges of the manger.
10            And subtly the amber
              has grown wherever
              has grown the joy
              of he who knows not how to speak
              except to recognize
15            his own dark marriage
              with the sky and the woods;
              the tables and the gardens
              overflow with curls of endive
              with sweetest snails
20            with precious sugars,
              a star from its villages
              of solitary crystal
              has dared to lean out sharper,
              the insect rises to the pure visage broken
25            and becomes a butterfly
              and deceives the cold dust,
              safe fires and scarab beetles
              encamp with the new Alps
              and with the sky tomorrow has shaped.

30            In the valley doors and trapdoors
              creak, in the valley
              they have made a cherished meal for me,
              they have again made up my bed
              of raw endive and mistletoe.]
```

An aside: the door that is the object of the first prepositional phrase here presages the image to follow, a calendrical setting for an ending that is also a beginning. The door is thus a Janus door, for Saint Sylvester's day is the end of the old year, the eve of the new. The endings marked here are not only those of *Dietro il paesaggio* but also those of a unit of time (*le ultime colline / dell'anno*) and of history (*e della guerra*). Since one of Zanzotto's two notes to the book states, "Questa raccolta comprende liriche scritte tra il 1940 e il 1948, in gran parte inedite" [This collection contains poems written between 1940 and 1948, most of which have not been published elsewhere], we may assume that the *guerra* mentioned here, in an iconoclastic intrusion of historical actuality (one which occurs at only one other place in the book, the poem, "Notte di guerra a tramontana"), is World War II and, further, that whatever was the order in which the texts of *Dietro il paesaggio* were written, this one, "Nella valle," is quite purposefully placed at their apparent end. Since World War II ended before the completion of *Dietro il paesaggio*, we might assume that Zanzotto found in this text something so much in the nature of an ending that, even if it had been occasional and hence from 1945, orderings based on a chronology of composition were passed over in favor of affective or thematic propriety.

There is certainly no reason to assume that the order in which the poems are arranged in the book in any way indicates the order in which they were written. Since the order in which they appear carries semantic value, however, as we have seen while following the *io* through these landscapes, it is impressive to find a possible indication that the final poem may have been written at the actual end of the war and used as a conclusion, along with its precedent, "Dietro il paesaggio," to a set of texts whose preparation continued for several years afterwards.

In any case, the war that was raging while Zanzotto was writing *Dietro il paesaggio* makes no specific literal appearance in the book. In fact, *le ultime colline / dell'anno e della guerra* could refer to any war, figurative or literal. The coincidence of the end of the *guerra* in the text with the ending of the book itself tempts us nonetheless to recall the political circumstances in which the book was written. If, given those circumstances, we marvel at how small a role the contemporary World War plays in *Dietro il paesaggio* (and if we recall in contrast how large a role the Great War plays in a book which has become a classic of modern Italian poetry, Ungaretti's *L'Allegria*), we should perhaps question our penchant to search for literality as we read. The persistent themes of reduction, minimalization, and regression stand, even if implicitly at this point, as antiheroic impulses, as reactions to the grand rhetoric of historical hubris, and as lowly refuge from the coercive will of nations to be mighty. These considerations, however, will gain more centralized attention in other of Zanzotto's works, especially the *IX Ecloghe* [IX Eclogues], which we shall treat in our final chapter here, and *Il galateo in bosco*, the latter written thirty years after *Dietro il paesaggio*.

In "Nella valle," a figure appears straightaway, initially lacking any specification other than that suggested by the date, December 31, the day of Saint Sylvester. This *uomo* does not obey night's laws and so may be assumed to wander about rather than give himself over to the mortal need for sleep. He may be read as a kind of contaminatory theological association with the strong-armed god of poetry and the plurality of gods we recently met. In any case, his golden finger ring and the gifts his presence foretells remain enigmatic suggestions of a future wealth and hint at other figures traditionally associated with midwinter holidays. The emphasis in this image seems to be on change, passage, a portal in time, a winter version, if you will, of what the formerly elegized Easter might have been. Although there is reason enough for this assumption in the calendrical setting, a more remote echo is also possible. Saint Sylvester was, in fact, the fourth-century pope who accepted for the church the (infamous, for Dante at least) donation offered by the Emperor Constantine, a gift which obscured the previous separation of church and state. With that donation began a new era in church-state relations—in a way, a new kind of historical time. Furthermore, it was the very same pope, Sylvester, who set the date upon which Easter would henceforth be celebrated each year.[18] The historical papal figure thus detracts not at all from the portrait of the *uomo* with which "Nella valle" opens: he is a figure of changing time, of endings which are also beginnings.

In the ninth line, the *io* appears, although not without preparation as in the preceding poem, for here we have already learned of his presence in the first line's possessive, *la mia porta*. The door between the years, the opening in time, he now claims as his own. And, even though it is titularly clear that the *io* is no longer scaling mountain (or tropical) peaks, he nonetheless, in this opening in time, is going somewhere: *io vado*. His destination, unlike that of the *uomo*, is what might seem, were they to remain metaphorically in the landscape, to be Hölderlinian bridges. That is, in a setting of *le ultime colline*, one might imagine bridges as sustaining structures which cross over chasms. Here, however, the landscape metaphor is telescoped abruptly to a calendrically appropriate image of infancy, and we learn that the *io*, after his fall, is making his way to a cradle. The regressive movement back to beginnings leads to the *presepe*.

The arrival at a cradle, together with the notion of gifts and, a bit further on, that of rejoicing (*è cresciuta la gioia*), brings another figure to mind, that of the Magi. Associations of magianism with magic, astrology, and oneiromancy are in keeping with Zanzotto's *uomo* here, as is the fact that the Magi are not subject to night's laws in any usual sense. In the most famous instance of their wanderings, they traveled by night, following a star, and upon seeing the child they had been seeking, rejoiced. Thus, in an appropriately Zanzottan locus, epiphany is suggested as part of the subjective situation "Nella valle."[19]

What follows may be the closest thing to a direct statement by the *io* of his own situation that the story provides. Paradoxically, it appears as an impersonal statement which, however, by its very impersonal nature, implies a generalization, a universalization:

10	E l'ambra sottilmente
	è cresciuta dovunque
	è cresciuta la gioia
	di chi non sa parlare
	che per conoscere
15	il proprio oscuro matrimonio
	con il cielo e le selve;

After the multitude of shadows which occur throughout *Dietro il paesaggio*, it is striking to find this light in "Nella valle." What was *ombra* in variants throughout the book (one of the most recent being an *ombra taciturna* in "Immacolata," the poem that directly precedes "Dietro il paesaggio") now appears as *ambra*, as golden light itself, in a phonic similarity almost impossible to ignore. The differences which formerly appeared were seen to be tenors of a metaphoric vehicle dependent on the sun as a source of radiance which, when interrupted, left a trace. What now appears as the *io* makes his way to a cradle is a radiance which has grown all around. Sources are unclear; heterogeneity seems to have given way to an encompassing glow, a suggestion, perhaps, of inclusion, perhaps even of likeness.

And likeness marks the iterated *è cresciuta* in a pattern which at first seems to be anaphora, especially after the rhetorical insistence on that device in the preceding poem. The reading continues, however, to discover that the subject of the second *è cresciuta* is not *l'ambra* but *la gioia*. The structure is therefore less anaphoristic than chiasmatic, hinging as it does on a syntactic and semantic turning point. The subjective shift makes the verbal iteration as close to being a literal mirror image—one bearing, that is, the mark of inversion—as our linear phonetic writing will permit. And the syntaxes of this mirrored *è cresciuta* go both backwards, so to speak, and forwards on the linear track: the growing of the amber light in the line above and of the joy in the line below mirrors itself as it looks both behind and ahead. Here once again the "form" illustrates the "content"; technical means are structurally similar to thematic material, signifiers and signifieds become reciprocally referential.

This *gioia* is not claimed uniquely by the *io*, however. It hovers in the landscape, as in the text, in an impersonal singular. The assumption of the *io*'s grammatical function by the *chi* is appropriate, nonetheless, because what follows is a generalized solution to

AFTER THE FALL

speechlessness, as if the *io* has discovered a proverbial maxim, a sort of principle: that any *io*, by joining in some obscure way with the alterity that the landscape has here come to mean, will find his own ability to speak. Speech, therefore, is shown in this metaphoric ensemble to come from a relation—a marriage, a long-term contract—with an other.

Our arrival, in *Dietro il paesaggio*, at this joyful statement prompts us to jump ahead momentarily. Just as it would have been easier to start our readings of Zanzotto at the "middle," it is now tempting to compare, at the "ending" of these "beginnings," the lines we have just considered with a well-known statement of Lacan:

> L'Autre est donc le lieu où se constitue le je qui parle avec celui qui entend, ce que l'un dit étant déjà la réponse et l'autre décidant à l'entendre si l'un a ou non parlé.[20]

❏

> [The Other is therefore the place where the I who speaks constitutes itself with the one who listens, that which the first of them says being already the response, and the other of them deciding to hear it whether or not the first one has spoken.]

Without wishing to impose a specifically Lacanian reading on Zanzotto's early work, we may nonetheless note, in passing, a structural similarity. Lacan says that the essence of the Other is determined by a sender-receiver relation, by a "place," to use this terminology, where both the speaking first person and the listener are constituted by the fact of speech. Their positions thus bear, in this "place," a structural similarity rather like that of a mirroring: the speech of the one is already its own response, and the listening of the other occurs whether the first has spoken or not. Each, that is, determines the other *via* the possibility of language. The relation established, and not the "message" sent, is the key here: the ambi-constituent *je/autre* structure is shown to be effectuated through a linguistic field. If we place this explanation of the place of speech in the relation of the first person and otherness alongside the metaphoric structures we have seen throughout *Dietro il paesaggio*, we may find that the Lacanian pattern is not unfamiliar to readers of the *io*'s adventures in the landscape. "Le lieu où se constitue le je qui parle avec celui qui entend" is quite a bit like that landscape; it may be found, even, in the subjective *proprio oscuro matrimonio con il cielo e le selve*.

Upon recognition, in "Nella valle," of the speech-producing union with an otherness (although it would not suit our purposes at this time to discuss Lacan's distinction between the *Autre* and the *autre*), the landscape—the otherness itself—overflows not in rushes of water as it potentially does in "Primavera di Santa Augusta," not, in other words, in eruptions of threatening difference where earlier there was familiarity, but instead in bountiful midwinter plenty, a superfluity of little things connected somewhat in the manner of Pascoli, or the *crepuscolari*, to the small ceremonies seen to lend sweetness to everyday life in a multitude of detail. What previously appeared, in "Primavera di Santa Augusta," for example, as the *io*-threatening capacity of the usually familiar landscape to break forth in sudden, devastating strangeness or change of form, has thus been resolved at the book's end by a wedding of the subject and that very landscape. The result is a subjective speech that exists only as knowledge or witness of that union.

In the text, there then follows the familiar imagery of *mense* and *giardini*. The *indivia*, even etymologically, is a fruitfulness in the midst of seasonal scarcity (Webster's traces *endive* to the Egyptian for January, when the plant is said to grow in Egypt). A (Christmas?) star also appears in a traditional signal, like the *presepe*, of beginnings and promise, recalling the endings and promise of Easter in "Elegia pasquale." In this landscape, beginnings and endings are perhaps all the same. But here, there is no paschal lamb, no figure of "windy Easter" going up to crucifixes as in the elegy. Here there is an even more lowly beast, an insect, though the verb is still *salire*. This small creature goes up to a *volto* that provides a homonymic echo of the *volto* in "Primavera di Santa Augusta": *e dal tuo volto vinto da morte / il mio conosco*. Now, however, not death but metamorphosis leads to recognition of the insect in a new form (*farfalla*) that can delude, if not elude, death (*e delude la fredda polvere*). And little signs of life, the secure fires and the beetles, find the landscape changed in a way now determined by the future: *si accampano con le alpi nuove / e col cielo formato dal domani*.

We may recall, at this point, that the relation of *io* and landscape in *Dietro il paesaggio* began harshly: the *io*, struck by an unknown force, was sent headlong down the mountain slopes. He was frustrated in many efforts to penetrate the superfice of landscape that then surrounded him. There was an ambiguity in the terrain: Alpine peaks were simultaneously tropical atolls, and nature's signs could not always be read in sure ways. Promises of fulfillment of desire, for example, disappointed him, and, when faced with a deluge of the very otherness he sought, he feared for his own identity, taking refuge in solitude or the company of beings with whom he could willfully identify but who were not like him. Finally, some pluralized version of the force that had initiated his experience in this landscape caught up with him once again, bringing this time a kind of ascendency and showing him panoramas of what lay *dietro*: still more landscapes! But these "gods" also enabled him to read signs or inscriptions in the landscape, and his next descent was not a passive one. The *io*, once abruptly knocked into a realm of superfice which tantalized him with what it hid, now weds himself to that superfice in the knowledge that it hides nothing, that all its secrets are already present, that *parlare* can have no meaning other than what it derives from an otherness from which it can never be separated.

If we wanted to use terms that will perhaps more appropriately apply to later books of Zanzotto where their literal presence is significant, we might forego the rather mystical lexicon we have just utilized and speak instead of the *Dietro il paesaggio* story as one of a subjective linguistic trauma when the subject is suddenly struck with an uncanny awareness that the signs he thought familiar are in fact also quite strange, that his control over them is determined simultaneously by their control over him. Or we might speak of a subjective crisis of identity, when the subject becomes aware that his very individuality depends on and is simultaneously threatened by his resemblance to an other. In the linguistic context, a resolution to the crisis is attempted by regression to an imaginary original state in which all signs were trustworthy because no schism had yet developed between them and their referents; dialect is assumed to be a system of such signs, and individuality, no more than a continuity with a (maternal or dialect) body not yet fixed as the other.

The mirror stage at which, according to Lacan, an infant recognizes the existence of its own separate body by becoming aware of the complete body of the other and finding in that the *imago* of its own, would seem to present an analogy to aspects of the subjective crisis traced in Zanzotto's *Dietro il paesaggio* if in this book we were to insist on a reading of the other as principally maternal, or in any case, from the *io*'s childhood.[21] The analogy is strengthened by a comparison of the *ambra* section of the last poem and Lacan's tenet that the mirror stage allows for an accession, in the child, to an awareness of symbolic processes of signification, the prerequisite to language acquisition.

By a similar token, the notion of the *unheimliche* or the uncanny, as described by Freud and found in so many literary texts (especially of the nineteenth century), would seem analogous to the distress of the subject in *Dietro il paesaggio* when faced with a sudden change, such as that occasioned by the arrival of spring floods, in the familiar landscape. In an article first published in 1919 in the journal, *Imago*, Freud establishes the origin of *unheimliche* in its opposite, *heimliche*, a lexical ambiguity which at a purely semantic level leads to coincidence of signification: only the familiar (*heimliche*) can at times give the peculiarly frightening sensation of strangeness which is termed the uncanny (*unheimliche*).²² In an effort to explain uncanny sensations, Freud postulates the existence of an unconscious repetition-compulsion and suggests that whatever reminds us of this instinctual compulsion is perceived as uncanny. Strangely enough, Freud's text itself contains an example which reminds us of the settings in *Dietro il paesaggio*:

> Other situations . . . also result in the same feeling of helplessness and of something uncanny. As, for instance, when one is lost in a forest in high altitudes, caught, we will suppose, by the mountain mist, and when every endeavour to find the marked or familiar path ends again and again in a return to one and the same spot, recognizable by some particular landmark.²³

How like the *io* in Zanzotto's mountains, who is often confused in his directionality and often lands in the same low place!

The *unheimliche* quality of the *io*'s springtime distress in "Primavera di Santa Augusta" would also be found in the very nature of language, and an awareness of this potential strangeness would be a prerequisite to the poetic use of language, as Zanzotto's technical tinkerings prompt us to realize. *Volto*, for example, allows a vast expanse of sky also to "be" a face. Both in the case of the *io*'s situation *vis à vis* the other and in that of the nature of the linguistic sign, what previously seemed familiar may suddenly become strange in a changeability which undermines assured notions of identity. Both the *unheimliche* and the mirror stage elucidate the relation of the subject and the other and bear structural analogies, as we have seen, to the story of the subject and otherness in *Dietro il paesaggio*.

Other psychoanalytic terms, especially some developed by Lacan in his study of Poe's "Purloined Letter," could be applied to *Dietro il paesaggio*.²⁴ For example, what he terms the moment of "realistic imbecility"—or the conviction that the signifier has a direct correspondence to reality—bears a striking resemblance to the nature attributed to dialect by the *io*, or to the mutterings of infancy (which, in the *io*'s case, are also dialect). These attributions remain at a rather implicit level in *Dietro il paesaggio*, however.

In the previous chapter as well as in the present one, we have endeavored to present a view of the early book that points out thematic bases—such as the unspecified *io*, minimalization, regression, dialect, desire, otherness, holidays, literature, and landscape—and stylistic practices—such as the use of rhetorical devices, traditional meter and stanzas as well as free verse, internal and external rhyme, suggestive homonymy, the insistent semanticization of grammar. We have especially tried to show how a reading of Zanzotto leads to the recognition that "style" and "theme" are inseparable—that the landscape metaphor is thematic, for example, or that an iteration may also be an illustration of the "story," or that a possible homonymy may add rather than confuse signification.

Our emphasis, therefore, whether through paraphrastic interpretation, mimetic recording of a subjective encounter with the text, thematic analysis, the discernment of metaphorical lexicons, etymological considerations, rhetorical analysis or any other of the tools we have used, has first of all been on the process of reading Zanzotto as a paradigm for possibilities and problems of reading in general. We have proceeded in linear fashion for the most part, taking a great deal of time to trace what we have termed the story. This procedure may have lent Zanzotto's book a linear appearance, but such an impression, perhaps prompted by an *après-coup* recognition of *Dietro il paesaggio* as one of Zanzotto's more narrative books, is misleading.

By choosing to discuss those texts which we felt most illustrate this story, furthermore, we have neglected others that stand as eloquent statements of different aspects of Zanzotto's work: "Quanto a lungo" [For how long], for example, which, though it partakes of the same metaphoric lexicon as many of the poems we studied (*sole, le ustioni della luce, voi, ombra unica nell'inverno, aurora, confini* [sun, the light's burnings, you, sole shadow of the winter, dawn, borders], among others), is a statement of the subject's relation to writing. It thus represents a likely hiatus in the nonspecificity of the *io* and remains, to a certain debatable extent, and in spite of all the interest it holds, outside the story it was our intention to trace.

Our option for the story arises from a wish to demonstrate that, even though this is Zanzotto's first published book, it already manifests many thematic and stylistic elements that continue throughout his work. By discerning these at an early stage of Zanzotto's production, we hope to aid our readings of what comes later: false etymologies, switches from Italian to Latin, as well as future plays of rhetoric, grammar, and syntax lose some of their mystificatory aura. When understood as being thematic, as being rooted, that is, in a practice which from the start consciously manipulates and attributes a great deal of significatory possibility to such play, these elements, traditionally reserved for discussions of style, may be seen as an integral part of the story—as, in fact, its very letter.

Without wishing to seem exalted, we might hazard to suggest that in choosing to trace this story we have been in some way mimicking a traditional practice in Italian literature, one rendered forever illustrious by Alighieri in the *Paradiso*: the story, of course, is not all, but it is at least something that may be told. And, to the extent that it is readable, it is not a ruse. We have attempted to show the beginnings of several structures that continue, perhaps in other guises, in later books. But we have not yet come to the end of the story, the final line group of "Nella valle." It is with this, then, that we would draw our own expository beginnings to a close.

The Janus door which opened the poem is now plural and varied, in an enjambment remarkable for the comma which sets it off, the only punctuation mark in this text which occurs somewhere other than at the end of a line. Here the comma marks a line or threshold already passed. In the valley, the low, inhabited part of the landscape (indicated, once again, by anaphora), we find not only a potentially sinister variant of *porte-botole*, or "trap-doors," but also a *loro* which, in context, may be read both as the valley's inhabitants (and therefore some familiar, everyday others in relation to the *io*) and as the gods we took *loro* to signify, under Hölderlin's aegis, in the preceding poem. The images of *il caro pasto, il mio letto,* and *indivia*, the latter of which literally repeats an image of bounty occurring earlier in the poem, constitute a fragmentary interior rather than a landscape, an interior suggesting family, everyday activities, security, the *heimlich*. But the adjective *cruda* perhaps renders the *indivia* image somewhat ambiguous, and our eyes may suddenly note the anagram *invidia*. The barest suggestions of unease that began in *botole* are thus continued in *cruda*, and the homey atmosphere is undermined by what these perfectly nice words could also mean.

Finally, the bed has been laid, in an identification with Christ-child beginnings, not only with *cruda indivia* but also with another winter plant, *vischio* [mistletoe]—or is it a trap [*vischio*, a snare]? Here again is a homonymic potential, a sudden appearance of possible strangeness in what seemed quite familiar. The image of return, of a cradle-home for the *io* after his conjugation with the landscape, contains in the very words that at one level suggest village architecture and the winter verdure associated with nourishment, decoration, and the manger of the baby Jesus, another level of significance: traps, harshness, snares. There is perhaps no one sure reading. Only the text is sure; readings are many. And the *io*'s status, like that of the reader, is still bound to the multitudinous signifying possibilities of the signs which surround him. With these we now close this door on *Dietro il paesaggio*: this is where the beginnings end, and this is what the story is about.

THREE

GATHERINGS OF POETRY AND MUSHROOMS
A Landscape Elegy

> Ce soir, du haut d'une tour, l'immense
> forêt sous les nuées basses et la pluie,
> la guerre en atteint les limites, du
> sud-ouest à l'est, un grondement sourd.
>
> Bataille, *Sur Nietzsche*

◘

> [This evening, from the top of a tower,
> the immense forest beneath low clouds
> and rain, the war reaches its edge,
> from southwest to east, a dull
> rumbling.]

> Solo d'un lauro tal selva verdeggia
>
> Petrarch

◘

> [Only with the laurel does such a forest
> shine green.]

This chapter and the two that follow are concerned with three books that titularly lend themselves to a grouping under the rubric of Poetry. *Elegia e altri versi* (1954), *Vocativo* (1957), and *IX Ecloghe* (1962) each have an independent significance in the itinerary of Zanzotto's poetics, a fact well recognized by much critical writing.[1] But we would draw attention to them as a group, for a moment, in order to consider them as a tripartite unity of engagement with the notion of Poetry undertaken by Zanzotto during the 1950s and early 1960s. It is an engagement in which Zanzotto subjects his processes of textual production to a detailed critique by a self-awareness that shows up as the flesh and bones—sometimes lively, sometimes moribund—of Poetry.

Lest our grouping be found surprisingly exclusive, let us briefly consider the titles of Zanzotto's first five published books. The first presents the metaphor of the landscape and an implicit subjective situation with which we are by now familiar. The fifth, which remains outside the realm of our study, presents a metaphysics of aesthetics not unknown to readers of Leopardi. Both *Dietro il paesaggio* (the first book) and *La beltà* (the fifth) may therefore be seen by virtue of the images their titles conjure up to be indirect references to some aspects of poetic discourse: namely, metaphor in general and precedent poets in particular. The case with the three intervening titles, however, is distinctly more direct: each is a literal reference to a specific kind of poetic utterance. In fact, each names itself, in turn, as elegy, vocative, and eclogue. These three books delineate a period of extreme textual self-referentiality when Zanzotto's themes converge toward an examination of their existence in a singularly poetic discourse.

Further, in these three books in particular, an attempt is made at a readable though not exactly literal self-definition of a "space," as Zanzotto calls it, which stands not only in opposition but actually in contradiction to the "space" of historical narrative. The poetic discourse in the *Elegia e altri versi*, in *Vocativo*, and in the *IX Ecloghe* accedes to conscious (and verbalized) responsibility as the "mondo Autre" that Zanzotto evidently felt pressed to chart during the 1950s.[2] The connections between grammar and history suggested in these books are connections of opposition or contradiction and, also, of subversion. The rapport of opposition or contradiction exists between the spaces of poetry and history; the subversion, as we shall see especially in *Vocativo,* is that of poetry by itself effected through a thematic voiding of certain aspects of standard and traditional grammatical usage. This voiding is less a negative procedure, however, than an unrelenting and unrepentant investigation of essentially two grammatical constructs: (1) the division of being into subjectivity and objectivity as determined by personal pronouns (along with the concomitant ontological confusion of any linguistically aware identity calling itself by the first person singular) and (2) the multifaceted referential ambiguity engendered by any textual use of the vocative case.

As we consider these three volumes, our analysis will concentrate on three central issues. Concerning *Elegia e altri versi*, we shall take a cue from critical neglect; of all of Zanzotto's works, this is the one about which the least has been written. This relative silence may imply that critical attention subsumes *Elegia* to *Dietro il paesaggio* as a kind of *coda* that would have appeared with the main *corpus* had the landscape's door not shut so soon, giving the elegy a semblance of separateness. We are curious to know, on the one hand, to what extent there may be validity in seeing this work as a kind of postscript to *Dietro il paesaggio* and, on the other, to what extent it distances itself from the first book. Our look at *Vocativo* will next bring us to considerations which will utilize some tools borrowed from the study of linguistics. For example, we shall analyze the extent to which the vocative case may be considered, in linguistic terms, a performative speech act—namely, one which might be classified as illocutionary—in an attempt to see how Zanzotto's use of that particular device holds implications about the nature of poetic discourse itself.

Finally, as we turn to the *IX Ecloghe*, we shall trace both the guise salvaged by a textual subjectivity for itself and the use made by this surviving subjectivity of poetic patterns bearing traditional implications. We shall also try to discern the ways in which those patterns are broken in a subversion of the very implications they inevitably carry.

> O natura, o natura,
> perché non rendi poi
> quel che prometti allor?
>
> Leopardi, "A Silvia"
>
> ◘
>
> [Oh nature, oh nature,
> why did you not give then
> what you had promised before?]

In his 1973 anthology of Zanzotto's work, Stefano Agosti includes only four texts from *Elegia e altri versi*.[3] This sparse selection is justifiable in a proportional economy of representation, since Zanzotto's second published book, in its entirety, consists of only thirty-one pages. But even in his extremely helpful and otherwise thorough Introduction, Agosti foregoes any mention whatsoever of *Elegia e altri versi*. This lapsus, we should note, is not Agosti's alone. In two of the most detailed critical texts tracing the path of Zanzotto's poetic discourse from *Dietro il paesaggio* up to or through *La beltà*, both Amedeo Giacomini and Luigi Milone completely ignore the little book that nonetheless did appear in 1954.[4] It would seem that, in a bit of a rush to arrive at the perhaps more weighty matters of such issues as grammar, subjectivity, trauma, and the ascendance of medico-scientific lexicon in Zanzotto's work, critics have been distracted from the little book that arrived in second place. But to ignore *Elegia e altri versi* might be to miss Zanzotto's *Secretum*: there is an old saying about small packages....

In any case, such critical distraction with regard to *Elegia e altri versi* is understandable to some extent because several aspects of the *Elegia* texts suggest an almost automatic association with *Dietro il paesaggio*. Thematically, for example, the discourse in *Elegia* is still sylvan, or in the town, or on the mountain: the landscape remains the essential metaphor. Moreover, what the thematic landscape setting does include, as was the case in the first book, is the play or interaction of subjectivity and otherness, or *io* and *tu* or its variants. Furthermore, the *Elegia* metaphors of seasons, as well as those of silence, the sun, and descent, are all familiar to a reader of *Dietro il paesaggio*, and, even stylistically, the most evident rapport between the two books is one of similarity, though not homogeneity. A significant stylistic difference between Zanzotto's first book and his second occurs, for example, in the versification. *Elegia e altri versi* contains no persistently short verse schemes and in this differs from *Dietro il paesaggio*. And except for the first, in quatrains of unrhymed hendecasyllables, all of its texts are composed in free verse. We may thus note a lesser degree of emphasis on traditional formal patterns of versification than exists in the first book, a lesser presence of rhythmic regularity, and a greater presence of long breaths, slow lines, run on in streams. Yet for all its other reminders of *Dietro il paesaggio*, *Elegia e altri versi* is defined by its author as a separate entity from the first work; its independence as a published unit perhaps merits more attention that has yet been paid it.

When asked how he determines what for him comprises a book, or how he decides when a book is ready for publication, Zanzotto speaks of the drawers in his desk at home in Pieve di Soligo.[5] These drawers serve as repositories for Zanzotto's works-in-progress. At any given time, there are many texts at many stages of "completion" in Zanzotto's desk drawers, where they grow almost on their own, like mushrooms in a forest, at different rates and with different appearances depending on climatic conditions and the engendering agents.

At some point, it occurs to Zanzotto that there are certain relations between some of the texts coming to fruition in his drawers. We know from the end results that these are not always relations of correspondence. They are, as often as not, relations of opposition, variation, contiguity, substitution. Notably, thematic patterns tend to be foremost among associative characteristics, however, and it may perhaps be assumed that such patterns contribute to Zanzotto's intuition of which texts should eventually come together under the same cover. Thus, a book begins to take on definition for Zanzotto in a manner more aptly characterized as layered than as linear. Such second-stage multi-level genesis—this drawing-from-the-drawers—demonstrates a significant authorial "stance" which is actually more a sitting back, a refusal to stand.

Evidently, Zanzotto's texts exist independently of a certain degree of traditional authorial intention—the intention that might envision them as filling a spot in a predetermined structure before they have even come onto a page. On the contrary, their eventual formal assemblage seems to have almost hidden beginnings, as if their author were not conscious of their silent growing together. The texts themselves gradually appear to him in a pattern that seems, for one reason or another, to appropriate the ontology of an interdependent unity which will in turn make a certain set of texts separate from all others: the book. Those poems sit in the drawers like unconscious desires or instincts that, more or less displaced, come into conscious structures independently of subjective will, producing readable symptoms in the book. The drawer-maturation of his texts, in any case, supports Zanzotto's own attitude as participant in, rather than director of, the processes of textual production.

This fact may be surprising to a reader acquainted with Zanzotto's *opus,* for the stylistic commitments of each of his volumes would seem to imply, on the contrary, a very conscious effort at control. What we learn from the story of the drawers, however, is that Zanzotto is not an experimental poet moving from one controlled and documented attempt at innovation to another with specific results always in mind. Instead, he exercises selectivity at various moments in the process of text-production in response only to the exigencies of his own ambiguous rapport with the signs in which his enunciation is simultaneously actuated and trapped. To the extent that each of the books resulting from various moments of this involvement is unique, each may be seen as the record of its own peculiarity. Further, what we call a moment is not necessarily temporally exclusive: several moments might occur simultaneously and later be situated by the author in a topical rather than a chronological pattern (as seems to be the case with the synchrony of inscription and the diachrony of publication dates of *Dietro il paesaggio* and *A che valse?*). To a great extent, and unavoidably, in any case, the books are chronologically determined. But how many texts lie in the drawer past the gestation period of their synchronic siblings? How many texts of *Vocativo* were already in the drawers at the time of *Dietro il paesaggio? Elegia e altri versi* itself could be a bridge built when its author already had one foot on either side of a ravine. The possibility that several books may begin to appear to their author as units more or less simultaneously is the case recently: *Il galateo in bosco, Fosfeni,* and *Idioma* are three books that Zanzotto says have matured more or less in tandem, presenting themselves as a triptych whose panels we readers are now able to view in any order we please.[6]

Whereas Zanzotto assumes a consciously passive attitude at early stages in the structural determination of the books, there is nonetheless—in fact, all the more—a great deal of significance in the divisions into books that Zanzotto's work finally takes, for it is with this division that the beginnings of our readings are set. The criteria that determine which texts appear to him not only as being independent at an initial stage (that of the individual poem) but, at a later moment, interrelated (as units of a book) first become readable in the very book groupings which result. With these, at least the beginnings of our readings are encouraged to mime Zanzotto's own.

This leads us back to a tautological assertion of the evident: *Elegia e altri versi* could have been appended to *Dietro il paesaggio* without seeming an inappropriate swelling had Zanzotto recognized it as part of the first book, but he did not. *Elegia e altri versi* exists as a separate entity and thus exhibits a conscious authorial determination it is our purpose to examine.

We would like to suggest that *Elegia e altri versi* shows its differentiation from *Dietro il paesaggio* in two main respects: the first is related to a thematics of narration and the second to a thematics of technique or style. Not only is the independent existence of *Elegia* after *Dietro* retrospectively meaning-productive as a kind of ending to the story in the first book, it is also significant as the beginning of a textual engagement with the potential meaning of poetry itself, a beginning that is already more than a prophecy to be fulfilled at some later date, a beginning that, in a flurry of critical distraction, has been somewhat overlooked.

Whereas the most immediate comparison is *Elegia e altri versi* with *Dietro il paesaggio*, we have already made another when we hinted that the *Elegia* is something of a *Secretum* in its author's *opus*. This simile holds to the extent that both are *libelli* in a production usually more voluminous and both contain secrets. In the *Elegia* the secret is a kind of confession of a depression into which the *io* has been induced in his dealings with otherness—a marked departure from the exalted ascents and descents of the first book. But a tenuous simile could also be made with the *Canzoniere* on the basis of Zanzotto's efficacious use of the turning point of thought initiated by Petrarch in his sonnets. Such a pivot is most often effected by Zanzotto in the *Elegia* with a *ma* [but] that suddenly creates a neatly proportioned thought progression in verse forms which themselves are far removed from the delicate divisions of Petrarch's octaves and sestets. "Storie dell'Arsura II" [stories of the drought II] and "Elegia" [Elegy] are cases in point.[7]

But if we wish to trace the story of *Dietro il paesaggio* beyond its own seasons and landscapes, our Petrarchan simile would have to be made, more appropriately, with the *Trionfi*. It is in his *Trionfi* that Petrarch tells us what becomes of Laura after the narrative of the *Can-*

zoniere and how the love-death story of the vulgate fragments finally ends. This general scheme is remarkably like what happens to the *Dietro* story in *Elegia*, where we read a kind of second ending in a mode very different from the first. For example, at the end of *Dietro il paesaggio*, the *io* finds a conjugal resolution, the *proprio oscuro matrimonio con il cielo e la selva*, to some aspects at least of the subject-object division which to a certain extent torments but which mostly discombobulates him.

The second ending presented by *Elegia e altri versi* is much less assuring than that union. In the *Elegia*, while the objectivity of *tu* is given several identities, its sudden, central occurrence as *Tu, morte*, to which we shall turn shortly, has a striking ring of finality. This death is associated, by means of the multiple identities of *tu*, with other instances of alterity as perceived subjectively. *Tu* is love, for example, in "Martire, Primavera" [Martyrdom, springtime], where we find:

	Tanti scoscesi terrori
40	e pietrose distanze violando
	rompi tu solo al petto, amore.[8]

◻

	[Violating so many steep terrors
40	and rocky distances,
	you alone break into the breast, love.]

Elsewhere, *tu* is some aspect of the landscape or the sky. In "Partenza per il Vaud" [Departure for Vaud], for example, we read:

	Riposo potrò chiamarti, cielo? E vento
	te, piangere concorde di pendici e di liane
15	verso il freddo Montello, parallele
	ombre e certezze della mia giornata?[9]

◻

	[Might I call you repose, sky? And you,
	wind, the slopes' and lianas' concordant crying
15	toward the cold Montello, parallel
	shadows and certainties of my day?]

Finally, in "Storie dell'Arsura I," *tu* is the town itself: *Da tanto a te, Soligo, mi conformo* [I've resembled you for a long time, Soligo].[10] But in a metaphoric current that returns more often to the season than to the landscape (in one of the significant variations on the metaphoric structure of *Dietro il paesaggio*), the season is most often winter, and the other evoked in central position is, as we mentioned above, primarily death.

These metaphorical attributions braid together at the center of *Elegia e altri versi*. There, "Storie dell'Arsura I & II" establishes first a season of drought that, for lack of water in a river bed, also implies silence (by itself a threat to the *io*'s identity inasmuch as it suggests the absence of any interlocution). The imagery then moves from a faraway *Pasqua dell'Angelo* [angel's easter] sun to the unhappy sun of a winter noonday, testimony that there is nothing *dietro*. This winter scene is one side of the *Elegia*'s central conjunction of winter setting and final alterity. Here is section II, one side, so to speak, of this braiding:

       Dai miei poveri giorni mi svio,
20   salgo con lena primaverile
       verso i boschi di Lorna
       e benefiche valli e grato verde
       d'aprile acerbamente sogno.
       Nulla per dorsi spenti
25   e per cavi torpori mattutini
       nulla dietro il ventaglio del meriggio
       che soffocate sere scopre
       per tramiti gessosi e stecchi e brividi.
       Negli altri anni a queste ore
30   sulle mie pene invernali
       grande e madido il bosco
       era cresciuto, mansueto limo
       aveva popolato il mio cortile.
       Ma ora un sole infelice mi fa scuotere il capo,
35   or si fende la creta, sbigottito è il ruscello,
       e le tue care labbra
       sento umide solo
       per un'avara dimenticanza
       dell'immenso risucchio dell'arsura.[11]

◘

       [From my poor days I stray,
20   I go up with springtime breath
       toward Lorna's woods
       and I bitterly dream
       of April's generous valleys and welcome green.

GATHERINGS OF POETRY AND MUSHROOMS

>   Nothing on the spent ridges
> 25   and in hollow morning torpors
>   nothing behind the fan of noontide
>   that exposes suffocated evenings
>   on chalky pathways, twigs, and tremblings.
>   In other years at these hours
> 30   the woods had grown
>   large and damp
>   upon my winter pains, gentle mire
>   had populated my courtyard.
>   But now an unhappy sun makes me shake my head,
> 35   now the clay cracks, the river takes fright,
>   and your precious lips
>   I feel moist only
>   because of my greedy forgetfulness
>   of the draught's immense whirlpool.]

The misleading humidity of this text's final kiss depends on subjective forgetfulness. The following text, the other surface in the interfacing where winter and death meet in one place, begins with memory, a major theme of *Elegia e altri versi*, as the title itself implies. This poem is "Ore calanti I, II, III" [Declining hours I, II, III]; we cite its first section here for the identification of the intimate other, the *tu*, as death, a perhaps logical conclusion in the gnosiology or cognitive phenomenology of subjectivity, but one at which *Dietro il paesaggio* never arrives:

>   Quale lento riflesso, quale vitrea memoria
>   di sè ai prati affranti va tentando
>   questo scorcio di maggio calante?
>
>   E a me tu sempre nell'angolo oscuro
> 5   della mia sorte distruggi quel lume
>
>   Tace il fianco beato del colle,
>   guarda incerto il papavero
>   le dissolte forze delle erbe
>
>   Prati affranti, affranti di tante acque,
> 10   grilli residui dello spazio vinto,
>   e non raggiungeranno il crudo azzurro
>   nè il felice giro dei monti
>
>   Tu, mia morte, fredda riporti
>   e cara quest'ombra di maggio

15   ed una sera divenuta un raggio
        che triste si sfibra a illimpidirsi.¹²

◘

[What slow reflection, what vitreous self-memory
is this tag end of waning May
trying for on the crushed fields?

And in the dark corner of my fate
5   you always destroy that light for me.

The blissful flank of the hill falls silent,
the poppy gazes uncertain
at the dissolved strength of the grass.

Crushed fields, crushed by so many waters,
10 left-over crickets of the vanquished space,
and they will not reach the raw azure
nor the happy circle of the mountains.

You, my death, bring back cold
and dear this May shadow
15 and an evening become a ray
that for sadness dims to transparency.]

This is the innovation and the quiet depression of the *Elegia*: the *io*'s recognition of the ultimate alterity as that which is closest to him, that which is his interlocutor in a setting that hides—or promises—nothing.

Going *dietro* here, unlike in *Dietro il paesaggio*, takes on figurative significance as an effort of memory, elegy, sad recollection, and singing about something behind not a surface or evidence, but a moment of time, the present. The constant and varied identification of *tu* as so many different things is implicitly subsumed in the identity of *tu* with death. The implications of the shifting identity of the other and its central appearance as a final alterity associate all alterity with a fruitless stasis, as if all chance for differentiation need flirt with annihilation, as if all were already over and the most that could now be expected were some internalized accounts of what had already happened. Take, for example, lines in which the dependence on the past is evident grammatically as well as thematically as *Ormai m'apparve il senso dell'estate* [By now the meaning of summer appeared to me], *Di tutto ho vuotato le mie mani* [I have emptied my hands of everything], *Arrischiata luce / prati che v'induceste / lungi nel grembo di una sera* [Daring light / fields that led you deep / into the lap of an evening].¹³

In "Martire, Primavera" the season is more promising, but the identity of *tu* is left in an ambiguity of spring / death that corresponds, as it did in the "Elegia pasquale" of *Dietro il paesaggio*, to the events preceding Easter renewal. Here are some excerpts:

>   Il monte scende, paese diviene,
>   qui con te cede il monte
>   [. . .]
>   Tu sei custode e causa
>   dei pochi nostri pensieri d'infermi
>   chiusi nel denso maggio
>   da calve piogge e ghiacci di Golgota
>   [. . .]
> 15 Nessuna svolta di tante strade
>   si attarda per te
>   per rifarti tra noi
>   altro dal ferreo stupore
>   dall'oscuro limite ove esisti
>   E noi ti proteggiamo
>   dall'essere ciò che ora sei.[14]

◻

>   [The mountain descends, becomes a village
>   here with you the mountain gives way
>   [. . .]
>   You are custodian and cause
>   of our few sickly thoughts
>   closed in the thick May
>   of bald rains and Golgotha freezes
>   [. . .]
> 15 Of so many streets not one turn
>   tarries for you
>   to bring you back among us
>   as anything other than the ironclad stupor
>   of the dark border where you exist
>   And we protect you
>   from being what you now are.]

In the book's final poem, the "Elegia" proper, we find, at last, the ambiguous but death-related *tu* merging with memory:

>   Pullula invano la sera di dolente
>   verde e di tardi monti,

>   la tua terra si vela di amori profondi,
>   fiumi e vallate divengono memoria;[15]
>
> ◻
>
>   [The evening swarms in vain
>   with mournful green and lingering mountains,
>   your land mists over with deep loves,
>   rivers and valleys become memory;]

Next, in a difficult winter wedding of an architecture signalling accomplishment (the past) and a landscape emblematizing presence (the present), the joining of what is over with what is now may suggest that the present is as much done with as the past, or that the past is as present, subjectively, as the present:

> 5   sta la mia sorte con te, con la tua
>   che già di grigie note punge i capelli stanchi,
>   e fervono i pianeti dal calore d'arancio
>   oltre mozze rovine pei cieli invernali,
>   celebra il vuoto dei cortili scoperti
> 10   le ardue nozze delle colonne e dei colli.[16]
>
> ◻
>
> 5   my fate rests with you, with yours
>   that already plucks grey notes on tired hairs,
>   and the orange-colored planets blaze
>   beyond mutilated ruins in the winter skies,
>   the uncovered courtyards' void celebrates
> 10   the arduous marriage of the columns and the hills.

This nuptial bed is a deathbed. A subjectivity comforted by traditional signals of goodwill is distracted from its watch just as terror is about to take hold by the very signs (*una stella di pace*) its vigil remarks:

>   Questo è il talamo tuo che precorre la selva
>   quello è il vitreo giaciglio della brina,
>   e Vespero, natura umana,
>   e una stella di pace e di volontà buona
> 15   tocca i primi terrori, soggiace
>   alla fosca vigilia che in sè già ci distrae.[17]
>
> ◻
>
>   [This is your bridal bed, it foretells the woods,
>   that is the hoarfrost's vitreous pallet,

and Vespers, human nature,
and a star of peace and goodwill
15   touch the first terrors, succumb
to the dark vigil which itself already distracts us.]

A second *Vespero* occurs in the second stanza of "Elegia." The canonical evening hour and its (Christmas) star recur as death signals of an alterity itself distracted to the point of being lost even to memory (*le tue spalle cui preme l'oblio*), an otherness that now ignores the sign-rich landscape:

Tu stai, nè più cura hai dell'umile
palpito ovino che ha la tua strada
se da notte a notte la guardi languire,
20   la tua nuca non cura
me e l'oriente ove vibra
l'illusorio vigore del frumento;
le tue spalle cui preme l'oblio
la tua mente che infrange altra legge
25   già da tanto giacquero, e trema e s'abbassa
l'oro natalizio della stella
di Vespero tra i capelli
tuoi che nota furtiva la morte.[18]

◘

[You hold still and no longer care about the humble
ovine pulsating in your street
when night after night you watch it languish,
20   the nape of your neck doesn't care about
me and the east where
the wheat's illusory vigor vibrates;
your shoulders, where oblivion presses,
your mind, that another law breaks,
25   have already lain low for so long, and the evening
                            ⌊star's natal gold
that stealthily takes note of death
trembles and settles
in your hair.]

With the elimination of temporal differentiation, and with the other's refusal of the landscape and even its illusory promise, the *io* becomes insensitive to the other's speech and to his own vision, thus blocking two channels of communication. This occurs along with what amounts to a renunciation of seasons as well in a generalized refusal of one system of signification after another.

The third line group of "Elegia" shows how in this situation nonetheless, and by means of an obstinate Petrarchan reversal, the *io* conducts a stubborn, if fruitless, nighttime search. In a synesthetic suggestion of great subjective dismay (*l'alba nera con acide palpebre*), the *io*'s insomniac quest for memory leads only to a dark dawn and to the *incipit*, long anticipating the more notorious instances in *La beltà*, of a lexicon of pathology:

```
        Non puoi dirmi la ruvida pioggia
30      che di sè ci stordiva
        e che improvvisi spazi e primavere
        ci rovesciò vive negli occhi,
        non puoi dirmi la grandine fresca
        che in fuga volò dalla nube
35      a pettinare paesi frettolosi,
        nè l'erba grande nei giardini
        nè i grandi pomi dell'agosto,
        nulla puoi dirmi nulla so nulla vedo;
        ma di quel cibo ora il seme perduto
40      lungo cieche ansie notturne ricerco
        nel campo dissestato e le ore vanno e nera
        sarà più l'alba che i grumi dei monti,
        l'alba nera con acide palpebre
        ci secernerà nella valle del mondo.

45      E da ghiacci orgogliosi a iride levando
        spoglierà il vento le nari,
        le viscere stente, la tosse,
        e tra poco lo stretto petroso
        focolare che ignora la fiamma
50      rabbrividirà di lumache e di crete
        cerule all'orlo della solitudine,
        gemerà di stanchezza la campana
        che offesa trapela dal cielo,
        l'iride irrisa tremerà
55      tremerà nell'inverno
        su chine e chine avide di paesi.[19]
```

◘

        [You cannot tell me the coarse rain
30   that was deafening us with itself

and that spilled sudden spaces
and living springtimes into our eyes,
you cannot tell me the cool hail
that in flight flew from the cloud
35 to comb hurried villages,
nor the grass tall in the garden
nor the big August apples,
you can tell me nothing I know nothing I see nothing
but now I seek that food's lost seed
40 along blind nocturnal anxieties
in the ruined field and the hours pass and the dawn
will be blacker than the mountains' clots,
the black dawn whose eyelids are acid
will secrete us into the valley of the world.

45 And, rising from proud ice to rainbows,
the wind will strip our nostrils,
our weakened viscera, our cough,
and soon the narrow rocky
fireplace that knows no flame
50 will shiver on the edge of solitude
with snails and cerulean clay,
the bell oozing offended from the sky
will moan with fatigue,
the scorned rainbow will tremble
55 will tremble in the winter
upon slopes and slopes that are yearning for villages.]

Next, the final stanza of "Elegia," and of *Elegia e altri versi* brings a past gloss for these predictions:

Ho coinvolto sole e luna nella mia sorte,
ho seguito le aperte promesse dei fiori
e la stagione che tutto presume, la bocca
60 rossa, gli occhi e il profilo che stimola e schiara
il mutevole margine delle radure
ed il pesco boschivo,
ho seguito la tua
piccola casa dall'ombra
65 riconosciuta familiare
anche tra i denti raggianti impetuosi
delle estati che saranno,
tra i pensieri implacati

```
              tra le moltitudini e i giorni. Ma stanche
70            ora le mani sul parapetto a luci
              di logge s'esalano, inverno
              senza requie logora presagi
              e moti d'alberi tristi lunghi affila.²⁰
```

◻

```
              [I have implicated sun and moon in my fate,
              I have followed the open promises of flowers
              and the season that presumes everything, the red
60            mouth, the eyes, and the profile that excites and
                                                    └brightens
              the changeable border of the glade
              and the forest peach tree,
              I have followed your
              little house from the shadow
65            familiar to me
              even among the gleaming impetuous teeth
              of summers to come,
              among relentless thoughts
              among multitudes and days. But tired
70            now my hands breathe forth their last
              to loggia lights on the parapet, and winter
              unremittingly wears out omens
              and sharpens long sad movements of trees.]
```

The anaphora here is a familiar one to readers of *Dietro il paesaggio*'s penultimate, namesake poem. A pattern of titular repetition ("Elegia" in *Elegia e altri versi*, "Dietro il paesaggio" in *Dietro il paesaggio*) is carried over in the rhetoric of this text to the inexact repetition in the preterit anaphora, *Ho coinvolto . . . / ho seguito*, and, later, an exact repetition, *ho seguito*. Within "Elegia" itself, this anaphora resembles the series of negative assertions in the third stanza: *Non puoi dirmi / . . . non puoi dirmi . . . / nulla puoi dirmi.*

In a multi-level play of similarity (titular, rhetorical, inter-stanzaic) that presages the poem's thematic conclusion, both the third and the final stanzas are serial in structure: the third lists what the *tu* cannot say; the fifth lists what the *io* has done. This is a seriality of progressive accession to silence at first objective (*non puoi dirmi*) and then, we would suggest, subjective. In the final line group, we find familiar images of sun, moon, flowers, seasons, the woman in the landscape, the *tu*, the house, the shadow; these are the signs that were the readable promise in *Dietro il paesaggio*, but here they are relegated to the past tense by a subjectivity whose silence perhaps consists of no longer finding anything to read. This second ending finds a final *Ma* that speaks the conclusive subjective alienation: the signs were there (all that was *riconosciuta familiare*); the future will vampirize them in its own historical version (*anche tra i denti raggianti impetuosi / delle estati che saranno*). But now, *ora*, the signs are worn out, and what was once the edge of *dietro* is now simply *tristi*, like a Sibelius waltz.

A note on verse groupings: since the four preceding stanzas alternate in length between sixteen and twelve verses, one might expect that the fifth would contain sixteen lines and thus preserve the pattern of alternation. Such is not the case: this final stanza contains seventeen verses. The extra line, the shortest, occurs in an anticipated central position in the line group. There, we find what might appropriately have been a fifteen-syllable verse—a length not at all uncommon in this text—*ho seguito la tua piccola casa dall'ombra*, broken into two lines. This break creates the shortest verse in the entire text (prompting us to identify it as the "extra" one) as well as a marked enjambement that leaves *tua* at the end of the verse, like an unreachable jewel glimmering at the bottom of a deep pond: *ho seguito la tua / piccola casa dall'ombra* (vv. 63–64). Even in this listing of past signs and subjective efforts at reading them, even in a moment of elegy for the passing of those signs and those efforts, the central, magnetic presence of the other is the fulcrum on which everything turns. The *tua*, simultaneously the familiar and the strange other (*dall'ombra / riconosciuta familiare*), would persist at an edge somewhere between woodland and shadow, but all is past.

Then, in the final four and one half lines, the turn of the thought swings on a Petrarchan *ma*: logical resistance as sign of resignation. The (writing) hands are tired; the setting is a parapet or windowsill, not an adventure-promising precipice. The elegy of past desire, of the search, of the other, of what was behind the landscape now draws to a close in the signless, sad dead of winter.

In a narrative economy, as we mentioned earlier, *Elegia e altri versi* may be seen to resemble Petrarch's *Trionfi* since both present a kind of second ending of a story written earlier and appearing elsewhere. Both, moreover, present a final association of alterity with death, a story of desire thwarted by mortality (though in Zanzotto's *Elegia* the death is subjective, *la mia morte*). Both show the transposition of signs once readable in a context that reserved some promise of fulfillment to a context of the willful evocation of a past standing as witness that promises were not fulfilled. Both present a subjective discourse about an absent object.

But here is precisely where the analogy breaks down. Petrarch ends his story of his love for Laura with a triumph, the victory parade of death which sweeps her away where he could not. Whatever the philosophical or theological implications, the vehicle he uses is one borrowed from returning conquerors. To the victor go the spoils, and the honor, and the vindictive last laugh. To the victor, especially, goes power over the vanquished: Petrarch's triumph is to show death victorious in his place.

Zanzotto's little *Elegia* stands in stark contrast to such triumphal sentiments. The mode is the sad lament of elegy rather than the glaring trumpetings of the *trionfo*. Zanzotto's tone is minimal, not grandiose. His verses are irregular; there is not even a rhyming vestige of drumbeats here. His sentiment is regret, not pride or vindictiveness. In the circumstances of the *Elegia*, the loser is not the other but the longing subject, alone.

Our initial question here, however, was not how *Elegia e altri versi* resembles or differs from Petrarch's several works, but how it distinguishes itself from *Dietro il paesaggio* to the extent that published manifestation of authorial intention determines the *Elegia* as a separate book. From our brief readings, we have already noted several significant points of differentiation. The condensation of the multiple identities of the other to a central, finalizing identity as death occurs only in *Elegia e altri versi*, for example. Furthermore, if *Dietro il paesaggio* may be considered as primarily formed upon a metaphor of landscape, and secondarily upon one of season, *Elegia e altri versi* would seem to present the inverse situation, for in this work seasonal metaphors take precedence over those of landscape. The shift from the implied (though at times contradicted) stasis of landscape to the temporality of seasons emphasizes the thematic importance of time in the second book. The very choice of elegy as the mode of expression implies a temporality that situates the subject in a present, taking most of its definition from the past via the function of memory. In *Elegia e altri versi*, moreover, the future barely exists. This is quite a different ontological situation from the one even of the "Elegia pasquale" in *Dietro il paesaggio*, where the present views itself essentially as a dividing line between a determinate past and a projected different kind of time to come.[21] Signs have foregone their projective referents and now depend more on a regressive pattern of signifieds.

A temporality circumscribed by memory is one of the marks of elegy; it is the earmark distinguishing Zanzotto's second published book from his first. The shift from a dependence on metaphor and narration to one of the oldest modalities of traditional poetic utterance has the consequences mentioned above and also leads to the oft-remarked grammaticalism in Zanzotto's following works, as we shall see. Thus, in *Elegia e altri versi* we may find the beginning of Zanzotto's simultaneously serious and ludic manipulation not only of the fragments of his myriad predecessors—the *operazioni decontestualizzanti* of *Dietro il paesaggio* as described by Luigi Milone[22]—but of the bones of poetry itself, of the privileged space it claims for itself in language. In other words, Zanzotto is now playing very seriously with the signifying possibilities of traditional forms or modes that he uses as semantic elements in a lexicon where signs now quite intentionally include all the implications associated with those modes.

This plunge into the realms of poetic modalities hallowed as far back as the Greeks suits very well Zanzotto's avowed purpose of creating *un mondo Autre*.[23] In the case of elegy, there can be no thematic claim of superiority or victory. There is memory and regret, but not exhortation or triumph. The elegiac mode, with its more or less resigned lamentations, creates a space for itself which traditionally has existed in counterpoint and even opposition to the discourse of history; the telling of subjective regret for the past is never the telling of the presumed fact of the past.

Elegy thus seconds the anti-historicism of Zanzotto's notion of poetic discourse in general, where words are not just symbols of facts or events but are themselves events, factual in their equivalence only to themselves. These poetic signs are manipulated in ways outlawed by everyday usage in attempts to find new and consequently always contemporary possibilities of meaning based on an eventfulness of the signs themselves. Such a technique does not carve in some figurative slab of marble what generations to come, limited by the letter, will read as the truth of any given time. The simultaneous multiplicity of signification that Zanzotto taps in his production of poetic texts exists instead as a vantage point from which history is revealed as but another discourse—one bent on a kind of persuasion, perhaps, or captured by its own desire to capture a past for a captive present, but a discourse nonetheless, and thus like all discourse susceptible to whatever analysis and scrutiny may obtain, and as feeble as any signs held in the shackles of narrative exclusivity, of one version of "truth."

The ending in *Elegia e altri versi* is, therefore, like all endings, simultaneously a beginning. With this book, Zanzotto begins his involvement with the semantic potential of poetry per se—of poetry, that is, as apart from other kinds of discourse, as traditionally, originally, an other kind of speech. He recognizes the internal alterity of his own poetic discourse; as *tu* dies to its old existence as the unattainable, it appears here as the very letter of a subjective *terminus*. This recognition continues in the following two books, turning around one facet or another of itself first with *Vocativo* and then with *IX Ecloghe*, both evident banner-titles in Zanzotto's rummagings through traditional poetic practice. In the book of eclogues, as we shall see, the notion of poetic discourse is problematized far beyond the degree present in the *Elegia*. But it is only after these three volumes of Poetry, so to speak, that Zanzotto's *beltà* will appear at stage center.

As concerns the *Elegia e altri versi* itself, we may conclude that, even though Zanzotto's most impressive stylistic innovations of the three Poetry books perhaps occur only midway through *Vocativo*, his little book of elegy may be seen as a first movement toward a textualized consciousness of poetic utterance as an antihistorical space, one in which subjectivity, though bound in this *libellum* perhaps more than anywhere else to temporality, may engage in a speech which, by beginning to make of itself the event it describes, takes its significance from a very different realm than that of linear narrative. The elegy elegizes the exaltation of poetry and therefore of itself; in so doing, it perpetuates the possibility both of elegy and of poetic utterance. It would hardly be possible to imagine anything more self-referential.

FOUR

ZANZOTTO'S *Grammaticalismo:*
Positions and Performance

> O endless vocatives that would still
> leave expression slipping helpless from
> the measurement of mortal folly!
> George Eliot, *Middlemarch*

> ma ancora eccedderebbe il sole
>
> ◻
>
> [but still the sun would go beyond]
> Zanzotto, "Prima del sole,"
in *Vocativo*

In the course of Zanzotto's middle "Poetry" book, *Vocativo* (1957), a reapportionment of stylistic motivation gradually asserts itself. As the book's title would imply, there is an insistence on the vocative case that places that case foremost among the thematic elements of the text. Now there is also the sur-motivation of the first person pronoun as the enunciation of a subjectivity determined only linguistically, and, hence, the concurrent implication that an authentic subjectivity can never be expressed. The emphasis, in *Vocativo*, on these two grammatical institutions, one a case with a long history of poetic usage, the other the originating term of enunciation, has been recognized by several critics as the most significant innovation in Zanzotto's third book. It is dubbed *grammaticalismo* by Michel David, who, in 1967, wrote:

> le sue ansie di catastrofi, il suo aggrapparsi al grammaticalismo per proteggersi dalla nevrosi erano inconsapevolmente prelacaniani.[1]
>
> ◻
>
> [his worrying about catastrophies and his clutching at grammaticalism in order to protect himself from neuroses were unconsciously prelacanian.]

In 1973, Stefano Agosti quotes David's statement in his Introduction to the Oscar anthology of Zanzotto's works but refers the textual practice in *Vocativo* to a more possibly conscious influence, the "concetto saussuriano di 'arbitrarietà' [Saussurian concept of "arbitrariness"].² Agosti's suppositions do not extend to any personalized authorial trauma. Instead, he provides an analysis, remarkable for its detail, of grammatical motivation in the text as an indication of a kind of material, everyday, nonindividual terror, one determined culturally (that is, collectively) rather than subjectively.³

Having once given what he considers the external motivations for what he aptly calls the "disturbance of the semantic universe" in *Vocativo*, Agosti proceeds to indicate instances of that disturbance, especially in the "disgregazione dell'Io," the thematic desecration of the landscape, the syntactic complexity (the long sentences and the interruptions), and the vocative, which, along with nominal constructions, he says, "non comportano, nemmeno *in absentia*, l'istanza della voce verbale" [do not allow for any verbal instance, even *in absentia*], and thus, "esautorano, in definitiva, la 'logicità' del discorso inteso come articolazione chiusa e fondante della realtà" [conclusively weaken the "logic" of the discourse understood as a closed, endowing articulation of reality].⁴ Agosti's assertion of the totally nonverbal nature of the vocative is the single weak point in his argument, since that verbal case, in any case, does carry the *in absentia* imperative, "hear me." One calls out in the supposition that one will be heard, even if the hearing ear is only one's own.

A final introductory step towards *Vocativo* is made for us by Luigi Milone, whose lexicon differs from both David's and Agosti's:

> Il *grammaticalismo* (l'*Io*—il pronome che organizza la rappresentazione dell'esperienza—e i *vocativi*—gli schemi anteriori e universali, più profondi e motivati della comunicazione—) si sovrappone alla superficie verbale istituzionalizzata ed emerge come *nucleo originario di verità* in confronto al livello superiore, ma estenuato ed astratto, del linguaggio illustre che si presenta ora come *sintomo di inautenticità*: il senso vero (*a parte subiecti*) degli enunciati si contrae decisamente nelle formule della *vocatività*, dell'interrogazione e dell'interiezione.
>
> In altri termini, il grammaticalismo di *Vocativo* può essere al limite interpretato come un primo, forse inconsapevole tentativo di colmare la lacuna corrispondente all'assenza di un grado zero della comunicazione, senza ricorrere ad un'istituzione linguistica data *a priori*, ma spostando invece la rappresentazione, la forma dell'espressione verso una *dimensione intersoggettiva*, verso il cosidetto *discorso pieno, concreto*. Se quest' ipotesi non è azzardata, si può affermare che facendo emergere le strutture grammaticali del *preconscio*, Zanzotto percorre la prima tappa di avvicinamento alle modalità linguistiche inconsce che saranno alla base delle sue più recenti esperienze, a partire da *La beltà*.⁵

◻

[*Grammaticalism* (the *I*—the pronoun that organizes the representation of experience—and the *vocatives*—the previous and universal, deepest, most highly motivated patterns of communication—) superimposes itself on the institutionalized verbal surface and emerges as *truth's originary nucleus* when compared to the higher, but exhausted and abstract, level of the illustrious language. This, in turn, now presents itself as *a symptom of inauthenticity*, and the true meaning (*a parte subiecti*) of the enunciateds decisively contracts into formulas of *vocativity*, of interrogation and interjection.

In other words, the grammaticalism of *Vocativo* can be interpreted, finally, as a first, perhaps unconscious, attempt to fill the lacuna corresponding to the absence of a zero degree of communication. This attempt is carried out without recourse to a linguistic institution given *a priori*, but instead shifting the representation, the form of expression, towards an *intersubjective dimension*, towards the so-called *full, concrete discourse*. If this hypothesis is correct, one can state that by causing the grammatical structures of the *preconscious* to emerge, Zanzotto takes the first steps on the road to the unconscious linguistic modes that will be the basis of his more recent endeavors, beginning with *La beltà*.]

Milone's emphasis on the first person pronoun and the vocative case as the most significant components of the motivation of grammar in *Vocativo* coincides with a starting point of our own reading. It is the *grammaticalismo* of that book we would like to investigate here and, specifically, the way in which the pronoun and the vocative demonstrate the motivation with which many readings recognize them to be charged.

We may begin with the situation of subjectivity in *Vocativo*. In a holiday chronology which places the earlier *Elegia e altri versi* between implied calendrical parentheses, *Vocativo* opens with "Epifania" [Epiphany], the celebration that follows Christmas by twelve days and by six the day of Saint Sylvester, where *Dietro il paesaggio* closed its Janus door. The revelatory appearance here is of no god, however, but of the *io* in all its worth. And that worth, the value attributed to subjectivity by itself, is declared to be as minimal as the smallest units, as the almost unimaginable sensations, like the wave of a squirrel's thirst, in a landscape that now is left behind by the same vehicle that provided the fortuitous, accidental encounter of the *io* and the *dio* some long time ago.

> Punge il pino i candori dei colli
> e il Piave muscolo di gelo
> nei lacci s'agita, nel bosco.
> Ecco il mirifico disegno
> 5 la lucente ferma provvidenza
> la facondia che esprime

        e rianncda e sfila
        echi gemme correnti.
        Tra voi parvenze e valli appena
10   sollecitate dal soffio del claxon,
        mormorate dall'alba,
        valgo come la foglia che riposa
        col vivo cardo col bozzolo e l'oro,
        valgo l'onda minuscola
15   che fu tua sete scoiattolo un giorno,
        valgo oltre il dubbio oltre l'inverno
        che s'attarda celeste ai tuoi balconi,
        valgo piú che il tuo stesso
        venir meno con la neve
20   che il motore per sempre, fuggendo
        dietro al sole, tralascia.⁶

        ◻

        [The pine pierces the hills' candours
        and the frost-muscled Piave
        fidgets in its snares, in the wood.
        Here is the wondrous design,
5   the shining still providence,
        the eloquence that explains
        and renews and displays
        echoes, gems, currents.
        Among you, appearances and valleys barely
10   quickened by the claxon's breath,
        whispered forth by the dawn,
        I am worth the leaf that rests
        with the living thistle, the cocoon and the gold,
        I am worth the minuscule wave
15   that was your thirst one day, squirrel,
        I am worth more than the doubt, more than the winter
        that lingers blue at your balconies,
        I am worth more than your own
        fainting away with the snow
20   that, fleeing behind the sun,
        the motor forever interrupts.]

The car drives off behind the sun to some other, more summery place while the *io* remains as part of the landscape which that vehicle has no power to call forth except barely, *appena*. His address to the landscape is no vocative, either, but direct: each pole of the message, both the subjective originator and the at first pluralized objective receiver, are on the same lowly plane. Here there are no gods; in fact, in a series of early signals of the importance the subjective gaze takes in these texts, the elements of the very landscape which gives the *io* its value are called appearances, *voi parvenze*. Three levels of visual perception are established prior to the *io*'s first declaration: the first sentence describes the winter landscape as it appears to an anonymous, omniscient eye; the *ecco* of sentence two establishes subjective rapport with that setting as one of presence; the third and lengthy final sentence sees the *io* immersed within the setting and then taking its own value as minimal entities of it. In another movement of reverse telescopy, the initially vast otherness (*voi parvenze*) is reduced to that of the tiny squirrel with its minuscule thirst-wave. The last vision is a landscape minimalized as the squirrel's *balconi* and the faintness of the little beast in the snow, a vision interrupted only by a sound as the motor's noise flees the scene. This initial reduction by degrees of what once was the sign system of the gods is another epiphany in a moment where not only subjectivity, but also perceived objectivity, is revealed as being much less than it might earlier have seemed, or been seen, to be.

The revelation of the *io*'s minimal value and the landscape's reduced scale provide tendential opposition between that *io*, which is proclaiming its existence, several times in fact, as a series of positive though minimal values, and the landscape, which might disappear from perception entirely were the reductive visual progression carried further. The risk of objective disappearance and the impetus to assert minimalized subjective being are simultaneous movements in a discourse which takes as its general epigraph Éluard's "Ce qui est digne d'être aimé / contre ce qui s'anéantit."[7]

An abrupt rejection of a subjective discourse about love appears partway through the third poem, "Piccola Elegia" [Little elegy], which nonetheless titularly and otherwise contradicts that rejection. The title recalls Zanzotto's second book, with its lament for a past when desire for the other was still possible. And the opening lines of the text echo in dyadic variation the desperate loneliness of Petrarch's attempt to leave love behind, while at the same time they attribute to *amore* a deeper validity than it had for the younger Zanzottan *io*:

> Giovane ed infelice
> qui torna l'anima mia,
> piú valido e fosco l'amore.[8]

ZANZOTTO'S GRAMMATICALISMO

> [Young and unhappy
> here my soul returns,
> more valid and darker the love.]

The reversal occurs after a hopeful signal that the future will hold the collective possibility of speaking the name buried in life-giving but inaccessible crevices, the sign lost now beneath the blossoming landscape:

>   Ti ridiremo, nome sepolto
> 5   tra questi clivi dove nuziale
>   s'apre la rosa ai pergolati
>   e giugno appannato d'acque e funghi
>   stillicidi insensibili protrae
>   per la festa delle api e delle zinnie.⁹

◘

>   [We shall say you again, name buried
> 5   among these hillocks where
>   the nuptial rose opens itself to the bowers
>   and June misted by waters and mushrooms
>   prolongs unfelt drippings
>   for the party of the bees and the zinnias.]

It is almost as if the *io* were taking what it lamented as being past in *Elegia e altri versi* and placing it in a future just as distant: this future of past impossibilities is perhaps just as much the topic of the little elegy as is the *io*'s own youth.

The discourse next turns, on a familiar Petrarchan *ma*, to an image of landscape self-annihilation like Éluard's *ce qui s'anéantit*:

> 10   Ma perpetuo il torrente nel fondo si divora.
>   Io sto solo e non parlo dell'amore.¹⁰

◘

> 10   [But the torrent is perpetually devoured in the depths.
>   I am alone and do not speak of love.]

The perpetual annihilation of the most constantly kinetic entity in the landscape is followed hard upon by the *io*'s statement of its own situation and its negative declaration about its own discourse. The torrent is devoured in a deep, perpetual motion; in stark contrast, the relatively static *io* accedes to solitude and a kind of silence.

But he does speak, if not of love; and he tells about his dottering young unhappiness and his self-repeating cry:

	Io membra incerte
	occhi sfibrati
	dall'aspro moto delle cose, avvinti
15	come residue vive contraddizioni
	al moto stesso della sera.
	Ah giovane ancora e infelice io sono
	e nulla posso
	e nulla posso dare.
20	E scopro nel mio cuore
	scritta l'elegia,
	e non ho pudore del mio pianto
	né dell'eco invocata.[11]

◻

	[I, uncertain limbs,
	eyes weakened
	by the harsh movement of things, enthralled
15	like live residual contradictions
	by the evening's very movement.
	Ah still young and unhappy am I
	and nothing can I
	and nothing can I give.
20	And I discover an elegy
	written in my heart
	and am not ashamed of my crying
	nor of the echo I invoke.]

So we see that this is an elegy for youth only in an inversion of time sequences: youth is not past, but present. The lament is for present puerile unhappiness as well as for a future which all too suspiciously resembles a shining past, the one when the *io* perhaps found the *nome* not buried but sparkling on the very leaves of what surrounded him. This *io* states its being now not as value, not even as what might be considered youthful; its self-description is more one of decrepitude, of tremblings caused by too much experience with the harsh movement of things, even of usually reposeful evening, than by youthful anticipation. And in its heart there is writing.

The elegy itself is perhaps not even any of what we are reading, in fact, for the *io* says he discovers it within himself. We cannot be sure he has transcribed for us the text in his heart; we only

ZANZOTTO'S GRAMMATICALISMO

know he is telling us it exists and that his discovery of it is preceded by a *recusatio* which, in its iterative insistence, renders abulic this old young man whose potency is nullified. Such a subjectivity early bound to its own demise feels it has nothing to give but also nothing to be ashamed of as it cries out, in the book's second signal of a vocative (which is nonetheless not yet a vocative but only a sign of a vocative elsewhere), only to its own echo. Solitary, solitary subjectivity: two times alone as it reads an elegy written only for itself and invokes only its own echo. The *io* we encountered in *Dietro il paesaggio* is already reduced here to a linguistically determined subjectivity: he no longer has an other-directed discourse (there is no *tu* in this elegy); but he still reads to himself, and he still cries out.

Then both the *io* and the landscape lose directionality as they eternally come apart like the syntax of this final sentence which never ends:

<blockquote>

Senza meta
e senza inizio, in quale
25   contraddizione, in quale
valle che stride e scivola e si spezza
nei millenni, che tuona
di querce in agonia . . . .[12]

◻

[Without aim
and without beginning, in which
25   contradiction, in which
valley that screeches and slips and shatters
through millenia, that thunders
with death-rattling oaks . . .]

</blockquote>

We may see *Vocativo* opening, then, in a kind of double movement. On the one hand, the *io* attributes to itself an ambivalent essence: it is first depicted as having a certain value on a minimal scale of integration with the landscape; soon afterwards, however, as the landscape disintegrates and as the *io* is no longer able to read the *nome* which is now buried in some source place and projected into an indistinct and collectivized future speech (*ti ridiremo / nome sepolto*), the *io* suddenly grows decrepit, impotent, dumb. On the other hand, with the disintegration of the landscape, we read the disappearance of the language of surrounding signs, the language which, in *Dietro il paesaggio* and *Elegia e altri versi*, allows the *io* to find its place, the relatively traditional poetic language which creates the space for subjective self-regard.

Here, then, the identity of subjectivity—what will soon, in the same book, be crystallized as pronominal enslavement or the purely linguistic nature of a subjectivity which finds no other space in which to be than that allotted it by deixis—depends entirely on the possibility of reading, of finding meaning through signs. As the external signs disappear, the subjectivity loses its claim to its own sign-determined place, the footholds that formerly provided its support. Gone are the little gods who in Hölderlinian swarms could infuse the landscape with significance. Going now, too, is the landscape, in an endless apocalypse where once there was syntax. And where does all this disintegration leave the *io*? Its discourse breaks like that of Hölderlin in his madness. Next, it will cry for its mother.

As subjective identity is reduced to dependency on linguistic functions (pronouns, vocatives, reading texts which are difficult to situate), it seeks refuge in origins. The first actual vocative uttered textually by this subjectivity suffering its own loss is for the mother, in "Altrui e mia I" [Others' and my own, I]. A doubly regressive movement occurs, first of the *io* wishing to find again its beginnings, and then of the *io*'s proffered image of his mother as an infant herself. This *mise-en-abyme* of origins, this zoom lens view erasing anything but beginnings in a potentially endless succession of starts that never finish, disintegrates the linear proprieties of narrative temporality. All proportion is unglued by subjective confusion in a Japanese-box series that, immediately upon uncovering something of the *io*'s origin, opens as well onto the origin of *io*'s originator.

Furthermore, since "Piccola elegia" revealed the *io*'s vocative as addressing an echo, we now associate the mother, object of the grammatical vocative, with that echo: origins are doubly confounded, both in temporal simultaneity and in singularity of discourse. The infantile mother is an echo of her child's invoking cry. By showing the mother herself as a baby, the *io* not only presents her as a linguistically circumscribed image of the life source in which he would perhaps find the *nome sepolto* itself, but also as the innocent, even immaculate genetrix, pure, unread text, without the marginalia of an external hand: thus the half-orphaned, linguistically defined *io* seems a product of continuity and similarity rather than of interruption and copulation.

(A reproductive aside. The purity of the infantile mother is an exact analogy to the innocence attributed to dialect speech in Zanzotto's general scheme. The mother tongue is corrupted by no images of contamination. Therefore, its only method of reproducing its purity untouched would implicitly be a kind of parthenogenesis. If there is a father, he is elsewhere, in some realm where things are contaminated, perhaps, touched and marked.

The father appears as a landscape painter, in fact, in "I paesaggi primi" [the first landscapes], which closes the first half of *Vocativo*. His link to the *io*'s identity perhaps lies in this: the landscape (*di Lorna che creasti e che ti crea* [of Lorna, which you created and which creates you], v. 16) and the *io* are both products of the paternal artifex (*tu artefice / di me, di un mai sopito amore* [you, artifex / of me, of a never-lulled love], vv. 17–18). Later, in the final pages of the eclogues that precede *La beltà*, we shall find the father within a metaphor of semantic heritage not limited to dialect or landscape. The father and the mother eventually come together in a union of poetic utterance and universal signification.)

"Altrui e mia, I, II" is, moreover, the first double text in *Vocativo*: where the *io* speaks to no one, where even thought fails him (*Ma la mia mente fallisce e non parlo / non parlo a nessuno*), there is still an impetus to call out to a mother and to say things twice. Perhaps by almost repeating (and by repeating quite literally in the vast system of iterative rhetorical devices used throughout *Vocativo*), the enunciating subjectivity can convince himself that he is finding authenticity or imbuing the discourse with it, somehow miming it by repetition. Or perhaps the repitions work more like returns, regressions themselves to some originary, more authentic place. (*Vocativo* is full of these stammerings at formal levels: there are ten double texts in *Vocativo* and one triple). Or perhaps the *io* is simply creating its own distorted echo, taking care to make sure some response will occur, even if it comes from no other, even if it only repeats the invocation that elicits it, even if "no other" disintegrates some original "mother."

The image of the mother in *Vocativo* seems closely connected both to the subject's speech situation and to his identity. We shall concentrate on the mother for a while longer, therefore, in order to observe closely how the *io*'s involvement with origins throws him back on the purely linguistically defined nature of his identity, the *grammaticalismo* in operation.

The *immondo calore* of summer, its *viscosa confusione*, perhaps birth images themselves, are the first glimpses we are given of the setting for the *io*'s return to the birth of the mother:

> Dalla viscosa confusione
> dall'immondo calore
> sempre invano accenna, sempre torna

```
                    tuo figlio, o madre, per le curve
     5              strade, per infiniti avvolgimenti¹³
```

◻

```
                    [From the viscous confusion
                    from the filthy heat
                    your son, o mother, always beckons
                    in vain, always returns over the curved
     5              roads, through infinite windings.]
```

Like mountain roads, the way back to origins—of origins—is not straight. Several lines on, the constancy of this crooked return is iterated next to filial infidelity mitigated by minimal landscape gifts (including the little cricket, sweet sign of summer and mother, for mother's July birth). Chronologies and temporalities now fold into each other like anniversaries:

```
                    Io sempre a te ritorno, a te ch'eri bambina
                    oggi: e nessun dono il mio cuore
                    dimentico t'ha offerto.
                    Nulla se non la popolosa luce
     15             e la cicaletta sul melo del cortile,
                    nulla per te sul desco
                    di scintillante e amabile.¹⁴
```

◻

```
                    [I always return to you, to you who were a child
                    today: and my forgetful heart
                    offered you no gift.
                    Nothing but the populous light
     15             and the cricket on the apple tree in the courtyard,
                    nothing sparkling and loveable
                    on the table for you.]
```

But the folding time sequences are interrupted by a faltering presence of mind of which muteness will be the isolating result. Now, the *io* extricates itself from a vague, cyclical consciousness as it descends without speech, out of breath and sightless, in an utterance that, like dialect, runs things together and anticipates adjectives. All this is present:

```
                    Ma la mia mente fallisce e non parlo
                    non parlo a nessuno. Veloce
```

20　　　　　　e sordo scendo dal frumento
　　　　　　　arso a monti, mi distolgo
　　　　　　　da cicli oscuri e porto
　　　　　　　afa e chiusi occhi.[15]

◻

　　　　　　　[But my mind fails and I do not speak
　　　　　　　I do not speak to anyone. Fast
20　　　　　　and deaf I descend from the wheat
　　　　　　　burnt in the mountains, I give up
　　　　　　　dark cycles and bring
　　　　　　　sultry weather and closed eyes.]

The question to follow presents the problematics of another *terminus* of identity than that of birth when it mimics Ungaretti's traditional Petrarchan concern with fame after death as it appears in "Canto primo" of "La morte meditata" in *Sentimento del tempo* [the feeling of time]: *Nella malinconia dei vivi/volerá a lungo la mia ombra?* [in the melancholy of the living, will my shadow fly for long?][16] The voice of Ungaretti, poet of a feeling of time, questions the *sorella dell'ombra*, death.[17] Here, in Zanzotto's text, however, the sphinx figure is not contemporary sister but originary mother, the subjective concern not identity-prolonging fame but a temporal exchange of distress, the feeling for time not a tradition musing on mortality but a jumbling-up of what might commonly be expected to hold some relationship of precedence and sequence or even cause and effect:

　　　　　　　Lascerò le mie pene di ieri
12　　　　　　per il tormento di questo
　　　　　　　oggi che tu volevi
　　　　　　　farmi felice
　　　　　　　narrandomi di te?[18]

◻

　　　　　　　[Shall I leave my yesterday's pains
12　　　　　　for the torment of this
　　　　　　　today that you wanted
　　　　　　　to make happy for me
　　　　　　　by telling me stories of yourself?]

The other's discourse thus specified as the mother's narration about herself is recognized as having been intended to produce a happy effect. But this maternal intention, this narration, her word, has somehow been deviated from its addressee. Subjectivity has no happy alternative in a choice between past pains and present torment; the *io*'s question is a kind of nightmare dilemma dependent on past narrations.

Or it would be, that is, if the sweet awakening that follows were not itself only a memory, a citation redoubling the unlikely chronologies of the *io*'s attempted return to origins and/or echoes:

> "Svegliati bimbo, la cicala ha cantato,
> 30   io sono nata, è luglio"[19]

◘

> ["Wake up, wee one, the cicada has sung,
> 30   I am born, it is July."]

The present narration is always subjective; it is never the desired word of the mother present but only the remembered word of the mother past. And the poem—or the double poem's first section—closes with an opening and a dolorous dawn of daily reality as the *io*'s oneiric evocation of maternal, linguistic beginnings ends like a repeated past action:

> Aprivi le finestre, io respiravo
> tutto il dolore dell'alba di luglio.[20]

◘

> [You were opening the windows, I was breathing
> all the pain of the July dawn.]

Here are some subsequent considerations regarding maternity, subjectivity, and linguistic determination of persons in *Vocativo* that will draw us further into Zanzotto's poetics.

1. The mother tongue in Pieve is dialect. In "Altrui e mia I, II," the mother's word appears not in dialect, but in the public language of the Italian text. The return to the mother is shown as a return to a disappearing point, as if to a disappearance of dialect itself. But the original (the mother) and the linguistically authentic (dialect) are unattainable, unpresentable. They are not present here.
2. The vocative in "Altrui e mia I" is empty of effect on its object. The invoked mother responds only in quotes, in a speech interpolated via memory and punctuation into subjective discourse.

The mother's word is only an echo in and of the subjective—and, by implication, inauthentic—utterance.
3. The only recognizable reality in this ruinous search for origins and authenticity is that held by the sign. All is sign in "Altrui e mia I," beginning with the unspecified possessives of the title. Even the "origin" is immediately a sign of itself multiplied *ad infinitum*. Significance is dramatically shown, therefore, as being doubly arbitrary: first, in its ordinary way, it depends on convention; second, with the crisis of subjectivity and the silence of the other, convention itself is threatened, and signs once trusted lose their meaning. They weigh heavily, like a too-bright dawn, on one who dreams of, but cannot grasp, origins or authenticity.
4. Nonetheless, invocation in "Altrui e mia I" is an act that, though without its intended effect, remains an act and therefore may be seen to alter a situation by its simple self-assertion, by its simple insertion of its self within that situation. How is this so, if the only response is subjective, a memory-echo of the speech of the other?

The emphasis here is perhaps not yet on the possible workings of the vocative, but on the implications its use has for the invoking subject. First, by calling to what is buried and will not respond or to a no longer present mother, the uttering subjectivity expresses a kind of desire for or even faith in the existence of a hidden maternal or authentic *nome*. Simultaneously, it also establishes its own position vis-à-vis that desired authenticity as a linguistically determined position like that of a supplicant who must use in his prayer the very linguistic signs that would be rendered unnecessary were that prayer to have a response or were the *nome sepolto* to prove utterable. But, as the search for subjective identity in maternal origins results in a progressive linguistic reduction of that identity, the *io* gradually turns from the mother to the landscape once again, and he seems to find in poetry a possible bridge between his linguistically ensnared (and thus inauthentic) person and the nonlinguistic (and thus authentic) landscape reality.

The poems that follow "Altrui e mia I" and precede "Caso vocativo" [Vocative case] give increasingly evident signals of the realization of this subjective situation. In "Altrui e mia II," for example, the vocatives addressed to the mother continue, but no response is represented. A more narrative mode appears instead to describe the sun-induced blinding of the subjective gaze which opened *Vocativo* by diminishing degrees:

>   Dove madre m'acceca
>   l'estate, dove io sono?
>   La mia strada s'inerba e dispera.
> 15   Dove, tra crepe di nuvole
>   negre, che sempre mi tolgono
>   libertà, io penso e non mi vedo?[21]

◻

>   [Where, mother, does summer
>   blind me? Right where I am?
>   My road grasses over and gives up.
> 15   Where, between cracks of black
>   clouds that always steal my
>   freedom, I think and see myself not?]

In the following text, "Elegia del venerdí I" [Elegy for Friday, I], *tu* (which may be an objectivization of the *io* or a personification of dialect in crisis) provides the point of view for an image of landscape harshness in a temporality delineated by canonical hours, hours of prayer, of faithful invocation (as are all times given in *Vocativo*):

>   Torna il monte, scalfisce un canto ad attimi
>   calcinati riposi,
> 15   a valve aperte il crepuscolo attende,
>   o ardente l'ora sesta
>   sugge rugiade e fragole
>   al cupo bosco. Ritorna il tuo sguardo
>   e il grande pianto e come
> 20   di flabelli e di nuvole e di torce
>   verde ribolle il luglio
>   nella stretta dei ghiacci, nel pugnace
>   nel non placato azzurro d'una notte
>   scaturirai
> 25   cometa soffocata.
>   Ansimante di fieni ti rivedo
>   ti rivedo perduto
>   nelle tue povere scritture
>   su cui piove equivoca la morte.[22]

◻

>   [The mountain returns, a song now and then
>   breaks into the calcified quiet,
> 15   with open valves it awaits the twilight,

```
             or, burning, the sixth hour
             sucks dew and strawberries
             from the dark wood. Your gaze returns
             and the great cry and how
     20      July bubbles up green
             with flabella and clouds and torches
             in the ice's grasp, in the pugnacious
             in the unappeased azure of a night
             you will gush forth,
     25      a suffocated comet.
             Panting from the hay I see you again
             I see you lost again
             in your poor writings
             upon which death ambiguously rains.]
```

The second part of the elegy of the last day before the Sabbath that is never to be (*il sabato d'oro e di rame che non sarà mai* [the Sabbath of gold and brass that never shall be], v. 3) contains a literal identification of subjectivity with an endless everyday of nearnesses or silences that never becomes more:

```
     10      Sei, venerdí di cereo sole
             e di tetre lusinghe di vallate
             intorno alla mia mente come un gemito,
             sei, stretto come tomba, errante come scala
             percossa da un mattino che rispecchia follia.
     15      Sei me, sei questa ebete lena
             di muco e d'astenie,
                —vicinanza che gli occhi cauterizza
             o silenzi che offendono
             anche il piú scarso monte del meriggio—
     20      sei la povera casa ed il povero cibo
             ch'io consumo agitato da terribili cieli.²³
```

◘

```
     10      [You, Friday of waxen sun
             and the gloomy enticements of valleys,
             are around my mind like a groan,
             you, narrow like a grave, wandering like a staircase,
             are struck by a madness-mirroring morn.
     15      You are me, you are this dull strength
             of mucus and asthenias,
                —eye-cauterizing nearness
```

> or silences that offend
> even noon's scantiest mountain—
> 20 you are the poor house and the poor food
> that I consume troubled by terrible skies.]

"Esperimento I" [Experiment I], the poem that follows "Elegia del venerdí I e II," continues the summer setting and presents a bridge image (*torno al sole del ponte / a te avaro arco su acri correnti / fredde che sempre mi turbano*) [I return to the sun of the bridge / to you, miserly arch over harsh, cold currents that trouble me always] (vv. 10–12) which is developed extensively in "Esperimento II." In the first "Esperimento" text, it is a bridge over a Dantesque river of final good-byes leading to a familiarly mechanically situated, if ephemeral, identification of the *io*:

> Si sperpera gigante, si risucchia
> e sfonda l'Acheronte.
> E alla forza degli addii
> 20 irreversibili, al fragore
> sovrano del motore
> arretro, esile fisima, e deterso
> presto è di me il petrigno bosco.[24]

◻

> [Gigantic, the Acheron
> dissipates, sucks itself back, and bursts open.
> 20 And, accompanied by the strength of irreversible
> good-byes, and by the sovereign
> din of the motor,
> I fall back, a feeble fancy, and soon
> the stony wood is cleansed of me.]

In the second "Esperimento" poem, the *io*, just now fleetingly self-defined as *esile fisima*, attempts a futile escape from constitutive *torride finzioni* by burying itself in surroundings of physicality, equating that very physicality, perhaps, with an authentic reality that has no need or tendency to go beyond itself or to signify:

> All'estate all'essudarsi
> di me dell'essere in torride finzioni
> alla luce immedicabile

volgo invano le reni,
5   m'interro in fisiche verdi lentezze.²⁵

◻

[On the summer, on the exudation
of myself of being in torrid fictions,
on the unhealable light
I turn my back in vain,
5   I bury myself in green physical slownesses.]

But the *io* immediately realizes that these *fisiche verdi lentezze*, these long-term nonverbal growths in which he would evade pretense and inauthenticity, themselves contain, as does a sign, that which surpasses them. There are strong reminders here of the Pievan landscape, with its rivers and old churches, and of the Montello wood, scene of many bloody battles not all in the distant past and consequently itself a graveyard now. But even this landscape, perhaps illegible in its *luce immedicabile*, contains some assiduous excess that seems to demand a kind of reading. The landscape contains and is constituted by, place, time, and blood: harsh surroundings, an hour screaming with songs, prayers, and reciprocal murder:

Ma pure è vostro questo greto assiduo
che eccede, vostra è l'ora
che stride di canzoni e di preghiere,
vostro il sangue premuto dalle nuche
10   uomo da uomo²⁶

◻

[But still this assiduous gravelly shore that goes too far
is yours, yours is the hour
that shrieks with songs and prayers,
yours the blood pressed from the nape
10   man to man]

In surprise and alienation, the *io* notices, via familiar synesthesia, another bridge, which, by use of the equivocal *scansione*, is also verse. In the preceding line group, the notion of poetry is suggested by the mention of both song and prayer; it appears there between an image of location and one of death in a kind of anaphoristic assimilation that might imply a serial association of those three notions. In this line group, however, the bridge, to whatever extent it may also be read as poetry, shows itself as a connective, the way, the life, and the truth, the support over ravines, the quasi-scriptural link which here itself seems in need of an opening or something to connect:

>   A bocca aperta mi sento remoto
>
>   E giá zampeggia il ponte
>
>   O scansione sospesa
>   via vita verità
> 15   ponte chi t'aprirà
>   tra informi tenebrose onuste erbe,
>   ponte chi ti darà
>   alle armate ombre sul greto
>   alle erte acque in rovina?²⁷

▄

> [Open-mouthed I feel remote
>
> And the bridge is already pawing the ground
>
>   O suspended scansion
>   way life truth
> 15   bridge who will open you
>   among formless shady burdened grasses,
>   bridge who will give you
>   to the shadows at arms on the gravelly shore
>   to the ruined waters on alert?]

Finally, the poem ends without closure, appositively identifying a bridging both vortex and void as the location of indexed alterity, a *tu* no longer simply identifiable, as it is in the vocative just preceding, as the bridge itself:

> 20   E tu nel vuoto nel vortice del ponte,
>   tu la cui bella fronte
>   soggiace al verde squamoso del mondo . . . ²⁸

▄

> 20   [And you in the void in the vortex of the bridge,
>   you whose beautiful brow
>   lies subject to the world's squamous green . . .]

The earlier *fisiche verdi lentezze* now appear as a squalid reality to which some still clear idea of innocent or original alterity, the *bella fronte*, succumbs. But here, even when the other is no longer specifically identified as the mother, even when there seems to be no noun to attribute to the pronoun, *tu* persists simply as grammatically indicated otherness; in so doing, it reserves for the *io* the continued possibility of song and invocation, *l'ora . . . di canzoni e preghiere*.

With these considerations in mind of the progressive thematic reduction of subjectivity to a linguistically-determined essence, we may jump ahead a bit to several telling statements in the second part of the book, entitled "Prima persona" [First person].

The second poem of this first person second section, the poem from which the section takes its name, contains two *ios*: one is the giver of the message, the implicit speaking-voice subjectivity, and the other is the pronoun which is subject of no verb but only the nominal identity of the receiver also deictically indicated as *tu* (in verse three). So we read this text as the *io*'s address to his linguistically-determined self, the self that makes itself known by saying "I":

—Io—in tremiti continui,—io—disperso
e presente: mai giunge
l'ora tua,
mai suona il cielo del tuo vero nascere.[29]

[—I—in continuous tremblings,—I—dispersed
and present: never does
your hour arrive,
never does the sky resound with your true birthing.]

After this subjective recognition of the impossibility of speaking its own authentically original identity, the "speaking" subjectivity identifies the *io*, nonetheless, as a surrounding essence, figuratively a landscape:

5   Ma tu scaturisci per lenti
         boschi, per lucidi abissi,
         per soli aperti come vive ventose,
         tu sempre umiliato lambisci
         indomito incrini
10   l'essere macilento
         o erompente in ustioni.
         Sul vetro
         eternamente oscuro

ZANZOTTO'S GRAMMATICALISMO

<blockquote>

            sfugge pasqua dagli scossi capelli
15   primavera dimora e svanisce.
            Tu ansito costretto e interrotto
            ora, ora e sempre,
            insaziabile e smorto raggiungermi.
            Ora e sempre?[30]

5   [But you gush forth through slow
            woods, through shining abysses,
            through suns open like live suction cups,
            you lick, always humbled,
            you crack, unsubdued,
10   emaciated or erupting-in-scaldings
            being.
            On the eternally
            dark glass
            touseled-haired Easter flees
15   springtime dwells and disappears.
            You constrained and interrupted gasp
            now, now and forever,
            insatiable, pale catching-up-with-me.
            Now and forever?]

</blockquote>

In answer to this question, the text proposes an if-clause possibility of an ideated touch which would be able to write, so to speak, the landscape-season language upon the very *vetro* that has just been called *eternamente oscuro*. Such a touch, the *ombra* of some undefined *bene*, an *idea* may activate signification procedures which do not exclude the first person pronoun:

<blockquote>

                        Ma se di un bene
20   l'ombra, se di un'idea
            solo mi tocchi, o vortice a cui corrono
            i conati malcerti, il fioco
            sospingermi del cuore. E là nel vetro
            pasqua e maggio e il rissoso lume affondano
25   e l'infinito verde delle piogge.
            Col motore sobbalza
            la strada e il fango, cresce
            l'orgasmo, io cresco io cado.[31]

                      [But if the shadow
20   of a good, of an idea,

</blockquote>

>   even only barely touches me, oh vortex
>   my uncertain efforts, my
>   heart's faint propulsion, run to. And there in the glass
>   Easter and May and the quarrelsome light
> 25 and the endless green of the rains sink down.
>   Along with the motor the street
>   and the mud start up, the orgasm
>   grows, I grow I fall.]

In fact, it would seem that these procedures reveal the constitutive relation of interruptions—an idea, the bounding of a car, an orgasm—to subjectivity. It was said, earlier in the same text, *Tu ansito costretto e interrotto/ora, ora e sempre* (vv. 16–17). Now, with the bounding and the orgasm, *io cresco io cado* results: subjectivity defined grammatically as the pronoun which personalizes verbs of ascent and descent. This *io* is not in quotes, and so it may be seen as a moment of covenant between the speaking subject and its pronomial addressee counterpart.

The poem concludes with a statement of this covenant, this peace treaty, this identity-deal made by subjectivity with its linguistic determinant:

>   Di te vivrò fin che distratto ecceda
> 30 il tuo nume sul mio
>   già estinto significato,
>   fin che in altri terrori tu rigermini
>   in altre vanificazioni.³²

◘

>   [In you I shall live until
> 30 your distracted diety goes beyond
>   my already extinct meaning,
>   until you regerminate in other terrors,
>   in other thwartings.]

The entire first part of the "Prima persona" section of *Vocativo* may, in fact, be read as a story of the *io*'s ambivalent recognition of this treaty which holds no victory, no moment of original identity identifiable without language. Here are some fleeting examples:

>   E tutte le cose a me intorno
>   colgo precorse nell'esistere.
>   ("Idea," vv. 1–2)

◘

[And I gather all the things that are around me
which have gone before in existence].

> Anche per te, mio linguaggio, favilla
> e traversia, per sconsolato sonno
> per errori e deliqui
> per pigrizie profonde inaccessibili,
> che ti formasti corrotto e assoluto.
> Anche tu mio brevissimo nitore
> di cellule mentali, tronco alone
> di gridi e di pensieri
> imprevisti ed eterni.
> ("Idea," vv. 8–16)

[For you, too, my language, spark
and mishap, for disconsolate sleep,
for errors and swoons,
for deep unreachable laziness,
you who trained to be corrupt and absolute.
You, too, my brain cells'
briefest brightness, truncated halo
of unforeseen and eternal
cries and thoughts.]

Chi, luce, a te mi conferma,
chi alla sostanza al tangibile al folto?
("Ineptum, prorsus credibile II," vv. 1–2)

[Who, light, bears witness of me to you?
Who to substance to the tangible to that which is thick?]

Madre, dondo il mio dirti,
perché mi taci come il verde altissimo
il richissimo nihil,
che incombe e esalta, dove
beatificanti fiori e venti gelidi
s'aprono dopo il terrore—e tu, azzurro,

a me stesso, allo specchio che evolve
nel domani, ancora mi conformi?
                ("Da un'altezza nuova I"
                [From a New Height], vv. 8–15)

[Mother, whence my saying you,
why like the highest green do you not speak to me,
like the richest nihil
that impends and exalts, where
beatifying flowers and icy winds
open themselves after the terror—and you, azure,
do you still shape me to myself,
to the mirror that evolves in tomorrow?]

Un senso che non muove ad un'immagine,
un colore disgiunto da un'idea,
un'ansia senza testimoni
o una pace perfetta ma precaria:
questo è l'io che mi désti, madre e che ora
appena riconosco, né parola
né forma né ombra?
                ("Da un'altezza nuova II," vv. 1–7)

[A sense that does not move to an image,
a color detached from an idea,
an anxiety without witnesses
or a perfect but precarious peace:
is this the I you awoke to me, mother, and that now
I scarcely recognize, neither word
nor shape nor shadow?]

    It is in light of this reductive process of subjective self-identification that we may understand the pronominal parameter of the *grammaticalismo* in *Vocativo*. The *io* recognizes that its only signification as self is a linguistic one. On the one hand, such a recognition then extends to surrounding identities. But, on the other hand, this recognition reinforces a subjective desire to find some kind of awareness, nonetheless, of a prelinguistic self: an unspeakable *io* somehow temporally *dietro* a worded self-consciousness. We may read "Esistere psichicamente" [Existing psychically] as a statement of these situations:

>   Da questa artificiosa terra-carne
>   esili acuminati sensi
>   e sussulti e silenzi,
>   da questa bava di vicende
> 5   —soli che urtarono fili di ciglia
>   ariste appena sfrangiate pei colli—
>   da questo lungo attimo
>   inghiottito da nevi, inghiottito dal vento,
>   da tutto questo che non fu
> 10 primavera non luglio non autunno
>   ma solo egro spiraglio
>   ma solo psiche,
>   da tutto questo che non è nulla
>   ed è tutto ciò ch'io sono:
> 15 tale la verità geme a se stessa,
>   si vuole pomo che gonfia ed infradicia.
>   Chiarore acido che tessi
>   i bruciori d'inferno
>   degli atomi e il conato
> 20 torbido d'alghe e vermi,
>   chiarore-uovo
>   che nel morente muco fai parole
>   e amori.[33]

◘

>   [From this artificial earth-flesh
>   slender sharp senses
>   and starts and silences,
>   from this slaver of events
> 5   —suns that struck eyelash strands
>   scarcely fringed ears of corn on the hillsides—
>   from this long moment
>   swallowed by snows, swallowed by the wind,
>   from all this that was not
> 10 springtime not July not autumn
>   but only sick spiral
>   but only psyche,
>   from all this which is nothing
>   and is all that I am;
> 15 so does truth moan to itself,

>   wish it were an apple tree that swells and rots.
>   Acidic glimmer that you weave,
>   hell-stings
>   of atoms and the restless
> 20   retchings of weeds and worms,
>   egg-gleam
>   that in the dying mucus you make into words
>   and loves.]

In a departure from attempts at paraphrase, we would like to offer here, as a kind of minimally commented commentary, several quotes from Émile Benveniste in "De la subjectivité dans le langage."[34] Benveniste sees humanhind as inseparable from language and thereby challenges the notion of a prelinguistic state which might be seen as the variant phylogenic counterpart of the *io*'s ontogenic fallacy or hope in *Vocativo*:

> Le langage est dans la nature de l'homme, qui ne l'a pas fabriqué. Nous sommes toujours enclins a cette imagination naive d'une période originelle où un homme complet se découvrirait un semblable, également complet, et entre eux, peu à peu, le langage s'élaborerait. C'est là pure fiction. Nous n'atteignons jamais l'homme séparé du langage et nous ne le voyons jamais l'inventant. Nous n'atteignons jamais l'homme réduit à lui-même et s'ingéniant à concevoir l'existence de l'autre. C'est un homme parlant que nous trouvons dans le monde, un homme parlant à un autre homme, et le langage enseigne la définition meme de l'homme.[35]

◘

> [Language is in the nature of man, who did not invent it. Our inclination is always toward this naive image of an original period when a complete man would discover for himself a likeness, equally complete, and between the two of them, little by little, language would develop. This is pure fiction. We never get back to man separate from language and we never see him inventing it. We never get back to man reduced to himself alone and contriving to conceive of the existence of the other. It is a speaking man that we find in the world, a man speaking to another man, and language teaches the very definition of man.]

With Zanzotto's line *tale la verità geme a se stessa* in mind, we follow Benveniste further:

> C'est dans et par le langage que l'homme se constitue comme *sujet*; parce que le langage seul fonde en réalité, dans *sa* réalité qui est celle de l'être, le concept d' "ego."[36]

◘

> [It is within and by means of language that man constitutes himself as *subject* because only language founds the concept of "ego" in reality, in *its* reality which is the reality of being.]

And, with the Zanzottan title "Esistere psichicamente," as our beacon, we proceed with Benveniste:

> La "subjectivité," dont nous traitons ici est la capacité du locuteur à se poser comme "sujet." Elle se définit, non par le sentiment que chacun éprouve d'être lui-même (ce sentiment, dans la mesure où l'on peut en faire état, n'est qu'un reflet), mais comme l'unité psychique qui transcende la totalité des expériences vécues qu'elle assemble, et qui assure la permanence de la conscience. Or nous tenons que cette "subjectivité," qu'on la pose en phénoménologie ou en psychologie, comme on voudra, n'est que l'émergence dans l'être d'une propriété fondamentale du langage. Est "ego" qui *dit* "ego." Nous trouvons là le fondement de la "subjectivité," qui se détermine par le statut linguistique de la "personne."[37]

◻

> [The "subjectivity" of which we are speaking here is the capacity of the speaker to set himself up as "subject." It is defined not by the feeling everyone has of being himself (this feeling, to the extent that one can ascertain it, is no more than a reflection), but as the psychic unity which transcends the totality of the lived experiences it assembles and insures the permanence of consciousness. Now, we hold that this "subjectivity," whether one considers it in phenomenological or in psychological terms, is no more than the emergence within being of a fundamental property of language. He who *says* "ego" is "ego." There we find the basis of "subjectivity," which is determined by the linguistic status of the "person."]

The *io* who says *io* in Zanzotto's book is also one who hesitates to let his essence be drained by the vampiristic determinism of the pronoun. This is nowhere so evident as in the complex poem that follows "Esistere psichicamente." "L'impossibilità della parola" [The word's impossibility] is inspired, a note tells us, by Dreyer's classic film *Nosferatu*. With its series of hypothetical subjective identifications with the vampires, it gurgles with familiar imagery. In another context, such figures from "L'impossibilità della parola" as *dal basso / dolce e pauroso, bisbigli / di campane e il compianto di novembre, la vostra / umile apoteosi* would perhaps bring to mind the *io*'s trajectories on the surfaces of the Pievan landscape. As do many others, this too would seem to be a poem about signs, signs which vampirize subjectivity. The "Impossibilità della parola" may be read as a charitable if gory meditation by subjectivity on its own linguistic captivity. In this expressionist text, where the impossible is the only reality, the *io* who says *io* now identifies himself with a worded denial of that self, *io-non-io*:

Se con te, sorella, se in tua vece
giacendo corpo di vetro, dal vetro
della bara dal basso
dolce e pauroso, il mondo
5 veduto avessi, ieri, tra bisbigli
di campane e il compianto di novembre
—come in un vecchio film venne narrato—
se il tuo silenzio col mio mutato avessi,
non maggiore l'affanno, non la morte
10 maggiore: e consumato
lo stanco equivoco ora mi dorrei?
E se per te compagno, se in tua vece
i folgoranti prati
la terra tagliente la neve
15 saziata avessi,
nel tuo grido quale grido mio
per te, dal cuore lacerato, quale
fatale e fosco giorno a lieto volto
a aperto petto salutato avrei.
20 Che mi trattenne lungi
da voi, dal vostro sonno
sterile o dalla vostra
umile apoteosi? Forse quella
che dicono sporca speranza—
25 e al gioco spinto ancora
da viscere agitate
di presente, di fisici conati,
non disertai da questo
esistere ove terra
30 tocca e beve la mente, dove il sole
è un lontano martirio.
Non disertai, né seguirvi mi fu dato
oltre l'accadimento
lo schema atono afoso delle lacrime.

35 Speranza e fede, virtú che dai cieli
discendono, assai piú che il fuoco offeso
di carità. Voci ed occhi traditi
assai, ma piú tu offesa
carità senza potenza, sgomenta
40 anima; né te volli salvare
per alla fine perderti, pietoso
non fui troppo di me se prime e verdi

```
                sempre, nelle ombre mie,
                speranza carità fede non foste
45              voi quella che pietà di noi si dice.
                E se un giorno dal fango,
                da una veglia impossibile,
                o da una sede non umana,
                o da un'innominabile certezza
50              io-non-io ripensassi a questo spazio
                gocciola, astuta pietra, a questa
                sacra e feroce brevità di cose
                e sensi e segni, se il fuoco di Marte
                cogliessi avvolto alle sue sere e mari
55              di salutari effimere salsedini
                e fanciulle protese ad abbracciare
                il luccichio degl'inferi
                e l'opera che edifica e ricade
                in sé come in un sogno, forse anch'io
60              —reo di speranza e d'amore—
                se tu fossi, sarei, tu ch'è da folli
                il nominare, da folli il tacere?
                Stipato avello, attesa, eco, di testa
                mozza: al piú blasfemo
65              dei silenzi equivale.
                Ma donde in suoni che nulla
                non di te colmi insegnano, non cieli
                né opere né volti né lo stesso
                adusto loro contraddirsi,
70              io mi trascino e tento?
                Dai mattini orribili tu liberami
                dalla luce infinita che non leva
                a sé le mie scomposte
                passioni, i gesti invano ripetuti,
75              ai mattini toglimi, ai risvegli
                nel raggiante terrore,
                tu risveglio perpetuo su te stesso.[38]
```

◘

```
                [If with you, sister, if lying, in your stead,
                a body of glass, from the glass
                of the coffin, from the sweet and fearful
                below, the world
5               I yesterday had seen, among whispers
                of bells and November's wail
```

—as it was told in an old film—
if your silence I had exchanged with my own,
the anxiety no greater, no greater
10 death; and, having used up the exhausted
misunderstanding, would I now feel regret?
And if for you, companion, if in your stead
I had sated
the dazzling meadows
15 the cutting earth the snow,
in your cry as my own cry
for you, from my lacerated heart,
what fatal and foul a day I would have greeted
with cheerful face and open breast.
20 What kept me far
from you, from your sterile
sleep or your
humble apotheosis? Maybe
what they call dirty hope—
25 and thrust again into the game
by viscera restless
with the present, with physical retchings,
I did not desert this
existence where earth
30 touches and drinks the mind, where the sun
is a faraway martyrdom.
I did not desert, nor was it given me to follow you
beyond the occurrence
the toneless sultry pattern made by tears.

35 Hope and faith, virtues which from the skies
descend, much more than the offended fire
of charity. Voices and eyes much betrayed,
but you the more offended,
powerless charity, dismayed
40 soul; nor did I wish to save you, soul,
to lose you in the end, nor did I indulge
in too much self-pity if,
always first and green in my shadows,
you—hope, charity and faith—were not she
45 who is called have-pity-on-us.
And if one day from the mud,
from an impossible wake,
or from a place not human,

```
                or from an unnameable certainty,
     50         I-not-I were to think again of this pendant
                space, shrewd rock, of this
                holy and ferocious brevity of things
                and senses and signs, if I were to gather
                the fire of Mars wrapped in its evenings and seas
     55         of healthful ephemeral salts
                and girls outstretched to embrace
                the glitter of the netherworld
                and the work that edifies and falls back
                upon itself as in a dream, perhaps I too
     60         —guilty of hope and love—
                I too would be if you were, you whose naming
                is for madmen, you who madmen leave unsaid?
                Crowded grave, wait, echo of a lopped-off
                head—worth as much
     65         as the most blasphemous silence.
                But why in sounds that, not being full of you,
                teach nothing, not skies
                nor works nor faces nor their own
                scorched self-contradiction,
     70         why do I drag myself along and keep on trying?
                Free me from the horrible mornings,
                from the endless light that does not raise
                unto itself my dishevelled
                passions, my vainly repeated gestures,
     75         loose me from the mornings, from my wakings
                in the radiant terror,
                you, perpetual awakening on yourself.]
```

The unnamable other. The other who it is crazy not to name. If this *tu* were somehow actually to exist, then so would the *io*, who in any case is dragged along and tempted by sounds which teach (or sign, *insegnano*) only a fullness of *tu*. The text culminates in an imperative: *tu liberami*. The *io-non-io* desires to be released from vain repetition, from *mattini* and infinite, terrifying light (elsewhere, we may remember, the initiator of significant differences, shadows, and signs). To this end, he paradoxically implores the very essence of repetition; but the vampire's dark and constant reawakenings do not resemble his own well-lit mornings. And so we see that the minimalized, grammatically-rendered *io*, the voided *io-non-io*, in fact, does not extend his own negation to the pronomial enslavement of the other. *Tu* never becomes *tu-non-tu* but is figured, instead, both in hope and in terror, as an essential *tu-autre*, different enough from *io*, and even from *io-non-io*, to hold the promise of some communicable self-consciousness: *tu risveglio perpetuo su te stesso*.

This vampire bite in which the self-negating, pronomial *io* envisions both its own essence and communication with otherness leads us from our considerations of the pronomial aspects of Zanzotto's *grammaticalismo* to a consideration of the verbal aspect, itself determined or vampirized by its pronomial poles: the titular and constitutive act of *Vocativo*, a verbal case.

One of the prime effects of verbality in this work as elsewhere is to situate pronomial agents in time. Our consideration of the *caso vocativo* [vocative case] begins with the double poem of that title which occurs halfway through the first section of *Vocativo* and clearly demonstrates a preoccupation with the passing of time; the realities of landscapes, sound, movement, love pass away as a future becomes. Although the text begins with a disparaging vocative, appositively one of the vocative itself, it seems that the subjective distress at the futile and temporal nature of its own language (and hence, its own self) may paradoxically provide a key to the insistence, nonetheless, in the texts that follow, on using that case. Our intention is to show how the vocative acts in those texts, to some extent enacting its own existence as at least (and at most) a grammatically determined entity, with an authenticity that at least (and at most) echoes that of the *nome sepolto*: a *carpe verbum* imitation of *carpe Verbum*. This act, exemplified in the paradoxical dialectic of a vocative addressed to that which will not respond by that which has no external definition other than a pronoun, constitutes the illocutionary nature of Zanzotto's *grammaticalismo*.

The *io*'s invocation of the vocative under the voracity of the summer sky opens the poem:

```
             O miei mozzi trastulli
             pensieri in cui mi credo e vedo,
             ingordo vocativo
             decerebrato anelito.
5            Come lordo e infecondo
             avvolge un cielo
             armonie di recise ariste, vene
             dubitanti di rivi,
             e qui deruba
10           già le lampade ai deschi
             sostituisce il bene.
```

>   Come i cavi s'ingranano a crinali
>   i crinali a tranelli a gru ad antenne
>   e ottuso mostro
> 15   in un prima eterno capovolto
>   il futuro diviene.
>   Il suono il movimento
>   l'amore s'ammollisce in bava
>   in fisima, gettata
> 20   torcia il sole mi sfugge.
>   Io parlo in questa
>   lingua che passerà.[39]

◻

>   [O my broken playthings,
>   thoughts in which I see and believe myself,
>   greedy vocative,
>   decerebrated yearning.
> 5   What a grimy and infertile
>   sky wraps up
>   harmonies of cut aristas, doubting
>   veins of riverbanks,
>   and here already steals
> 10   lamps from the dinner-tables,
>   substitutes the good.
>   How cables mesh with the ridges,
>   the snared craned antennaed ridges,
>   and the future becomes
> 15   an obtuse monster
>   turned upside down in an eternal "before."
>   Sound, movement,
>   love soften in slaver
>   in whim; the sun,
> 20   a cast-off torch, escapes me.
>   I speak in this
>   tongue that will pass.]

The forbidding noonday sun seems to be all that remains as the *io*'s jeremiad continues in "Caso vocativo II," where the locative tendency now supplants *il paesaggio* with *la mia vita* as the surface holding something *dietro*:

>   Anni perduti sotto la rotta vampa
>   pomeridiana dei cicloni,

anni dove l'attesa mi dissolse,
dove straziato il ritorno invocai;
5   là dietro la mia vita,
presso l'addentante
torrenziale condanna
che mezzogiorno ormai vieta e la vana
perennità del sole.
10   Tremo e piango tra i boschi?[40]

◻

[Years lost beneath the broken postmeridian
blaze of the cyclones,
years where waiting dissolved me,
where racked I invoked return;
5   there behind my life,
near the biting
torrential condemnation
that by now prohibits noontime and the sun's
vain perpetuity.
10   Do I tremble and cry within the woods?]

The *io* who questions the actuality of his own actions next invokes the earth itself, represented as a hostile thickness from which his tongue extricates itself, as if from the past tense of a tomb, to vacillate according to the shifting, sickened sky:

O grumi verdi, ostile
spessore d'erompenti pieghe,
terra—passato di tomba—
donde la mia
15   lingua disperando si districa
e vacilla; vacilla se dal dorso
attonito del monte
smuove le sue lebbrose fronti il cielo.
Ah passaggio mio fervido, accorato
20   amoroso passaggio. Vedo felci
avanzare e sciuparsi nelle nere
correnti, e tra vaganti
inferni, gorghi atomici, il pudore d'ortica
e il vino e il dolce lavoro di Dolle
25   deprimere il suo lume,
e la vite inclinarsi disossata

sventurata sulle case, e l'uva
chiudere il vento e il giorno.⁴¹

❏

[O green clots, hostile
thickness of erupting folds,
earth—past tense of tomb—
whence my despairing
15   tongue extricates itself
and vacillates; vacillates if from the mountain's
stunned ridge the sky
shifts its leprous brown.
Ah my fervent passage, my heartbroken,
20   amorous passage. I see ferns
get left over and go to ruin in the black
streams, and I see the nettle modesty
and the wine and the sweet work of Dolle
turn down their light among rambling
25   hells, atomic whirlpools,
and the vine bend boneless
and wretched over the houses, and the grapes
close off the wind and the day.]

The landscape, *paesaggio*, no longer legible, nor either the last hope of authenticity, has given way to subjective, implicitly temporal, passage, *passaggio*. This two-letter difference marks a shift in emphasis in the *io*'s discourse regarding subjectivity and utterance; it marks a move from landscape to some kind of internally measured temporality as a central metaphor; it marks a shift from the signifying potential of surroundings to internalizing attempts at signification; it marks, perhaps, a shift in subjective sensibility from context to text.

(We arbitrarily choose this moment to note a phenomenon which, though it does not occur in the poem we have just been discussing, may have significance at any point of a discourse concerning *Vocativo*. It is, in other words, a clue, appearing in a sparse but powerful pattern of distribution throughout the book: the use of Latin quotes. In itself, the appearance of Latin, either literally or in syntax formations, is not uncommon in Zanzotto's work, as we have already noted. In *Vocativo*, however, the Latin words are quotes; moreover, they are biblical quotes: the *montes exsultastis* of "Dove io vedo, II" [Where I see, II] is from Psalms 113:6; the *gloria in excelsis* of "Ineptum, prorsus credibile, I" is from Luke 19:38; the *surrexit* of "Io attesto" [I bear witness] may claim many sources in the gospels, perhaps especially in Mark.

These biblical quotations do more than provide a citation practice in keeping with the use of canonical hours for time telling in *Vocativo*. Two of the Latin quotations are from the New Testament, a new covenant in a new time, to echo the subjective covenant established in the story. Somewhat iterative, they total three, and we can hardly help but notice that this trinity, with its theological associations of fullness, describes one of the *io*'s most familiar directionalities and modalities: ascent and exaltation.

What are we to make of this Latin retelling, *in nuce*, of what we earlier came to recognize as part of the story of the *io*, encountering poetry, reading landscape signs, and becoming confused in its own subjectivity? It may be that these three little clues are most easily decipherable if we look at what they in some way displace. Now we are given hints from the Bible, whereas previously the *io*'s story was inscribed in Hölderlinian hints from the gods. The notion of the word of the deity has not been discarded. But now the word is quite literally scripture, while earlier it was landscape superfice.

A movement from surrounding landscape signs to the textual word par excellence has occurred. The Latin in *Vocativo* may thus be read as another instance of the shift from context to text, from *paesaggio* to *passaggio*, so to speak. Subtly but surely, the notion of the sign turning up here and there in bursts of nominalism, the sign as decipherable identity tag for a reality other than itself, is being displaced or at least accompanied by the notion of the word as an event, as a scriptural sort of *fiat*. *Montes exsultastis, gloria in excelsis, surrexit* may be considered emblematic of the deictic force of subjectivity reduced to a pronoun and of the illocutionary force of the vocative case, banners of the story of *io*).

It is the shift of emphasis toward the word itself that brings us to a direct consideration of the use of the vocative in *Vocativo*. In spite of the temporal thematic implications which serve to illustrate a shift in thematic emphasis from *paesaggio* to *passaggio*, we should note that the vocative case is always in the present. The *passaggio*, therefore, to the extent that it may be associated with the use of the vocative, is a process in the present; like a text, it may contain an inscription of past events or that of predicted future ones, but its very existence as inscription or utterance is present, on the page, in a presence re-effectuated through reading.

We shall sidestep these metaphysical considerations of presence for a while, however, in order to attempt to delineate the illocutionary force of the vocative as Zanzotto uses it. Our remarks here are general; they draw from, but do not exhaustively represent, recent linguistic theory regarding speech acts. Our concern is specifically with the use of the vocative in *Vocativo*, however; we hope to illustrate not only that the verbal part of this book's *grammaticalismo* may be described in linguistic terms, but that this *grammaticalismo* itself is profoundly thematic, an aspect of style which is essential to what we have been calling the story. It is, in fact, the point in Zanzotto's work at which the style becomes the story.

When Austin proposed in the fifties the notion of an illocutionary linguistic force, he intended, essentially, those verbs which, when enunciated affirmatively in the first person singular of the present indicative, effectuate the act they describe at the same time they describe it: "I promise," "I command," "I request," "I baptise," and so forth.[42] Put another way, the performance of an illocutionary act, according to Austin, is "the performance of an act *in* saying something as opposed to the performance of an act *of* saying something."[43] He delineated three types of performative acts, later referred to by John Searle as speech acts: locution, illocution, and perlocution. Simply put, locution is considered an act that utilizes articulation and combination of sounds to link syntactically the notions expressed by words; illocution is considered an act that occurs simultaneously with the description of the act; and perlocution is an act that aims at eliciting a response in the receiver which is usually not literally described in the enunciation.[44]

As Ducrot and Todorov note, the performatives "have as a property that their intrinsic meaning cannot be grasped independently of a certain action they allow us to accomplish . . . but once this property has been discerned in the particular (and particularly spectacular) case of the performative, we can see that it belongs to non-performative expressions."[45]

The difficulty with Austin's scheme seems to lie in the confusion that arises, then, between performatives in general (the characteristics of which seem to be less specific than Austin maintains, however, to the degree that these characteristics may also be discerned in non-performatives) and the illocutionary in particular, which retains the most specific performative properties because it takes as its very definition the literal simultaneity of performance and description. As Ducrot and Todorov also observe, Benveniste is the first linguist to examine these questions. We should note that he accepts the notion of the performative[46] but rejects the notion of the illocutionary act.[47]

Ducrot and Todorov remark that Austin's analysis, nonetheless, "allows us to go further: much more than the Jakobsonian functions, the illocutionary puts into play the most basic interpersonal relationships."[48] They make his statement in the context of a description comparing Austin's research to that of other linguists, namely Bühler and Jakobson. However, our interest in Austin is in the play of interpersonal relationships within his own curious definition of a happiness/unhappiness dimension pertinent to illocutionary force.[49] Austin distinguishes this from a truth/falsehood dimension pertinent to locutionary meaning. Without concerning ourselves with truth and falsehood in locution, we would like to concentrate on the "happiness" or "unhappiness" dimension of an illocutionary act.

According to Austin, extra-linguistic circumstances determine whether an illocutionary act is "happy" or "unhappy." Put quite schematically, an illocutionary act, the performative par excellence, may be considered "happy" when extra-linguistic circumstances provide for its recognition as illocutionary and "unhappy" when those circumstances do not provide such recognition. "I baptise," "I command," "I promise," for example, are "happy" illocutionary acts when a witness is present to register the simultaneous performance and description of those acts. The witness could even be the subject himself if the verb were made reflexive, as in "I baptise myself," "I command myself," "I promise myself." One might also say, then, that such an act is "unhappy" if there is no person to witness the act or, more extremely, no situation to ascertain it.

However, the illocutionary is often defined as such only if it has "as its first and immediate function the modification of the interlocutor's situation."[50] We could imagine, then, that a non-reflexive promise made in a social void would no longer qualify as an illocutionary act. We could further imagine that a promise made within a literary text would not qualify as illocutionary, being bound by nothing more than the fiction of the text, or, to state it from another point of view, the reader's willful suspension of disbelief.

Our reading of Zanzotto's *Vocativo*, however, urges us to salvage the notion of the illocutionary act as possible within a literary text. Even though it may be textualized in a fabric of confused subjectivity (the *io-non-io*; the problem of authorship: who is *writing io*? is the narrator the author? is the author Zanzotto? who is Zanzotto?) the vocative may still be seen as an illocutionary act, with the condition of "unhappy" attached, perhaps, given the difficulties we would have in determining that its utterance "modifies the interlocutor's situation," but, formally, an illocutionary act nonetheless. We can avoid this condition of infelicity by showing that the vocative in *Vocativo* does, in fact, "modify the interlocutor's situation" and, moreover, that in so doing, it helps to create the space of poetry which Zanzotto has so often called *un mondo Autre* by an action of language.

Our first task is to move beyond promises most often used to exemplify the illocutionary and make a case for the vocative itself as an illocutionary act. It is evident from the examples we have given and from any definition of the illocutionary that verbal action is intrinsic to the notion of illocution. It has recently been accepted by linguists, however, that the illocutionary verb itself may be absent from an utterance which, nonetheless, maintains its illocutionary force, so that "I promise to arrive at eight o'clock" may be stated as "I'll arrive at eight o'clock" without losing its force as a promise.[51]

It seems clear, then, that a vocative may be considered illocutionary for the simple reason that the utterance of "O" followed by a name or a noun contains the illocutionary force of the implicit request or command, "hear me." In fact, two reasons may justify attributing to the use of the vocative case a doubly illocutionary value.[52] First, given its implicit nature as a directive, it is an attempt by the speaker to get the receiver to do something (to listen, first of all, and then perhaps also to answer or to grant a further request); therefore, the vocative alters the situation of both interlocutors by putting the speaker in the position of a giver of directions (either as supplicant or as superior) and by putting the receiver in the position of being a potential provider of a response or service. Second, by virtue of a kind of troping, the vocative may be seen to contain an expressive aspect: its use expresses a psychological state of the speaker in relation to the addressee—the speaker has a need which the addressee can fill—as it creates the situation delineating that state.

With regard to the persistently thorny question of whether a vocative appearing in a literary text maintains its illocutionary force, we would suggest that the simple inscription of a vocative meets the requirements of illocution by its capacity to create special effects, effects, for example, of the real. The textualized vocative, that is, imparts an odor of the real to the implication that the textualized subject recognizes someone or something other than itself and considers this person or thing capable of hearing and even of responding. This implication, reciprocally, lends a quality of enunciation to the inscription of the vocative. We might even call this special effect the special effect of faith. Further, this implicit subjective recognition, what we are calling the special-effects result of the vocative, places the enunciation in a hierarchy that reinforces the effect of that faith. This hierarchy is constantly reinforced in *Vocativo* by the thematic humility of the minimal *io*, or of the *io-non-io*, whose horizons are those of a squirrel and for whom such utterances as *O vita irraggiungibile o remota /*

passione che edifica il nulla [oh unattainable life oh remote / passion that edifies the nothingness][53] or *O scansione sospesa* [Oh suspended scansion][54] or *O grumi verdi* [Oh green clots][55] are equally the invocations of others always implicitly higher on the hierarchical totem pole than is the enunciating subject.

The literary textual use of the vocative, however, may be considered unnatural or, in Searle's terms, even "parasitic,"[56] precisely because it is literary. But this "unnatural" quality is another special effect. The vocative, when it appears in a literary text, may create by its simple fictional enunciation a character implicitly higher than the subject who appears real in the framework of the text simply by virtue of the special effects that go into operation when that character is called to. In a tautology of influence, subjective recognition and invocation in the text encourage a willful suspension of disbelief in the reader and place such ephemeral entities as "unattainable life," "remote passion that edifies the nothingness," "suspended scansion," and "green clots" at least momentarily among the cast of characters that peoples the text's story.

But are the special effects of the illocutionary force of the vocative strong enough to fulfill Austin's "happiness" dimension or are they merely a kind of Hollywood staging for a cry that, unhappily, goes unheard in an isolated textualization? The *io* invokes many things in *Vocativo*, from its mother, to the landscape, to its own *mozzi trastulli*.[57] Yet none of these characters created by the special effects of the vocative responds, not even the mother, as we noted earlier. We may thus see that these vocatives do not, even within the fiction of the text, meet Austin's condition of "happiness." Nor, perhaps, do they convince us unequivocally of their illocutionary nature, for even if we accept the arguments put forth above about troping, implicit verbality and special effects, we may find our case built on little more than a bundle of split hairs. After all, these vocatives do occur in a text which, being poetry, is superlatively literary. Can their illocutionary force possibly hold up to the willful suspension of disbelief upon which it seems to depend?

Until now, we have overlooked perhaps the most significant vocative of this book—the title, *Vocativo*. And this hitherto overlooked vocative not only provides the context which allows the textualized vocatives to persist with an illocutionary force, but it does so in a way which directly implicates us: we read *Vocativo*. Any book as an object is, after all, a kind of vocative, for its very existence implies a request for the hearing we give it by reading. The vocatives in the texts of *Vocativo* may be seen as miniaturized, textualized replicas of the intersubjective relations and subjective positions established by the very book itself. The book implies the existence of the reader to whom it calls; its existence also implies that of an author. We may have no other proof of the existence of someone called Zanzotto than that implied by the fact that *Vocativo* exists.

Structurally, this is an identical pattern to the one established in the textual story: the *io*'s existence, fraught with confusion though it be, is reiterated not only in each first person singular utterance but also in each vocative. The illocutionary force of the vocatives sets up a set of interlocutory relations resistant even to the paradoxical autonegation of pronomialized subjectivity: even the *io-non-io*, that is, persists as an entity in the web of the vocative. In fact, that self-negated originating pole of the vocative utterance may be viewed as emblematic of the ambiguity of authorship itself: we read that "Zanzotto" is author of *Vocativo*, but, to return to our earlier question, which Zanzotto? The Zanzotto who exists for us because of *Vocativo* may coincide to varying, questionable degrees with the Zanzotto who takes his coffee in the main square of Pieve di Soligo, or with the Zanzotto inscribed as author of *Dietro il paesaggio*, or with the Zanzotto whose desk is filled with mushrooms, or with any other Zanzotto we might imagine. We are warned, by implications of the story of *Vocativo*, to accept his existence as author without making assumptions. We are implicitly told that, if the *io* of the story is also *io-non-io*, then the "Zanzotto" given as author is also *Zanzotto-non-Zanzotto*, that both authorial signature and its potential negation are part of a story which, though inscribed within the book, also goes beyond the book.

The story beyond the book, the story of *Vocativo*, is accomplished in our reading of it. For by reading it we activate its illocutionary force: we hear its call, we recognize the ambiguous subjectivity of the enunciator of that call, we, the reader, provide the receiving recognition which, finally, makes the speech act of *Vocativo* not only eminently illocutionary, but also happily so, even if our action also puts "we" in quotes.

Our efforts at establishing the illocutionary force both of the vocatives in *Vocativo* and of *Vocativo* itself are not meant as an exercise in applying current linguistic theory like a veneer over poetic texts which would also lend themselves to any number of other critical finishes. As we mentioned earlier, our aim has been to delineate in concrete linguistic terms the ways in which the *grammaticalismo* manifests itself in *Vocativo*. But our brief forays into speech act theory are also aimed at what we have tried to do all along: to follow a story. And, as we said earlier, *Vocativo* may be considered the point in Zanzotto's work where the style most evidently becomes the story. Thus the appeal to linguistic theory is intended as yet another road map for our tracings of the adventures of the *io* who first met poetry in *Dietro il paesaggio*.

The pertinence of the illocutionary force of the vocative and of *Vocativo* lies in the simultaneity of action and description which characterizes illocution. This simultaneity differentiates an illocutionary act from all other sorts of utterances: it *is* what is says as it *says* what it is. Zanzotto's choice of the vocative as titular emblem and recurrent theme is thus doubly significant. First, the vocative, unlike other illocutions, is the traditional, characteristic utterance of poetry: *O fons bandusiae* and *O miei mozzi trastulli* may be read as variant appearances of the same utterance, the eminently self-referential *fiat* of poetic discourse. Second, the vocative, because of its illocutionary force, may be seen as a mimetization of an originary utterance unencumbered by signifier/signified or referential dismemberment. The illocutionary vocative returns us to the story by imitating the *nome sepolto* for which the *io* endlessly yearns. In itself, it is not the *nome sepolto* but, in its self-sufficiency, it does tease us with its structural apeing of an originary, essential word.

This imitative aspect may also be found in the use of the biblical Latin quotes we mentioned in parentheses above. In the three instances where these occur, the *nome* is mimetically buried twice: in Latin, the skeletal, persistant originator of Italian, and in quotes, literal liftings from the Bible, bedrock of scripture, of writing itself as illocution.

With this linguistic cartography, we may begin to trace the boundaries of Zanzotto's space of poetry. In *Vocativo*, the story seems not so much one of a subjectivity intent on deciphering signals coming from *dietro* and inscribed on the perceptible; here, instead, the textuality may be seen to assert itself as an imitation of origin, an attempt at inscriptively miming the force of an authentic word. The significant aspect of poetry, then, might be that the story per se is less important than the fact of its being told. And if the same could be said of history, for example, we should further infer from the dynamics of *Vocativo* that, while poetry may have a story to tell, it is the telling more than the story itself that implicates us. By bearing the earmarks of poetry, by eschewing the order of prosaic, perhaps even of linearly understandable, discourse, the text asserts itself as illocution, as an act consubstantial to its description, as an iconoclastic space in which traditional expectations of order are transgressed and the reader is situated in a position of analogical similarity to the very *mozzi trastulli, pensieri in cui mi credo e vedo* evoked in the text.

Put another way, the speech act of the vocative, when textualized, goes beyond the deixis of the text's narrative fiction and reaches the reader. In the other, but nonetheless real, world of poetry, the reader and the *io* are thus activated as members of a populace created by and dependent on language per se rather than any described fact or event. In this way, we participate in, although we cannot recuperate, something brushing on authenticity, the *nome sepolto* that creates by utterance a space in which we are led to recognize ourselves.

The *nome sepolto* of "Piccola elegia" stands for us, then, as an emblem of authentic utterance, that which, in being said, also becomes. In the story we are following, it would be the impossible but not unimaginable verbalization of subjective essence, an *io* speaking itself in a way unconstrained by pronomial reductivity. We have suggested that the *grammaticalismo* in *Vocativo* may be thought of in linguistic terms from at least two force fields: the deictic force of the pronoun and the illocutionary force of the vocative case. In terms of the story, the deictic force of the pronoun may be analogous to the recognition by subjectivity of its linguistic determinacy. The *io*, unable to escape being *io* in any attempt at communication, at least maintains an acute awareness of its linguistic determinacy, even to the point of denial, the *io-non-io*, which says that *io* is something more, or less, or at any rate other, than *io*. And, again in terms of the story, the illocutionary force of the vocative may be analogous to the subjective recognition of a way of manipulating its own linguistic determinacy vis-à-vis the other so that, in spite of everything, a dialectic may occur in which the other, the *tu*, or the addressee of the vocative, is situated in a place implying a reciprocal place for the subject.

But the extent to which the notion of desire for an irrecuperable authentic word permeates *Vocativo* is emblematized not only in its appearances in poems containing invocations of the mother but also in the book's second section, "Prima persona." Here, such desire clothes itself in a striking number of images not of the landscape or of the earth, traditional burial ground, but of the sky. Before we pass from *Vocativo* to the *IX Ecloghe*, we would like to follow the story of *Vocativo* further by tracing the metaphoric development of the sky in several poems. *Vocativo* figures the sky as burial place of this *nome sepolto*, as the space of opening beyond linguistic determinism, as the absence of sign-filled landscape which nonetheless surrounds that landscape and contains us, as well, in an encompassing which simultaneously recognizes, perhaps, that "we" are also something more than can be said.

A note tells us that Campèa, Dolle, Lorna, and Serravalle, placenames encountered in *Vocativo*, are *nomi veri o fitizi di località* [true or *fictitious place names*].⁵⁸ We would begin our sky tracings in one of these true or fictitious places, then, keeping in mind the unity of truth and fiction implied by the note's oxymoronic clarification. "Campèa I" begins to designate the sky as repository of (unspeakable) meaning by the curious indication that a certain kind of utterance may not only penetrate that sky but also have a devastating effect on a landscape image projected skyward. If we leave actual vocatives behind in "Campèa I," it is only to come upon a description of the equally illocutionary force of a curse. This curse is preceded by the main body of the text, which gives as context for the curse a series of suppositions concerning subjective and objective being in the past. Not surprisingly, the text begins with a landscape, a cold August of maximal and minimal entities, of ridges and batwings, of involuted light and mumbled nibblings:

> Nella fredda Campèa, dove i crinali
> vibrano alle nubi
> a piombo sulle spoglie
> sulle ombre del degenerante agosto,
> 5   il pipistrello allarga le ali
> e scatta, involuta la luce
> nulla piú annuncia, brucano
> sussurri oscuri le erbe
> nei vicoli sepolte.⁵⁹

◻

> [In cold Campea, where ridges
> vibrate in the clouds
> plumb above the spoils,
> above the shadows of deteriorating August,
> 5   the bat stretches its wings
> and takes off, light turned inward
> no longer announces anything, dark
> murmurings nibble on the grass
> in the buried lanes.]

In this cold, shadowed August time, in this place outlined by cloud-vibrated ridges and filled with minimal movements, a "perhaps" appears, the hypothesis of which recalls that of the title of the book's first section: "Come una bucolica" [Like a bucolic] and the *forse* that follows here both would seem to indicate a distancing from authenticity—a troping of the authentic:

10 Qui forse io fui, con la mano sorressi
   la mia fronte, al rifugio degli uccelli
   smagliante di miele e di vischio
   al bosco superbo d'affusolate lune
   sospirai.[60]

◻

10 [Here perhaps I was, I propped up my brow
   with my hand, I yearned for the birds' refuge
   shining with honey and mistletoe,
   for the woods haughty with tapered light.]

The hypothesis of a subjective past extends next to the *tu*, which here is sculpted, unlike the *io* in its shining birds' hideaway, in images of blood and stone (where *pietra* may induce a Dante-related suspicion that here, at least, the other is a woman):

   Forse qui sorressi
15 la tua fronte di sangue e di pietra
   forse qui conoscesti
   qui conobbi ciò che va scemando
   con noi oltre ogni morte.[61]

◻

   [Perhaps here I propped up
15 your brow of blood and stone
   perhaps here you knew
   here I knew what keeps declining
   with us beyond every death.]

The hypothesis that the other might have known that which diminishes *con noi* beyond any death brings us to a realm of minimalization not previously encountered. This may be the knowledge, so to speak, of the *forse* (and also, perhaps, the supposed subjective knowledge of *tu*, itself another sort of *forse* upon which much of *io* depends, as we have seen). The setting is specified further:

   Presso Dolle verdissima di meli
20 appena usciti da lunghe abluzioni,
   presso il bosco superbo d'affusolate lune,
   quando i funghi spuntano di tana
   e s'intramano i raggi i cardi i ragni.[62]

◻

	[Near Dolle all green with apple trees
20	barely emerged from long ablutions,
	near the wood splendid with the tapered moons,
	when the mushrooms sprout from their den
	and rays thistles spiders scheme together.]

Dolle itself, we recall, may or may not be an actual place. If it is, then we are told not to be sure. If it isn't, then we are told to assume it is. Its wood remains a superlative of tapering light. Inversely to this description of landscape indicating a time, verse 22 begins a series of temporal specifications dependent on entanglements of objects in the landscape, none larger than a mushroom. The chiasmus of imagistic procedure in these verses may suggest an inextricable articulation of temporal and spatial notions, a condition emphasized further by the passage from the remote past tense of *fui, sorressi, sorressi, conoscesti, conobbi* in the earlier lines to the present tense prevalent from *quando i funghi spuntano* of verse 22 to the end of the poem. The individualized past, in other words, has passed to a generalizing present, and the landscape witnesses this passage, is a party to it, constitutes itself within it.

The poem's final lines are both the final item in the series of temporal specifications and the place of the curse, which arrives unexpectedly as the final indication, perhaps, of when the moment might have been in which the *tu* might have known *ciò che va scemando / con noi oltre ogni morte*. (The diminishing beyond death here recalls the self-valuation of the *io* in "Epifania," with which *Vocativo* opens. There, subjective value is stated as going beyond even the smallest perceptible entities: *valgo oltre il dubbio oltre l'inverno / che s'attarda celeste ai tuoi balconi*, vv. 16–17.) If even death itself is here supposed to be something less than a signifier of finality, if even death itself is, in this turning from past hypothesis to present generalizations, supposed to be no *terminus* for the growing less of things, the moment of such supposed recognition is described as a burning of the sky by a word:

	Quando paralizzata
25	la mano regge la fronte e la fulva
	verticale bestemmia
	cieli di perlati atolli incinera.[63]

◘

	[When the paralyzed hand
25	props up the brow and the fulvous

> vertical curse
> incinerates pearly-atolled skies.]

A hand which, were it Ciacco's, would have gestured obscenely towards the heavenly realm is paralyzed here in the posture of supporting that which might be thought, in more mobile circumstances, to govern it. The *bestemmia* itself (absent from the text, we note, in a locutory dilution which recalls by its relative pallor the vivid tones of the actual vocatives) is vertical, capable of challenging horizontality, of miming the directionality of the *io*'s encounter with poetry, perhaps capable even of indicating the contradictory desire of poetic discourse itself to break through the linguistic horizons which would keep it tied to the world. It is, literally, a splendid curse, one shining with a light that sets the skies afire. And, if the skies encompassing Dolle, and the *io* and the *tu*, and therefore us as well, are also pearleate atolls, we may get an indication of where Dolle is: not simply below some pearly gates of a sky patterned geomorphically after terrestrial horizontality, but in the vertically defined nadir of sacrilegeous and sacred community between a void and an all-significant. In this metaphysical realm, the gesture of a self-referent word, the *fiat* of a curse, would simultaneously delineate its own trajectory from nothingness to meaning as it would turn to ashes the tropical, and trope-ical, landscape in the absent center of which it is visualized.

> ORA ULTIMA: Lascia andare cotesti dubbi. Tu non avrai a star molto in casa del Sole; e il viaggio si farà in un attimo; perché io sono uno spirito, se tu non sai.
>
> COPERNICO: Ma io sono un corpo.
>
> Leopardi, "Copernico: Dialogo,"
in *Operette morali*
>
> ◻
>
> [FINAL HOUR: Let go of these doubts. You won't have to stay long in the house of the Sun, and the trip will take only an instant, for I am a spirit, in case you didn't know.
>
> COPERNICUS: But I am a body.]

The axiomatic beginning of "Campèa II" shocks us into the recognition that hypothesis, when released from a horizontal condition of logic, may accomplish the feat sometimes referred to as a leap of faith:

> In fede evolve l'anima
> tutto accoglie e allontana.[64]

◻

[The soul evolves in faith,
it takes everything in and sends everything away.]

In this newly and abruptly stated condition of the soul's evolution in faith, totality is gathered as well as distanced, assimilated as well as rejected. Such an oxymoronic dynamic nonetheless leaves a space for the soul to evolve in a recognition of its participation in and identity with a past.

The singular *io* now begins, perhaps, to consider itself part of a more collective *anima*:

>   Antico e vivo è il ricamo che preme
>   e carda il sonno
> 5   delle mie tempie insoddisfatte:
>   foreste ed acque spettinate e fiere,
>   meli dagli aspri acini rossi
>   e il Soligo che cinge gli ostacoli
>   di colli e siepi con spume sommesse.⁶⁵

◘

>   [Ancient and alive is the embroidery that presses
>   and cards the sleep
> 5   of my unsatisfied temples:
>   tousled and bold forests and waters,
>   apple trees with harsh red seeds,
>   and the Soligo that girds the obstacles
>   of hills and hedges with soft foams.]

The landscape is embroidered on the *io*; it seems consubstantial to him, even, if we note the passage from *tempie insoddisfatte* in verse five to the synesthetic *acque spettinate* in verse six.

This headland is next presented as a plurality of architectures, and we see that the apostrophic cry here is for these structures to make themselves manifest: subjectivity desires to perceive the structures it knows are tenaciously, if tenuously, holding things together. Although the only sign of the sky here occurs in the terzultimate line with *il sole*, this text is a vivid expression of the faith that elsewhere will be shown as an aspect of the verticality through which language invokes meaning in the story of *Vocativo*.

Here, the anthill and beehive images, in their familiar reductivity as minimal structures, may further suggest that what is being evoked and implored is not entirely without similarity to the space of dialect utterance:

ZANZOTTO'S GRAMMATICALISMO

10   Tenui, tenaci architetture
            architetture di formiche,
            disarmonie d'alveari
            dove il miele si stringe
            in coerenza di raggi,
15   apparite, strutture risibili
            ma forza senza grazia senza nome,
            apparite, supreme
            ustioni, a ritroso dipanate
            la luce ieri inestricabile
20   gli equivoci grumi dei corpi,
            osate contro il cuore
            che appassionatamente
            vi palpita, contro il sole
            incommensurabile,
25   contro il grigio asilo della mente.⁶⁶

◘

10   [Tenuous, tenacious architectures
            ant architectures,
            beehive discords
            where the honey squeezes itself
            into a coherence of rays,
15   appear, laughable structures
            but graceless nameless strength,
            appear, supreme
            scaldings, untangle backwards
            the light yesterday inextricable,
20   the equivocal clots of our bodies,
            dare against the heart
            that passionately
            beats there, against
            the incommensurable sun,
25   against the grey shelter of our mind.]

The laughable, coherently unharmonic structures of faith, perhaps, must counter the passions (interruptive, like orgasm and other involuntary somaticisms) of the heart, the vastness of sun-defined reality (emblematic of the reality defined linguistically, as we saw in *Dietro il paesaggio*) and the grey (therefore shadowless, resistant to sign formation) into which the mind would retreat. The poem beginning *in fede* closes *contro il grigio asilo della mente*: the lines of faithful combat have been drawn against passion, language-bound clarity and the reclusive thoughtlessness of a cloudy *mente*.

In yet another instance of reflection at a turning point, "Colle di Giano I" opens with a landscape description utilizing images of light and little things. We reproduce here the final lines of the first line group, another hypothesis like those of "Campèa I," but this time without a verb:

>   Forse
> solo l'affanno e il gridio dei bambini
> 15   e la trombetta che scavalca i monti,
> forse solo l'amore.[67]

◘

>   [Perhaps
> only struggle and the whining of children
> 15   and the trumpet that scales the mountains,
> perhaps only love.]

Here is a series which, lacking a verb, might be read as a hypothesis of authenticity not dependent on verbalization. What follows leads us to view these entities as desired interlocutors, in any case:

> Oh come, come vi parlerò?
> Ma forzo il cuore, forzo gli occhi a accendersi,
> ad accendere vita.[68]

◘

> [Oh how, how shall I speak to you?
> But I force my heart, I force my eyes to set themselves,
> to set life on fire.]

The effort to light or to set on fire organs of visual perception as well as the heart and even life itself in spite of subjective distress at not knowing how to speak to a *voi* (which perhaps consists of *l'affanno, il gridio dei bambini, la trombetta che scavalca i monti,* or *l'amore*) is perhaps not without similarity to the incendiary capacities of the curse word in "Campèa I."

"Colle di Giano II" opens on yet another image of light, this time surrounding a deadening of life:

>   In una sede abbagliante
>   s'attutisce tutta la mia vita,
>   non piú che filigrana
>   a voce bassa piange la mia voce;
> 5   amaramente accanto
>   mi lascio la vita e in un dolore affondo
>   chiaro e senza domani.⁶⁹

◻

>   [In a dazzling place
>   my entire life is muffled;
>   no more than filigree,
>   in a low voice my voice cries;
> 5   bitterly I set
>   my life beside me and sink
>   in a clear pain with no tomorrow.]

This dolorous drowning, this clear pain which displaces a place of light, is a marking of time on the subject; the time he has left is also an indication of mortality, as in *A nessuno diró che il mio fuoco / in eterno durerà* [I shall tell no one that my fire will last forever] (vv. 8–9).

Further on, we find an oxymoronic apposition echoing the truth and fiction of place-names in this book: *Palpitante inganno / verità dissociata / aperta ai venti, ad erbe polverose* [Throbbing deceit / dissociated truth / open to the wind, to the dusty grass] (vv. 14–16). And then, the oneiric *mezzo del cammin* of verses 17–20:

>   Ah metà del mio sogno è consumata,
>   pervicace Febo come una piaga,
>   pervicaci colori
> 20 mie piaghe dolcissime pel mondo.

◻

>   [Ah half of my dream is used up,
>   Phoebus, obstinate as a wound,
>   obstinate colors,
> 20 my sweetest wounds for the world.]

The trickery and truth of life lived in language is felt to be at a halfway point; as in the "beginning," the encounter here is with the now obstinate Phoebus Apollo, god of love and poetry, persisting as a wound metonymically carrying the image to Christ-like allusion (an echo, perhaps, of the tortured Christ figures in Pasolini's Friulan poetry; a testimony, perhaps, to a shared Friulan heritage). The "Colle di Giano II" text perseveres to its edifying nonconclusion:

>   E cola il cuore al calore
>   di lente che infrollisce
>   le mura e i dorsi,
>   che lima il ripido respiro.
> 25 O vita irraggiungibile o remota
>   passione che edifica il nulla.⁷⁰

◻

>   [And the heart oozes in the heat
>   of the lens that tenderizes
>   the walls and the ridges,
>   that rasps our steep breath.
> 25 O unattainable life o remote
>   passion that edifies the nothingness . . .]

So both *passione* and *vita* remain to be called to as the foundation upon which the *tenui, tenaci architetture* are perhaps structured out of nothingness. The *nome sepolto* is a cornerstone; it is passion and life which are remote, unattainable, and yet which stand as the basis of all that displaces the void.

The final images of life and passion in "Colle di Giano II" are associated with the earlier, emblematic *nome sepolto* image by virtue of the distance of all three from the *io* in the story. In "Colle di Giano III," the final panel of the triptych Janus-hill text, a kind of imagistic condensation appears: space, light, a landscape reduced to colors, atoms, and a plurality of absence are the setting here for a subjective recuperation, of sorts, of the authentic, the *vero*. A familiar movement has the sun slipping by *un uomo* as the *io*, reclining in its *vera voce*, in its *stasi prima*, finds its *vero corpo* as well as an *amore* pulled from an inhospitable earth. A subjective truth seems present as this narrative begins in the present tense:

>   Spazio e spazio ancora mi confonde,
>   l'antipodo intendo della vita,
>   nel nitore profondo
>   sul liberato colle
> 5   monde e quiete erbe
>   colori atomi assenze.
>   Giaccio nella mia vera
>   voce, m'inoltro nella stasi

10   prima, nella luce mai saziata.
      Presso un uomo scivola il sole,
      uomo l'azzurro
      già velato dei boshi.
      Trovo il mio vero corpo
      le mie ossa e le lacrime,
15   trovo l'amore che sottrassi
      alla violenta terra,
      ortiche occhi aliti invetriati[71]

◻

      [Space and again space confounds me,
      the antipode, I mean, of life,
      within the deep brightness
      upon the liberated hill,
5   clean and quiet grasses,
      colors, atoms, absences.
      I sit inside my true
      voice, I penetrate the first
      stasis, the never-satiated light.
10   The sun slips away not far from a man,
      man, the woods'
      already veiled azure.
      I find my true body,
      my bones and my tears,
15   I find the love I snatched
      from the violent earth,
      glassy nettles, eyes, breaths]

Then, after a space which marks an abrupt interruption in this series of recuperated (or almost) authenticities, the *io* begins a shorter series of direct addresses in which the Campéa curse is not absent:

      Tu stolta eternità, mai vinta
      adorante bestemmia,
20   polvere che si ribella, cielo
      a me strappato, tu
      viscere sempre gemebonde, terra. . .

◻

      [You senseless eternity, never vanquished
      adoring curse,
20   rebellious dust, sky

> wrenched from me, you
> endlessly moaning viscera, earth. . .]

This indomitable curse, adjectivally designated also as an act of worship, is identified through apposition as *stolta eternità*, an illocutionary act of speech both foolish and eternal. Apposition next associates the terrestrial *polvere che si ribella* as well as the celestial *cielo / a me strappato* to this adoring sacrilege: dust and sky, more facets of foolish eternity. The *tu* is reiterated in final position in the penultimate verse to personify an always groaning viscerality, finally identified as *terra* when the poem ends with no finality but rather the trailing off of three dots, the fading away of utterance.

But *tu* is expanded in "Colle di Giano III" to encompass both life and language, as well as the *cielo* which implicitly once belonged to the *io* and now is *a me strappato*. The parade of images has now reached the sky.

> Diventa oggetto della poesia l'unica possibilità conoscitiva pensabile, sebbene anch'essa assurda, che è quella metafisica, l'interpretazione del mondo *sub specie aeternitatis* (si veda tutta la lunga poesia "Dal cielo").
>
> *Pier Paolo Pasolini, 1957,*
> now in *Passione e ideologia*

◘

> [The only cognitive, thinkable possibility (even though it too is absurd), the metaphysical possibility—the interpretation of the world *sub specie aeternitatis*, that is—becomes the object of poetry (see the long poem, "From the Sky," in its entirety).]

Coming near the end of *Vocativo*, "Dal cielo," with its oscillation between direct address of the *tu* and subjective declaration, is one of the most expository texts of the entire book. We would read this text with an accumulation of images going back to the minimalized subjectivity at the beginnings of *Vocativo*, the gradual disappearance of the landscape as context, the tantalizing *nome sepolto* and its illocutionary mimetization, and the recent verities found by the *io*.

In the rapport established here between *io* and *tu*, in these sunrise revelations of a constitutive reality, we find the sky as repository of faith as well as the source which enables the *io* to identify and to identify with both itself and the perceptible. The four long stanzas shift from direct address of *tu* in the first, to declaration in the second, to direct address of the *tu* again in the third, and to direct address of an expanded *tu*, a *voi*, in the final stanza. The first stanza begins with a pair of hypotheses, the "ifs" we have been encouraged by the awakenings of "Impossibilità della parola" to read as the most faithful statements of a sometimes terrifying quotidian reality, of a reality, that is, which includes faith:

    Se in te mi esprime il risveglio
    se io tutto
    avvampo e sono mente,
    io tuo seno, realtà:
5   brevi figure tra cui svolse
    il suo debole senso la mia vita,
    lieto e aspro rifugio
    che l'alba senza affanni e il sole
    già sommuove di pura meraviglia,
10 ecco il dono e l'azzurro
    usciti in forza dalla morte,
    ecco supero il corpo
    mio impoverito e il respiro
    e tutto da te riconosco,
15 cielo, felicità di fibre miti
    di felci e brine,
    conclusiva diafana ebrietà,
    intransigente e fulgida
    causa che stai nel vero.[73]

◻

    [If my waking expresses me in you,
    if all of me
    blazes and I am mind,
    I, your breast, reality:
5   brief figures among which my life
    worked out its faint meaning,
    gay and harsh refuge
    that already effortlessly stirs up
    the dawn and the sun with pure marvel,
10 here the gift and the azure are
    come out in force from death,
    here I exceed my impoverished
    body and breath
    and recognize that all comes from you,
15 sky, meek-fibered happiness
    of ferns and hoarfrosts,

> conclusive diaphanous intoxication,
> intransigent and refulgent
> cause that rests in the true.]

The *io*, perhaps, finds an explanation of its own repetitions (*il risveglio*, like the vampire mornings of "Impossibilità della parola"); it catches fire like the celestial atolls at the strike of a curse and becomes both *mente* and the very breast of the *tu* now designated as *realtà*. The brief figures in which the meaning of subjective life is recognized to have occurred are appositively associated, from this new nurturing-organ perspective, with a harsh and happy refuge that already stirs up an effortless dawn and a sun of pure marvel. This could be the subject's recognition that the linguistic determination of its *senso* is somehow a refuge full of marvelous potential.

The *ecco* of line ten presents this situation as a gift and an azure (the sky again) forcibly extricated from death. The presentation continues in line twelve: here and now the impoverished physicality is overcome and, in verse fourteen, all is known. The gift is from the sky, and the gift is knowledge. The sky is a *conclusiva diafana ebrietà*; it is the *intransigente e fulgida / causa che stai nel vero*. The sky is seen as authenticity, the open vastness which, in other terms, is the *nome* upon which all of the *io*'s knowledge depends.

From this encompassing, constitutive source of reality also comes a shadow in which persists the minimal faithfulness that enables the insect to touch a dipping star; it is the shadow of signification perhaps, that makes possible a minimal *sidera feriam vertice*. From the sky comes even the perceivable, readable order of the landscape and the *io*'s smiling, speechless past. From the sky, not surprisingly, is the road that once led the *io* to poetry:

```
20      Dal cielo è questa penombra
        dove senza termine è la fede
        anche dell'insetto che procede
        dalla foglia invernale alla stella
        che ardendo gocciò nella valle,
25      dal cielo è questo scrigno di paesi
        dormenti tra le presenze oscure
        e feconde dei monti,
        dal cielo è l'ordine tenace e leggero
        delle viti sui colli
30      dov'io tacqui e sorrisi,
        e dal cielo è la strada
        che già mi balza dalle mani
```

```
                verso il lavoro e la ventura
                mentre turge la fiamma dentro il vetro
35              e di tintinni brulicano i boschi.⁷⁴
```

◻

```
20      [From the sky comes this dim light
        where endless is the faith
        even of the insect that proceeds
        from the winter leaf to the star
        that, burning, dripped onto the valley,
25      from the sky comes this jewel-box of towns
        sleeping among the dark and fecund
        mountain presences,
        from the sky comes the tenacious and light order
        of the vines upon the hills
30      where I smiled and was silent,
        and from the sky comes the street
        that already leaps from my hands
        towards work and chance
        while the flame swells up inside the windowpane
35      and the woods seethe with tinklings.]
```

The *cielo*, behind this *paesaggio*, is the constitutive force *dietro* the landscape which itself is reproduced here via a stylistic procedure not unknown in Zanzotto's first *paesaggi*: like the landscape, the anaphora here hinges on the sky.

The oxymoronic leitmotif begun in verse seven with *aspro e lieto* appears to identify the sky further in another dyad in verse 37, after the third stanza, initiated as is the one preceding by the titular source preposition *da*, returns to an interlocutory mode:

```
            Da te azzurra remota corona,
            assedio e sostegno,
            è la mia noncuranza
            ed il grido onde volgo
40          le ormai facili spalle,
            da te s'irradia la mia pace
            al di là delle ortiche
            insonni, dei bronchi in agguato,
            e se m'adagio e ascolto
45          il sussurro di sagra che fa nostro l'inverno
            se porgo orecchio alla lusinga
            bisbigliata dai gerani
```

	giá oltre il ghiaccio di gennaio,
	dal cielo io dico ogni mio moto
50	ogni verde d'atti scintillanti
	ogni luce d'atti incerti e immaturi
	per pienezza d'amore,
	e in amore già accolte le colline
	io sempre rinascendo
55	insieme riconduco al cielo.⁷⁵

❐

	[From you, remote azure crown,
	seige and support,
	comes my nonchalance
	and the cry that lets me turn
40	my back, easy by now,
	from you my peace radiates
	beyond the sleepless
	nettles, the stumps lying in ambush,
	and if I lie down and listen
45	to the festival murmur that makes winter ours
	if I lend an ear to the enticement
	the geraniums already whisper
	beyond the January ice,
	from the sky I say each of my movements,
50	each green of glittering deeds,
	each light of deeds uncertain and immature
	for their fullness of love,
	and, forever reborn,
	I lead the hills already gathered in love
55	together again to the sky.]

Subjective nonchalance in the face of an environment waiting in ambush derives from the sky, itself both siege and support. The *io* here comes upon a sky-radiated peace in which the "ifs" may be read as "whens": faith has the illocutionary power to ritualize the harshest season as a collective possession rather than a threat. The promise of a spring to come leads to sky-given subjective speech: *dal cielo io dico ogni mio moto* (v. 49) is a hendecasyllabic climax and condensation of the *io*'s story in *Vocativo*. From the unattainable source-space comes the very language which, having been lived as a fetter, is now experienced as a totalizing logos of subjective being. This linguistic totalizing of subjectivity is now seen as a fullness of love which leads to rebirth of the *io* as well as the landscape. The evolving soul of cold

Campèa has faithfully regressed to a constant birth-iteration: *io sempre rinascendo* is both regressive and constantly repetitive, like a year of Christmases.

As the *io* earlier searched for a way to return to the mother, frustrated in all attempts by the inability of deixis to resuscitate an origin, this iterated restarting now leads the *io* back to the sky from which it recognizes itself to be constituted. The frustration of former attempts is overcome by performative faith. To the extent that *io* is a sign or a signifier, the *cielo* persists as a vast source of signification from which the *io* takes its "meaning," its "signified." And the "meaning" is a knowledge subjectivity can now claim of itself; the *io* recognized the deictic and illocutionary force of faith, its capacity to authenticize the subjective gaze turned on itself. The third through seventh verses of the final stanza, the *voi* stanza, begins with a constitutive series:

> Mani, lingua, respiro,
> dal cielo è questo mio conoscervi,
> dal cielo vita immemore
> ti componi al tuo sguardo e il tuo sguardo
> 60 dal cielo si compone.
> E in volto di mattina si riannuncia
> a sé quanto da sé fu oppresso:
> vedere, udire, ancora
> a me nuovi ritornano?
> 65 E questo io posso donde
> la faglia senza fondo mi divelse
> e, fatto sangue, nelle congiunture
> nuove che il mondo affermano,
> viventi sensi, muovere a me stesso?
> 70 Riproposte realtà
> qui dal vuoto che smuore
> vi attendo perché io sia. Dal cielo
> è la pietà che il mondo fa consistere.[76]

◘

> [Hands, tongue, breath,
> from the sky comes this, my knowing you,
> from the sky, forgetful life,
> you shape yourself to your gaze and your gaze
> 60 shapes itself from the sky.
> And all that had oppressed itself
> announces itself to itself again in morning's visage:

| | do seeing and hearing still return
new to me?
| --- | --- |
| 65 | And can I, having become blood,
move this from the bottomless fault that uprooted me
can I move this back to myself
in the new junctures that, as living senses,
affirm the world? |
| 70 | Reproposed realities
here from within the paling void
I await you that I may be. From the sky
comes the compassion that composes the world.] |

The *vita immemore* is situated here in an originary position structurally analogous to that of the *nome sepolto* in the mother poems. If we note the passage from *nome* to *vita* as emblem of origin and authenticity, we may get some idea of the degree to which subjective recognition of its linguistically determined self has now been extended, in a gesture of acceptance that later is defined as *pietà*, to a participatory self-recognition constituted elsewhere, *dal cielo*, for all life. In this metaphysical extension of the constitutive linguistic structuring of subjectivity, which we earlier saw in terms of deixis and illocution, may be found the scope of the story of *Vocativo*.

In the two poems that remain after this *credo*, the *io* addresses itself to two manifestations of language that have the most to do with faith, perhaps which have the capacity, that is, to tap the source space of meaning imagined just now as the *cielo*. "Bucolica" [Bucolic] begins after an epigraph from Rilke (*"Seit Jahrhundert ruft uns dein Duft. . . ."*) [For a century your fragrance has been calling us. . . .] with a woeful description of the line that both separates and conjoins the terrestrial and the celestial, the perceptible and the imperceptible, the signifier and the signified:

> Corrotto è l'orizzonte, né rinfranca
> poco cielo i pendii deboli e foschi,
> ma nella mente sei, fede mai stanca,
> —tu innocente con me nei vuoti boschi?—[77]

◘

> [Corrupt is the horizon, nor does the small sky
> hearten the weak and darkened slopes,
> but you are in my mind, tireless faith,
> —are you innocent with me in the empty woods?—]

The neat quatrains of Italian's aulic verses continue with what may be read as a description of the space of poetry, a bucolic Arcady persisting through centuries of separation of earth and sky. If *Vocativo*'s first section is "Come una bucolica," we find the unqualified "Bucolica" near the end of its "Prima persona":

```
5       E se intorno la terra è tempestosa,
        se premono laggiú le rupi acerbe,
        oltre i secoli amica a te la rosa
        pende al lembo d'Arcadia pingue d'erbe.

        Qui, se a pace tu inviti questo ambiguo
10      fondersi del respiro nel passato,
        questo, che altrove inclina, moto esiguo
        d'alberi, questo raggio abbandonato

        qui all'estenuata luce si compone
        della mia della tua congiunta vita
15      la voce risanata, la ragione
        irrealmente a dirsi fatta ardita.⁷⁸
```

[And if the earth is stormy all around,
if down there the harsh crags press,
beyond the centuries your friend the rose
hangs on the edge of rich-lawned Arcady.

Here, if to peace you invite this ambiguous
10   melting of breath in the past,
this elsewhere-leaning, meager movement
of trees, this abandoned ray,

here in the exhausted light is shaped
from my from your combined life
15   the healed voice, reason
made bold unreally to say itself.]

The dulcet acceptance of lives conjoined to the point of sharing one voice occurs in this place where *la voce risanata* is appositively named a reason not dependent for utterance on the real, *la ragione / irrealmente a dirsi fatta ardita*. But there is a kind of nonterminal *mors*, a dyadic appearance of tectonic stasis and shove, in this Arcady; it holds the promise of another, if not a greater, *vero* as the poem ends:

>   Ah, ma tra poco volgerà da fragili
>   dubbiose piogge l'ombra a noi, tra piante
>   e foglie, donde ieri bevvero agili
> 20   lepri in tremanti abissi acqua tremante. . .
>
>   Quel nimbo ci dissanguerà, quel furto
>   molle che tarpa con la rosa il mostro
>   fossile e il marmo piega: stasi ed urto
>   dove in un altro vero affonda il nostro.[79]

◻

> [Ah, but soon from fragile doubting rains
> the shadow will draw nigh unto us, among plants
> and leaves where agile jackrabbits yesterday
> drank trembling water in trembling abysses. . .
>
> That nimbus will bleed us, that moist
> theft that clips the fossil monster
> with the rose and bends marble: stasis and thrust
> where in another truth our own sinks down.]

The final poem of *Vocativo* is the double text of "Fuisse I e II" [Lat. to have been I and II]. The first text here addresses those dialect speakers who, in losing their sweet maternal tongue, have participated in a generalized disappearance of the landscape and the minimal flora and fauna associated with dialect. In this general bereavement, the *io* exclaims poetic modes, receiving a response of assurance that his nominalized verbality of past essence, his *fuisse*, will persist in the landscape. Then the *non-uomo* that *io* will become will await the *tu* that is also *nulla*, folded in the earth like its geology, blind to all the dawn has meant before:

>   Pace per voi per me
>   buona gente senza piú dialetto,
>   senza pallide grandini
>   di ieri, senza luce di vendemmie,
> 5   pace propone e supremo torpore
>   l'alone dei prati la cinta
>   originaria dei colli la rosa
>   dispersa il sole
>   che morde tra le tombe.
> 10   Ah la cicuta e il poco
>   formicolio, non piú, colà sepolto.

>   Ah l'acqua troppo tenue che mi cola
>   oltre la gola e gli occhi e di là di là s'invischia
>   in tiepidi miseri specchi
> 15   su cui l'ortica insuperbisce.
>   Ed ah, ah soltanto, nei modi
>   obsoleti di umili
>   virgili, di pastori castamente
>   avvizziti nei libri, nella conscia
> 20   terrena polvere,
>   ah ripeto io versato nel duemila.
>   —Ah—risuona il colloquio
>   in eterno sventato,
>   dovunque io passi, ovunque
> 25   l'aria mai sfebbrata mi sospinga,
>   la selva m'accompagni
>   e impari la vicenda non umana
>   del mio fuisse umano.
>
>   Futura età, urto di pietra
> 30   sulfureo sangue che escludi
>   che inintelligibili fai questi
>   fiori e gridi ed amori,
>   non-uomo mi depongo
>   ad attenderti senza nulla attendere,
> 35   già domani con me nel mio fuisse,
>   pieghe tra pieghe della terra
>   cieca ad ogni tentazione d'alba.[80]

◻

>   [Peace for you, for me,
>   good people now without dialect,
>   without the pale hailstones
>   of yesterday, without harvest light;
> 5   the halo of the fields, the originary
>   circle of the hills, the scattered
>   rose, the sun
>   that bites among the graves propose
>   peace and utmost torpor.
> 10   Ah the hemlock and the sparse
>   swarming, not more, buried yonder.
>   Ah the too thin water that oozes through me
>   beyond my throat and my eyes and way over there
>   ⌊gets ensnared

| | in wretched tepid mirrors
| 15 | the nettle lords it over.
| | And ah, only ah, in the obsolete
| | manner of humble
| | Virgils, of shepherds chastely
| | shrivelled in their books, in the conscious
| 20 | earthly dust,
| | ah I repeat, spilled into the year two thousand.
| | "Ah," resounds
| | the eternally thwarted conversation,
| | wherever I go, anywhere
| 25 | the never feverless air moves me;
| | let the forest come along
| | and learn the inhuman event
| | of my human fuisse.

| | Future age, you rock thrust,
| 30 | you sulphurous blood that excludes,
| | that makes unintelligible these
| | flowers and cries and loves,
| | as no-man I settle down
| | to wait for you without waiting for anything,
| 35 | tomorrow already with me in my fuisse,
| | folds among folds of the blind
| | earth at each temptation of dawn.]

After the bucolic reference here to humble poets—a prophecy, perhaps, of the Virgilian book to follow—and after the transcription of the colloquy that is eternally thwarted, as most seem to be here, *Vocativo* comes to its final pages with "Fuisse II," a statement of hope which is the *io*'s folly as well as its support. In the final sentences, one addressed to a *te* that is *speranza* and the other to a *voi* that echoes the initial *voi* of "Fuisse I," the *buona gente senza più dialetto*, we find two questions. The fact of *Vocativo*, however, its illocutionary, deictic force, directs those questions to us, as well, and the *io*'s story of invocation draws to a close by requesting our response. Although the questions remain open, the *io*, like the book, is now *chiuso*:

| | Chiuso io giaccio
| | nel regno della rovere e del faggio
| | che ondeggia e si rifrange
| | in ombra là dove piovvero folgori.
| 5 | Lontana ogni opera ogni umano

o sovrumano moto: e come or ora
incatenati gli strati della terra
nel silenzio ricadono.
Lontano ogni sospiro ogni furente
10   ogni smorto desío della vita.
Nel silenzio ricado.
Speranza dentro gli ultimi
dubbi insequita fin dove reagiscono
e urticano soli in formazione,
15   dove serpenti e uccelli covano
confusi in marmo,
mia stoltezza e sostanza,
in te guistificato
un nome avrò per quelle mani nude
20   nel bollore dell'acqua nel nitore
rodente della seta, per il volto
che arse la falce,
per il corpo che brancia
scalfendo abissi di carbone?
25   Qui riversato dal nulla o da violenta
onnipossente verità,
qui inarticolato contro luci
dure e squallidi dogmi—
anche por voi le labbra
30   mie dall'assenza
debolmente si muovono?[81]

[Closed I lie
in the realm of the oak and the beech tree
that sways and is refracted
in shadow there where lightning struck.
5   Far away is every work, every human
or superhuman movement: and how just now
the earth's chained strata
do fall back into silence.
Far away every sigh every mad
10   every listless life's desire.
I fall back into silence.
I followed hope within final doubts
even where forming suns
react and nettle,
15   where snakes and birds brood

```
             confused in marble,
             hope, my stupidity and substance,
             shall I have a name justified in you
             for those naked hands
    20       in the water's boiling, in the gnawing
             silk-brightness, for the face
             the crescent burned,
             for the body that gropes
             grazing carbon abysses?
    25       Here again spilled out from the nothingness or from violent
             omnipotent truth,
             here inarticulate against hard
             lights and squallid dogmas—
             do my lips move weakly
    30       from the absence
             also for all of you?]
```

Or almost closed. The 1981 second edition of *Vocativo* contains an appendix of six previously unpublished poems which were written from 1953–1955.[82] This *coda* of tardy appearances modifies the tale we have been tracing as a batch of late-rising mushrooms changes the taste of an entire crop.

One of the first modifications is striking for its concern with felicity or the lack of it. If we recall the condition of felicity posed by Austin for certain illocutionary utterances, we can hardly help but be tempted to read the first appended text as a troping of the subjective situation in the vocative by means of a metaphor of love.

Amo e sono infelice? [I love and am unhappy?], the first line of the poem, may imply two subjective attitudes. First, the simple conjunction joining two verbs provides a syntax of lapidary simplicity and suggests that the bond between love and unhappiness is not only serial but also causal: *Amo e poi sono infelice*? [I love and then am unhappy?], but also, *Amo e dunque sono infelice*? [I love and therefore am unhappy?]. Second, the interrogative mode implies that this causal sequence is surprising to the subject, as if the question were displacing not its declarative counterpart, *Amo e sono infelice*, but rather an opposing variant of it, *Amo e sono felice* [I love and am happy].

Further, the intersubjective relationship posed by this simple first person question may also be read as a gloss on the structure of faith or what we have called the subject's *credo* found earlier in "Dal cielo."[83] In that text, the subject seems to engage in a simple act of faith with no objective correlative, so to speak, an act motivated solely by the subject's need to conceive its own essence as being in excess of linguistic determination. This act of faith allows the subject to imagine a place of vital authenticity outside language but from which, rather paradoxically, perhaps, all signifying capacity derives. The imagined place, the *cielo*, thus provides the reassurance of a response (language) that may always be conceived as less than totalizing (the *io* of language as insufficient sign of subjectivity) and that also guarantees a modicum of authenticity since it arises from the place of the authentic itself. The linguistically determined subjectivity is thus reconstituted by the linguistic response imagined to emanate from this *cielo*. Faith, in "Dal cielo," thus works like a vocative, eliciting from the *cielo* a response which modifies the situation of the enunciator.

Love might be expected to do likewise. But in the first of the texts appended like a revising afterthought to *Vocativo*, the path of love leads not to a felicitous reassurance, as did the path of faith in "Dal cielo," but to an unhappiness which, in the second line group, is recognized as corporeal, and therefore undeniable even to a subjectivity desirous of being constituted from some other place. This state of subjective infelicity undermines the earlier metaphysics of faith and reduces the vocative to an address of shadows:

>   Amo e sono infelice?
>   Oggi o ieri in queste pause
>   anfrattuose dell'estate
>   che la grandine investe
> 5 —e mi rizzo sui gomiti
>   nel giaciglio ed ancora non so
>   che orrori sopra i miei capelli ruggano—,
>   in queste albe sorde di cannoni
>   di luminarie fradicie, di vetri
> 10 infranti a mille a mille.
>
>   Amo e sono infelice, questo dice
>   il corpo che con voi dispera,
>   ombre da me evocate,
>   antiperistalsi
> 15 che automi e behemot
>   trai dalla terra, dalla tetra mente.[84]

[I love and am unhappy?
Today or yesterday in these anfractuous
summer pauses
that the hail assails

    5   —and in my cot I rise up
　　　　　　　on my elbows and still don't know
　　　　　　　what horrors roar over my hair—,
　　　　　　　in these deaf dawns of cannons,
　　　　　　　rotten holiday lights and windowpanes
  10   smashed into thousands and thousands of pieces.

　　　　　　　I love and am unhappy, this says
　　　　　　　the body that despairs with you,
　　　　　　　oh shadows I've evoked,
　　　　　　　antiperistalsis
  15   that drags automatons and behemoths
　　　　　　　from the ground, from my gloomy mind.]

    Metaphysics are then challenged by a corporeal materialism that, in the following line group, seems to dictate that the terms of love and unhappiness are so inextricable that they can be negated only as a dyad. The condition of not being unhappy, here, is that one not love. The negation of love and, consequently, of unhappiness, displaces subjectivity from a position where it might be constituted as receiver of a response. Simultaneously, the earlier sky-writing of signification moves, perhaps, to *un'altra vita*, and assassination passes metonymically through blood to give rise to *altre rose*. Here, the blue of the sky is the cryogenic medium even for the interruptive corporeal spasms that might delineate subjectivity as if by punctuation. By now, the poem says, the celestial place is one of inaccessible fury. The line of dots with which "Amo e sono infelice?" ends is witness to the disappearance of the imagined authentic *cielo* as agent. It stands, perhaps, for an absence of the dependent clause which might once have contained a celestially motivated verb:

　　　　　　　Ma non amo e non sono infelice.
　　　　　　　Forse verso un'altra vita
　　　　　　　nuota il sole,
  20   il sangue assassinato sulle soglie
　　　　　　　fa strada ad altre rose,
　　　　　　　in azzurro s'aggela la tosse, l'orgasmo,
　　　　　　　l'ormai recondito
　　　　　　　celestiale furore
　　　　　　　. . . . .
　　　　　　　　　　　☐

　　　　　　　[But I do not love and am not unhappy.
　　　　　　　Perhaps the sun swims

                toward another life,
20   the assassinated blood on the thresholds
                makes way for other roses,
                in azure the cough freezes, the orgasm,
                the by now recondite
                celestial furor
                . . . .]

    The following three poems trace the passage of the discouraged *io* through autumn months in which he feels alienated both from himself and the landscape. In "Da un eterno esilio" [From an eternal exile], we read, *"e coi giorni mi volgo e mi confondo, / vado, da me sempre più lontano"* [*and I change and merge with the days, / I go, always further from myself*].[86]

    And, in the following poem, "Molle clivo, dove traluce a raso" [Soft slope, where, skimming dead dawns], the subject asks the landscape to guide him by means of the very signs to which he now recognizes it was useless to offer himself:

                Molle clivo, dove traluce a raso
                delle albe morte l'ora del mio cammino?
                Dove la stella il fragile novembre
                precede e scioglie al rivo tutto il clivo?
5   Ed io vivo per te, per te m'aggiro
                fuori e lungi dal mondo,
                fuori sospiro.
                Non è finito il mio destino
                anche se mi si lascia qui a perire
10   con le distese dell'autunno
                cui vanamente mi volli offrire.[87]

                             ◻

                [Soft slope, where, skimming dead dawns,
                does the hour of my pathway shine?
                Where does the star precede fragile November
                and release the whole slope to the brook?
5   And I live for you, for you I roam
                outside and far from the world,
                outside I breathe.
                My destiny is not over
                even if they leave me here to perish
10   with the expanses of the autumn
                to which I vainly wanted to offer myself.]

Then, in the mild December of the following poem, "Per il mite dicembre ove l'erba" [For meek December where the grass], the *io* questions whether the winter landscape promises the disappearance of devastation at the same time that he seems to view the crystalline, even angelic, surroundings as the place in which love is frozen numb. We cite from line seven to the end:

>   È dunque il fausto
>   il pingue inizio,
>   sparisce la devastazione?
> 10 Deviante per selve raggio ignaro,
>   per cristalline sedi, angoli angelici,
>   intirizziti
>   intirizziti amori?
>   . . . .
> 15 Non adulti i dolori?[88]

◻

>   [Is it therefore the auspicious
>   the fruitful beginning,
>   does the devastation disappear?
> 10 Ignorant ray deflecting through forests,
>   through crystalline places, angelic angles,
>   benumbed
>   benumbed loves?
>   . . . .
> 15 The pains, not adult?]

The landscape here takes on the freezing properties of the *azzurro* in "Amo e sono infelice?". But this poem, like that one, contains a missing line and thus buries in an absence whatever connection there might be between *intirizziti amori?* and the apparently sudden, and possibly regressive, doubt that the pains (of the subject, of the landscape) are not mature. The connection is buried in absence; unless, of course, absence is what makes the connection.

The final unraveling of subjective faith occurs in the following poem, "Là nel cielo, là nel terrore" [There in the sky, there in the terror].[89] This abjuration of the "Dal cielo" credo is inscribed and iterated in an oscillation of the remote past tense with the present; these two temporal poles are brought into contact in the present perfect of verse ten, when the faith of "Dal cielo" is redubbed *ossessione*. This obsession begins a syntax opposing a dice-throw image of singularity and syllabization to the enigmatic evidence of corporeal reality: once

187

again the body acts as witness to a non-linguistic, or extra-linguistic, subjective materiality. The subject, once the beneficiary of authentic definition imagined to exist elsewhere, has lost his title by some unknown inversion of decrees. A place is left in the final line for that which is not said but should have been. The subjective claim to a legacy of extra-linguistic being or authentic definition has been denied:

>   Dissi ieri "dal cielo," ma remota nell'ora
>   della notte, mutati i contorni
>   del mondo della casa del quaderno,
>   s'offuscò la parola, si pente la gola
> 5   Dissi ieri "dal cielo"
>   come rivo di sangue
>   dalle labbra—
>   e l'oscuro cemento
>   senza tregua dappresso mi guarda
> 10 Ossessione il tuo nome ho imparato,
>   dado che contro mi rivolgi
>   il pochissimo numero
>   la scena unica
>   la sillaba
> 15 sola
>   il mio corpo tessuto di enigmi
>   le membra viluppi di stento
>   la cellula che figlia
>   nel silenzio, che scatta
> 20 dalla macchina avara
>   Dissi ieri "dal cielo": sicuro amico,
>   erede, io
>   del piccolo campo azzurro;
>   ma per quale inversione
> 25 di decreti oggi
>   più non afferro il senso
>   che m'apparve sì chiaro
>   . . . .

◻

>   [Yesterday I said "from the sky," but, remote in the night's
>   hour, the contours of the world,
>   of the house, of the notebook having changed,
>   the word grew dark, the throat repents
> 5   Yesterday I said "from the sky"
>   like a stream of blood

```
            from my lips—
            and, nearby, the dark
            truceless cement watches me
     10     Obsession, I have learned your name,
            die that comes up against me
            with the smallest number,
            the only scene,
            the syllable,
     15     alone,
            my enigma-woven body
            my effort-ravelled limbs
            the cell that foals
            in silence, that snaps
     20     from the stingy camera
            Yesterday I said "from the sky": I,
            sure friend, heir
            to the little azure field;
            but by some inversion
     25     of decrees today
            I no longer grasp the meaning
            that seemed to me so clear
            . . . . . . . . .]
```

The final poem of the new edition of *Vocativo* may seem iconoclastically occasional and, hence, to have "no known function," like a physiological appendix rather than a literary one, according to Webster's. But "Per la morte della madre di L.G." [On the death of L.G.'s mother] may also be read as a circular, finalizing synopsis of the story of the subjective dilemma in *Vocativo*.

The titular indication of a person by reference to her maternity recalls the earlier images of the subject's own mother. This identification is reinforced by the epigraph and the first and fourth line groups which, with their summer setting, also echo the July birth of the subject's mother. The associations in earlier poems of the maternal figure with the *nome sepolto* contribute to a subjective personalization of the loss which occasions this text. The woman mourned for here is not simply an acquaintance of the subject, a *tu*; she is also seen by the subject as, specifically, someone's mother, *la madre di L.G.* The loss of the mother corresponds thematically, as we saw in the "Come una bucolica" section of this book, to the loss of origin and authenticity. There, this loss is revealed in a potentially endless regressive series when the mother appears as a child herself. Here, the lament for the death of another's mother immediately follows the earlier poem's *dissi ieri* declaration of a loss of faith in authenticity. The linguistic determination of subjectivity is thus depicted more than once in *Vocativo* as being closely related to the disappearance, either into childhood or death, of the mother.

The poem begins in a honeyed wood:

> *attraversando un ruscello, in estate*
>
> Quando nella calura
> nella selva di miele tutto giace
> e tutti
> il miele suggono del sonno[91]

> [*crossing a stream, in summer*
>
> When in the heat
> in the forest of honey everything lies down
> and everyone
> sucks the honey of sleep]

It continues with a direct address of the lamented *tu* in a syntax and with a lexicon that suddenly seem relatively traditional. An Ariostan abundance of adjectives especially characterizes the second line group. To whatever extent this syntax and this lexicon may hearken back to Italian writing of other centuries, we may perhaps suspect that the *io*, as if to acknowledge his own thrall to linguistic determination, has decided to take refuge in a use of language which is markedly that of others. And, perhaps, finding that it lacks neither beauty nor feeling, he either adopts it to express "himself" or adapts "himself" to what it expresses:

```
5        tu buona
         perché l'opera mite
         che ogni tuo giorno fu, non tralasciavi?
         Ahi prodiga
         troppo di te, che ai sussurri agl'inganni
10       del rivo discendevi.
         Perché il mal cauto piede
         allo specchio instancabile fidasti
         al capriccioso gelo?[92]
```

```
5        [good woman,
         why did you never neglect the meek work
```

>   that was your every day?
>   Alas, too prodigal
>   with yourself, you used to go down
> 10   to the whispers to the ruses of the river.
>   Why did you trust your incautious foot
>   to the tireless mirror
>   to the capricious frost?]

The figure of Diana appears in the third line group as a point of conciliation between tradition and subjectivity, since the woodland huntress of traditional myth has long been a talisman of the subject's relation to the landscape:

>   E non vista
> 15   ti saettava Diana, quando al varco
>   dell'acque, forse, altrove già toccavi—[93]

◻

>   [And Diana, unseen,
> 15   shot you with her arrow when, wading
>   through the river, you were already reaching the other
>   ˪side—]

Significantly for the story of *Vocativo*, this line group ends on a metaphor of death as the absence of response: on the riverbank of death there is no deixis or illocution to constitute a place for subjectivity, and the death of someone else's mother is structurally analogous to the subject's loss of faith:

>   e fu la riva donde non ha ritorno
>   sguardo agli sguardi, non il grido ai gridi
>   dei figli d'Eva.[94]

◻

>   [and it was the side from which no gaze
>   returns to the gazes, no cry to the cries
>   of the children of Eve.]

The penultimate line group of this text and the entire book wishfully eternalizes a rapport with the landscape for the deceased. But the landscape is not generalized; instead, it is both the setting of the death described and also the specific landscape of the subject's mother's July birth. A full circle from the maternal provenance of the *nome sepolto* to this summer drowning of a mother has now been drawn, and the accompanying chorus of cicadas and messengers seems to bespeak the subject's wish that this aqueous entombment hold a message:

20
>
> Eternamente ora di pace
> t'abbevera la grande estate, in coro
> di cicale e di messi.[95]

◻

> [Eternally now, in a chorus
> of cicadas and harbingers, high summer
> waters you with peace.]

The poem and the book now end with an inscription that not only defines what immediately precedes it as a prayer but also is a prayer itself. The *io*, finding himself crossing the river in summer, as the epigraph tells us, does not renounce his impulse to illocution and deixis even when faith has failed. Instead, he seems to ritualize it as, literally, prayer. The ranks of *ombre da me evocate* are increased by this mother's death, and the second ending of *Vocativo* quietly resounds with the fatalistic invocation of one who, having once been laid low by the god of poetry, has since wrestled with angels of faith and can somehow not admit that they lost:

> Che questa prece
> ti sia soave come l'ombra estiva.[96]

◻

> [May this prayer be soft for you,
> soft as the summer shade.]

FIVE

THE SEEING *"io"* AND THE BEAUTY OF POETIC VISION

> The first artificial satellite, Sputnik I (c.184 lb.), was launched on Oct. 4, 1957, by the USSR, as a part of the International Geophysical Year. It carried few scientific instruments except for a device to record any puncture by a meteoric fragment. It had a radio transmitter and batteries that sent out its characteristic "beep" for 23 days.
> —Columbia Encyclopedia

In the same year that the cry of *Vocativo* became public, a technological event of notable historical import occurred. The initial piercing of the skies by an object of man's making coincides chronologically with the "end" of Zanzotto's second "Poetry" book and the gestation of his subsequent *IX Ecloghe*, published in 1962. It is an essential, perhaps even a causal, coincidence, for this event inscribes itself in the poetry of the eclogues in such a way as to displace previous directionality of inspiration and crisis. Earlier trajectories of location and landscape, of deixis and illocution, are challenged by a rocket trajectory that rapes the space upon which distances formerly depended, from which things—and the *io*—took their measure. The event inscribes itself orbitally in the poetry; it turns around a space, so to speak, revealing an emptiness in which speaking, finally, is seen to be grounded. The linguistic identity of subjectivity is somehow subsumed within this space, which manifests itself emblematically, in the *IX Ecloghe*, in images of circularity (where an orbit is also that which contains an eye) and in the returning rhythms of dialogue. The determination by language of the *io* as subjective identity is less at issue here than the possibilities of perception in general, and, more specifically, the perception of poetry, or the essential nature of poetic perception and utterance.

The changing realms of metaphor do not depart from their grounding in language itself, however, as that which is finally at issue. But there is a departure in the *IX Ecloghe*, if we compare it to Zanzotto's previous books, *Vocativo* in particular, from an *io* whose main properties have to do with the determination of a subjective identity to an *io* which, though still maintaining those properties, appears as the functional (or non-functional—this, too, is at issue) grounding of the poetic voice: in short, as language.

We might indulge ourselves here in a bit of play on the first person singular Italian pronoun for what we hope will be purposes of illustration. (Our perception, as will be seen, is perhaps not free from the influence of the essential English pun, but even the phonic identity in our own tongue of the first person singular pronoun and the word for the organ of visual perception is to the point here.) We might, that is, characterize what we have called the changing realms of metaphor in a comparison of *Vocativo* and the *IX Ecloghe* as a shift in emphasis from what the first letter of *io* might emblematize to what the second letter might. The up-and-down linearity of the *i* would stand, then, for the directionality implied by the use of the vocative case where the request for hearing implicitly addresses itself upward and establishes a line that, in turn, implies the deixis of a point of emission and a point of arrival, if not reception. This vocative linearity may itself be seen as superimposed upon both the eventful directionality of the mountainous and tropical landscapes and the trajectory of poetic inspiration and subjective response in *Dietro il paesaggio*. These earlier ups and downs, these vaguely *i*-shaped linearities, are further superimposed upon in the *IX Ecloghe* by the trajectory of the rocket necessary to propel a satellite out of the close drag of earth's gravity.

At this point, we pass from the *i* to the *o*, for the satellite serves, in our scheme, as the transitional object. Propelled by a rocket, this object, round like the *o*, signals a metaphoric passage from a linearity in which subjectivity is implicitly at one pole to a circularity in which the grounding of perception is challenged or rendered ambiguous, unsure. The satellite orbits the earth. The satellite is a false moon. The moon's place is challenged. The moon reflects light from another celestial orb as it circles the earth in its no longer singular orbit. The eye rests in an orbit. The satellite pierces the heavens; the eye of Polyphemus is pierced by a sharp, pointed object. The eye socket, as orbit, encircles the organ of visual perception, holds in place the place from which such perception originates. The satellite, like the moon, turns in an orbit around the earth. The turning is a returning: *rursus*. The orbit is a circle; the orbit is an encircling, an encircling that is a returning. The *o* returns to its place in *io* as the shifting metaphoric realms traced here return to the linguistic emblem we have used for illustration. *Io* as language itself is not simply a point on a line or a circle, but, as language, it gives these lines and circles of heaven and earth their presence for us. In Heideggerian terms, language,

THE SEEING "io" AND THE BEAUTY OF POETIC VISION

in the *IX Ecloghe*, reveals itself as the presencing of heavenly and earthly beings for mortals. Through language, the mortal *io* experiences the worlding of world, the grounding of earth, the fourfold oneness in which mortals, the gods, earth, and world are mirrored and encircled.[1]

But language, in the *IX Ecloghe*, presents itself in Zanzottan terms, with many of which we are already familiar. Zanzotto's text, familiarly enough, takes as its terms, for example, the stuff of past poetry: Virgil, Dante, Petrarch, Leopardi, and D'Annunzio are several of the moonstruck aulic mentors present in these eclogues. Against their stately measure, a new lexicon appears: the lingo of medicine, biochemistry, physiology. This new ingredient of descriptive precision, grounded in the body, sets itself against the mechanical precision of modern technological history as emblematized by the rocket-satellite. Where technological precision seems to hold sway, somatic precision also occurs.

The value of language itself pervades these parameters of the text and is equally evinced in others: the presence of Latin and the bits and pieces of popular songs, for example. The reevaluation of language is perhaps the book's main theme. This is what we shall trace. And this, symbolized in part by the very sign that seemed so contentious a determinant in *Vocativo*, the *io*, is announced in the first poem, "Un libro di Ecloghe" [A book of Eclogues], where the *io* in quotes may be read as many things: as first person singular pronoun (with a history going back to *Dietro il paesaggio*), as this present book of eclogues, as language itself, as poetry in general. The negative declaration at the poem's outset turns upon itself (an early *rursus*) in the positive statement with which the poem closes. Negative measurements taken against Virgil (and the Renaissance epic poets) turn to a positive evaluation of present, though minimal and humble, possibilities. The book itself, and our selected readings here, will follow this inscription of a turning.

> Non di dei non di príncipi e non di cose somme,
> non di te né d'alcuno, ipotesi leggente,
> né certo di me stesso (chi crederebbe?) parlo.
> Né indovino che voglia tanta menzogna, forte
> 5   come il vero ed il santo, questo canto che stona
> ma commemora norme s'avvince a ritmi a stimoli:
> questo che ad altro modo non sa ancora fidarsi.
> Un diagramma dell' "anima?" Un paese che sempre
> piumifica e vaneggia di verde e primavere?
> 10   Giocolieri ed astrologi all'evasione intenti,

a liberar farfalle tra le rote superne?
Trecentomila parti congiunte a fil di lama,
l'acre tricosa macchina che il futuro disquama?

Faticosa parentesi che questo isoli e reggi
15   come rovente ganglio che induri nell'uranico
vacuo soma, parentesi tra parentesi innumeri,
pronome che da sempre a farsi nome attende,
mozza scala di Jacob, "io": l'ultimo reso unico:
e dunque dei e príncipi e cose somme in te,
20   in te potenze, cose d'ecloga degne chiudi;
in te rantolo e fimo si fanno umani studi.²

[Not of gods not of princes and not of highest things,
not of you nor of any other, reading hypothesis,
nor certainly of myself (who would believe it?) do I
ᒪspeak.
Nor do I divine what so much falsehood wants,
ᒪstrong
5   as the true and the holy, this song that goes out of
ᒪtune
but commemorates norms fascinates with rhythms
ᒪwith stimuli:
this song that still knows not how to entrust itself to
ᒪother modes.
A diagram of the "soul?" A town that always
plumes and raves about green and springtimes?
10   Jugglers and astrologers intent on escape,
on freeing butterflies among the supernal spheres?
Three hundred thousand parts joined on the edge of a
ᒪblade,
the sharp tricosal machine that scrapes the scales off
ᒪthe future?

Belabored parenthesis that isolates and supports all
ᒪthis
15   like a red-hot ganglion hardening in the uranic
vacuous soma, parenthesis among innumerable
ᒪparentheses,
pronoun that has been waiting forever to become a
ᒪnoun,
lopped-off Jacob's ladder, "I": the last, made singular:

and therefore gods and princes and highest things in
⌊you,
20   in yourself you enclose powers, things worthy of
⌊eclogue;
in you death-rattle and dung become human studies.]

The book's first poem, written in the late seventeenth-century *martelliano* verse, now practically obsolete, has all the prophetic assuredness of a preface, of the text that always gets written last. In our attempt to trace out the patterning inscribed in the book, the patterning compactly foretold in the turning of the first poem, we shall consider only five of the eclogues, the ones in dialogue, in some detail. It seems that the issues raised by the book in its entirety come most directly to points of confrontation in these texts; thus, they will serve, it is hoped, as an economical, though by no means exhaustive, illustrative reading.

A note on eclogues.

Virgil's ten eclogues serve as evident model and clue to Zanzotto's nine. The archetype of any eclogue is, of course, the Virgilian, and much of the textual proceeding in Zanzotto's book counts to a large extent on an evident intertextuality with Virgil. Concerning Virgil's *Eclogues*, we would do well to recall the main themes of pastoral, as opposed to urban, life, the frenzies and yearnings of love, and, throughout, the striving to achieve good poetry. The singing, or poetry, contests in Virgil's *Eclogues* are generally represented in dialogue form; thus, from the Virgilian model, we may infer a coincidence between the eclogue in dialogue and a concern with and a striving for a perfecting of poetic utterance.

As significant as these direct relations between Virgilian and Zanzottan eclogues may be, however, there is a reference to Virgil in Zanzotto's choice of eclogue form itself that works less directly but no less significantly. This is a negative reference: the choice of the Virgilian eclogue model is simultaneously a rejection of the Virgilian epic model. Zanzotto's main literary emblem in the *IX Ecloghe* is the Virgil of the pastoral world of the singing contests, the world most directly concerned with conscious and constant attempts at perfecting the poetic utterance; it is not the Virgil of the historic world and its epic narration.

Zanzotto himself has called his *IX Ecloghe*, in fact, an "omaggio presuntuoso alla grande ombra di Virgilio" [a presumptuous homage to Virgil's great shade].³ This is an homage not to the epic singer of pious Aeneas, but to the Virgil of the *Eclogues* who, taking up a theme of Theocritus, establishes an Arcady where poetry as such is of the essence. This Arcady corresponds, for Zanzotto, to the utopic space of poetry in which many great writers, Petrarch the first among them, come to situate themselves. The Virgil of the *Eclogues* thus emblematizes the choice of poetry over history. The Virgil of the *Eclogues*, according to Zanzotto, mirrors within himself all the contradictions of the meek man, of the man far from all forms of prevarication and violence who is drawn by circumstance to the center of power. The Virgil of the *Eclogues* is invoked in Zanzotto's *opus* at the moment when history most threatens, when technology everts the frames of human perception as it breaks into places formerly reserved for mystery and origin.

The persona in Zanzotto's eclogues is not at the center of power, however, as we shall see. Rather, this persona, in a modern twist of circumstantial inevitability, finds the language of power coming to him in spite of himself. Technology facilitates the invasion not only of sacred heavens but also of what would happily have remained a marginal space outside the standardizing language that, over the air waves, brings its version of history to all. Thus, snippets of popular songs or publicity slogans appear now and then in the *IX Ecloghe* as testimony to a modern reality which is an inversion of the situation in which Zanzotto sees Virgil. We would do well to keep in mind, then, that the eclogue signifies a choice of poetry when history is the alternative.

Our substitution of the word "persona" for what we have previously designated as the "subject" indicates a new referentiality of the pronoun *io* in the *IX Ecloghe*. Here, we encounter a subjective poetic voice that speaks itself as a voice striving for poetry, as a voice aware of and accepting its dependence on and its basis in language. This is paradoxically both broader and more specific than the *io* of linguistic determination in *Vocativo*. It is broader in an effective way, perhaps, because the persona of Zanzotto's eclogues is engaged in an activity which goes beyond the *Vocativo* agonizings over subjective identity in its attempts to come to grips with poetry. Yet it is more specific, perhaps, in what we might call an affective way, because the persona here, as it goes beyond the crisis of linguistic determination of subjectivity (the most anonymous specificity of which lends itself to rapid universalization) to identify itself as that voice which, specifically, would speak poetry.

Thus, where two *persone* are indicated in the dialogated eclogues,

THE SEEING "io" AND THE BEAUTY OF POETIC VISION

we may understand that each is an *io* at the same time that neither is overly concerned about pronominal entrapment. These *persone*, minimally indicated by the letters *a* and *b*, are functional, if not necessarily existential, first persons. Their function appears through their interacting utterances. Gradually, we come to read *a* as what we identified as the poet—or rather, as the guy in the car—in *Dietro il paesaggio* and as the reductive *io* in *Vocativo*. Here, *a*, this persona in search of a poetic voice, engages in dialogue with *b*, the voice, we shall see, of poetry itself. Each letter represents a role: poet and poetry are personified; each adopts an *io* for the sake of dialogue. And we shall perhaps not be surprised to learn that, given the precedents in occidental philosophy, this dialogue eventually brushes the realm of didactics.

But the first of these dialogated eclogues, *I lamenti dei poeti lirici* [The laments of the lyric poets], does not present itself as didactic. Nor does it even exactly formulate a question. Rather, it presents itself, as its subtitle indicates, as a pluralized lament of a plurality of lyric voices. Nonetheless, most of the text is contained in the opening monologue of the singular voice attributed to *a*, who describes those laments and adds his voice to them in a hesitant impetus of association which, as we see in verses 55–57, depends on the will of *b*.

The description of the poets' laments promised titularly begins only in verse 43; it is preceded by a description of a modern linguistic situation in which the landscape of lyric poetry, a landscape which almost touches some actual truth, is seen crystallized by simulated light in anthologies of oneiric readings, murmuring repetitively that which is useless to say:

> Persone: *a, b*
> *a*—Alberi, cespi, erbe, quasi
>   veri, quasi all'orlo del vero,
>   dal dominio del monte che la gran luce simula
>   sempre tornando, scendendo
> 5 a incristallirvi
>   in oniriche antologie:
>   mite selva un lamento
>   mite bisbigliate un accorato
>   ostinato non utile dire.[4]

◻

> [Characters: *a, b*
> *a*—Trees, bushes, grass, almost
>   true, almost at the edge of truth,

always returning, descending
from the domain of the mountain that the great
⌞light simulates
5   to crystallize
in oneiric anthologies:
meek forest, you murmur
a meek lament, a heartfelt
obstinate useless speech.]

This *ostinato*, or bass line, would seem, in the following lines, to be the place of a plethora of signifiers, and of a grounding of these within material itself, in turn associated, as well, with an initial linguistic movement of syllabification.[5] The most significant aspect of these lines is perhaps the coincidence of signifiers and originary syllables within the metaphor of the landscape: one could easily be led to read this metaphor as a strong suggestion that both the initial sound-producing material of language and the end products of language, both syllables and signifiers, that is, are based in a materiality represented by the landscape. This is not necessarily a comment on the notion of the arbitrariness of the sign. Rather, it confers a status of material reality on polarized aspects of language. Both the syllable, which exists but has no meaning, and the signifier, which means but, in some way, does not exist or has an ambiguous material existence, are associated here with *sensi* (sensations—physical—which are also meanings) and the lowest earth. The cry, designated not insignificantly in musical terms (*ostinato, unisono*), is called most perfect:

10 Significati allungano le dita,
sensi le antenne filiformi.
Sillabe labbra causole
unisono con l'ima terra.
Perfettissimo pianto, perfettissimo.[6]

◻

[Signifieds lengthen their fingers,
meanings, their filiform antennas.
Syllables lips clausulas
in unison with the vilest earth.
Most perfect cry, most perfect.]

Then, after a verse which is unwritten, its place indicated in Hölderlinian fashion by a row of dots, the corporeal metaphors of

THE SEEING "io" AND THE BEAUTY OF POETIC VISION

fingered signifiers and belipped syllables pass to that of the hand, the other hand, in fact:

```
10              . . . . . . . . . . .
                E tenta di valere, accenna, avvampa
                l'altra mano dell'uomo.⁷
```

◻

```
                . . . . . . . . . . .
10              [And man's other hand attempts
                to be of use, it signals, it blazes.]
```

In the lines that follow to the next unwritten verse, this *altra mano* reveals itself as the one that writes not with a pen but a rocket, the sinister manualization of the technology that now writes history:

```
        Da lei protesa
        rugge, accelera il razzo a dipanare
20      il metallo totale dei cieli.
        Per lei fibrilla il silenzio, incellulisce.
        Oh aquiloni orientati
        piú su dell'infanzia, piú del punto che brilla,
        mano da un fuoco a un altro, mano bisturi.
25      Mano dove gli strati serpeggiano nel coma,
        dove il ventre della terra accampa
        profili irriferibili,
        funzioni insospettate, osceni segni,
        foglie e corpi di sofismi, il libro
30      che non scrisse, la penna, non illustrò, il colore.
        Autopsie, autopsie.
        Mano da un fuoco a un altro, mano bisturi.
        . . . . . . . . . . . . . .⁸
```

◻

```
        [From this outstretched hand the rocket roars,
        accelerates in order to unwind
20      the total metal of the skies.
        Due to this hand the silence fibrillates, encells.
        Oh kites aimed higher
        than childhood, than the shining point,
        hand that passes from one fire to another, scalpel hand.
25      Hand where the layers snake in a coma,
```

> where the earth's belly asserts
> unreferable profiles,
> unsuspected functions, obscene signs,
> leaves and bodies of sophisms, the book
> 30   no pen wrote, no color illustrated.
> Autopsies, autopsies.
> Hand that passes from one fire to another, scalpel hand.
> . . . .]

This scalpel hand that writes autopsies where the other would write books is, for all its sinister associations, nonetheless not excluded from the metaphoric field in which the music of linguistic artifact (syllable, signifier, *sensi*) was earlier seen to be grounded. Verses 25 through 30 reveal that even this other hand is a place of *imo terra*, specifically, in verse 26, *il ventre della terra*.

The Petrarchan adversative which appears in verse 34 precedes a translated citation of Virgil:

> Ma pure, ecco, "le mie labbra non freno"[9]
>
> ◻
>
> [But yet, here it is, "I do not restrain my lips"]

The Virgilian line, "Ecce, labia mea non cohibui" (given in note), encourages more fanciful illustrative attempts on our part. To wit, the prefix *co-* of the Virgilian verb may contribute to our reading as emblem of a paradox that is arising in the metaphoric structure of the text. The *co-* indicates togetherness, commonality, much in the way the image of one hand implies that of the other. Further, the appearance in Zanzotto's poem of the landscape as both a kind of archetypal linguistic terrain and the humus of the *profili irriferibili, / funzioni insospettate, osceni segni* of technology may be seen to indicate that two "events" cannot be stopped ("non cohibui"): first, the speech of poetry and, second, perhaps, a kind of cohabitation in which the technology that here determines the fact of history depends on the same processes as does the language which would, as poetry, touch upon some truth that goes beyond mere fact.

The adversative introduces, in any case, an interlude—between technology's intervention and the appearance of the lyric poets' lament—of the landscape once again, the *selva* as source of insinuation, of implied meaning, perhaps, deriving from such differences as can appear in the movements of leaves within the *selva* itself. These small movements are associated by means of simile with a *lago / albuminoso*

THE SEEING "io" AND THE BEAUTY OF POETIC VISION

which, in turn, is associated appositively with a temporal play of light and the first appearance, in the book, of an eye. This eye, fluctuating between affective extremes, is set in a line that itself reaches no conclusion, unless one can imagine that the conclusion is missing in the line of dots which follows:

	Ma pure, ecco, "le mie labbra non freno"
35	insinui, selva,
	tu molto umiliata,
	tu quasi viva, piú che viva, quasi viva
	—le tue foglie movendo
	bagliori come d'insetto nel lago
40	albuminoso che fu notte fu giorno
	occhio in gioia occhio in lutto. . .
	. . . . .¹⁰

◘

	[But yet, here it is, "I did not restrain my lips"
35	you insinuate, forest,
	you very humbled,
	almost alive, more than alive, almost alive
	—you flash your moving leaves
	like an insect in the albuminous
40	lake that was night was day
	joyful eye mournful eye. . .
	. . . .]

But in spite of this lack of conclusion, in spite of this unfinished syntax, we may note that the terms of the simile associate the eye with the *selva* itself, through the intermediary image of the lake. The eye, organ of visual perception, site of the origin of the subjective gaze, is likened to the humble *selva* that, in minimal appearances of differentiation, insinuates nonetheless (*Ma pure*), in spite of the workings of *l'altra mano dell'uomo*. In the circlings of this simile, significance and perception are shown to be structurally related.

In verse 43, the persona indicated as *a* begins his description of the situation of the poets. These poets are nurtured, we read, at Lazarus' table. A note tells us that this is the Lazarus of the parable recounted in Luke 16:19–31, rather than the Lazarus raised from the dead. (The parable represents Lazarus, a beggar, starving at the door of a rich man's home, receiving not even the crumbs from the rich man's table. When both die, the rich man, suffering the torments of hell, wishes for Lazarus, whom he sees safe in Abraham's bosom, to

THE SEEING "io" AND THE BEAUTY OF POETIC VISION

cool his tongue with water. If the division which kept the rich man from nourishing Lazarus while they were alive was strong, the division of their eternal placement is even stronger, and, as Abraham informs the tormented soul of the rich man, no refreshment will be provided.) This Lazaran *mensa* is so minimal as to be nonexistent except as an unattainable object of desire. This biblical version recalls the tantalizing structure illustrated in classic myth by the metamorphosis of Daphne to which we had occasion to refer in our readings in *Dietro il paesaggio*. Here Zanzotto adds the notion of literal nurturing, whereas in the biblical parable nurturing never occurs.

These poets who live on desire grow pale but nonetheless engage in a serial invocation that culminates in that of *le orme / che s'addentrano al simbolo* [the tracks / that go into the symbol]. The parenthetical, aorist declaration in verse 49 of the death of the symbol gives a conclusion to the trajectory of *le orme*; the symbol in which the tracks invoked by the poets immerse themselves is void of life. If it died, it must once have been alive. This image of symbol as place, as *situs*, whose status is changed, may recall to our reading the "Dal cielo" poem of *Vocativo*, in which the *io* depicts the sky as a source-space of linguistic—or essential—significance. If this association is considered, we may read the result of sinister manual dexterity, the rocket that appears earlier in the present text to *dipanare / il metallo totale dei cieli* (vv. 19–20), as being structurally similar in its trajectory to the tracks leading into the symbol that appear in verses 47–49.

The underlying analogy of metaphoric structure is found, in all three instances (the *cielo* of *Vocativo*, the rocket trajectory here, and the tracking into the symbol here), in a directionality that intrudes upon a vastness associated with signification (*cielo*, *cieli*, *simbolo*). The death of the symbol in verse 49 may then be related to a changed nature of *cielo* after the intrusion of technology, of an unnatural object which, pen-like, "writes" only autopsies in the heavens. The result of the central manifestation of this structure, the rocket trajectory in verse 19, is, as we saw in verse 21, a fibrillation of silence, a cellular encapsulation, a rendering into organic units of that which speaks not. The oscillation of life and death images at the end points of these several trajectories bespeaks a confusion: which of the directionalities is the more fecund? The rocket fibrillates the silence and renders it in organic units but later produces only autopsies. The tracks invoked by the poets lead to a symbol which is already dead. Is the *cielo* the terminus even of these tracks beloved by the poets? Is the piercing of the heavens by man's technology the event that killed the symbol?

Verses 43–49 present something of an enigma to a reading which recognizes these recurrent directional similarities:

THE SEEING "io" AND THE BEAUTY OF POETIC VISION

45
   Chiedono, implorano, i poeti,
   li nutre Lazzaro alla sua mensa,
   come cigni biancheggiano.
   Invocano l'amata
   l'iddio la pia vittima le orme
   che s'addentrano al simbolo
   (morí quel simbolo, morí).[11]

◻

45
   [The poets ask, they implore,
   Lazarus feeds them at his table,
   they whiten like swans.
   They invoke the beloved,
   the god, the pious victim, the tracks
   that go into the symbol
   (it died, it died, that symbol).]

(We leave the Mallarméan *cigne* / *signe* aside here. But we should note that the swan simile does more than convey whiteness and a possible Gallicizing pun. The swan is the only living thing in this poem that can fly; it may thus stand as the signal of a natural sky-bound directionality. But more insistent, perhaps, is the notion of song that accompanies the image of the swan: the poets' search for symbol is given a tinge of pathos even before we learn that the symbol itself is dead; the swan's loveliest song is always its last. *Et in Arcadia mors.*)

The poets are recognized by *a* in the appurtenances of names and dates, file cards and diagrams, insect cadavers, finally, in anthologies now accessible in no waking moment. Verses 53 and 54 recapitulate in condensed version all that *a* earlier addressed as a landscape of signifiers, syllables, and *sensi*, the perfected conjunction of that which sounds and that which means:

50
   Nomi hanno, date con interrogativo,
   schede, schemi,
   cadaveri com'elitre
   in oniriche antologie.
   Perfettissimo pianto, perfettissimo.[12]

◻

50
   [They have names, dates with question marks,
   index cards, outlines,
   cadavers like elytrons

in oneiric anthologies.
Most perfect cry, most perfect.]

The *a* persona ends his monologue with a final identification of these poets. It is an identification that also reveals a competition: the rocket is not the only artifact of man's invention that would pierce the heavens; poetry was there first, with its desire to strike the stars:

55   I poeti tra cui
       se tu volessi pormi
       "cortese donna mia"
       sidera feriam vertice.[13]

◘

55   [The poets among whom,
       if you desired to place me,
       "gentle lady mine,"
       sidera feriam vertice.]

The Latin is a jumbled quote of Horace's "quodsi me lyricis vatibus inseres, / sublimi feriam sidera vertice" (the *Odes*, Book I, 1). The temporal ambiguity occasioned here by the use of the past subjunctive Italian in the hypothetical clause and the future Latin in the result clause serves as an ironic commentary on the contemporary relation of those languages themselves: Italian is the present, Latin, the past. The future as a present (Italian) which is past and hypothetical here (the past subjunctive) appears in its own skeletal basis (Latin) as the promise (future tense) made by a dead past (Latin, Horace).

But these verses serve not only to evoke great shades in a confusion of temporal placement: they also contain the first identification of *a*'s interlocutor. "*Cortese donna mia*," a formulaic address associated with the rhetoric of courtly love poetry, attributes to *b* a feminine identity maintained throughout the *IX Ecloghe*. This feminine persona, who we eventually know as poetry personified, is first addressed in an utterance traditionally determined to be poetic. We can ignore this association no more than we can ignore the familiar etymology of *donna*.

And, perhaps surprisingly, *b* does place *a* among the poets in a response that promises more. The poets, and *a*, will have what they yearn for. The condition of this satisfaction is confession according to a canonical rule:

>   *b*—Come per essi, basterà la tua
> 60   confessione, immodesta, amorosa,
>   e quasi vera e piú che vera
>   come il canone detta:¹⁴

◻

> 60   [*b*—As it is for them, your immodest,
>   amorous confession will be enough,
>   and almost true and more than true,
>   as the canon dictates:]

There is nothing *simply* true about such a confession. It will have to be, she says, immodest, amorous, both almost true and more than true. The idea, it would seem, is to admit that which does not subject itself to simple referential correspondences. If this condition of confession seems exigent, there is, nonetheless, a guide to or an indication of what it should be. And at this point, punctuation clearly indicates that both *a* and *b* are privy to this canon: *a*'s response to *b* is the syntactic completion of *b*'s illustrative clause; it is a citation both of what *b* would have said next and of a text that exists elsewhere, a text that both *a* and *b* know. This is the confession the poet must make before a *perfettissimo pianto* can be achieved. This was a condition for the ancients; it is still the condition:

>   *a*—"Ma io non sono nulla
>   nulla piú che il tuo fragile annuire.
> 65   Chiuso in te vivrò come la goccia
>   che brilla nella rosa e si disperde
>   prima che l'ombra dei giardini sfiori,
>   troppo lunga, la terra."¹⁵

◻

>   [*a*—"But I am nothing
>   nothing more than your fragile assenting nod.
> 65   Closed in you I shall live like the drop
>   that shines in the rose and scatters
>   before the too long shadow of the gardens
>   withers the earth."]

The confession will bring *a* and the poets back to an earthbound enfolding, back to their grounding.

THE SEEING "io" AND THE BEAUTY OF POETIC VISION

We might summarize, *grosso modo*, the first Zanzottan eclogue in the following way: the persona of the poetic subject characterizes the perfect *pianto* as a useless, obstinate speaking that derives from the reality of things, their "thingness," to borrow once again from Heidegger. From this reality also derive the polarized possibilities of language itself, from the elemental unit of vocalized utterance, the syllable, to the essential artifact of linguistic communication, the signifier. Thus, the oneiric anthologies of perfected poetic utterances share a common grounding with the very essence of language.

The horizon of this metaphysical terrain, which, as a linguistic earth, depends on a sky of mystery, origin, silence, is challenged by a product of man's other hand, the sinister artifact of technology. The technological sky-piercing inscribes with one hand the autopsies of what the other hand would write. As the source space of poetic utterance is intruded upon by the precision of technology, history writes itself in a way that seems to mark the death of symbol, the horizon upon which poetic grounding depends. The poets' distress seems to be occasioned by this changed status of landscape and sky.

Poetry tells *a* that the answer to his and the lyric poets' lament lies in a confession, a confession of minimal identity, a confession that identity derives from some other (*in te*, line 65) which is to the persona as the rose is to the dew drop. Finally, the first eclogue says, the possibility of poetry depends on a fragile, earthbound protection.

The second and third eclogues contribute to an identification of *b* as *poesia* herself if we associate the speaking persona in these poems (in which, since they are not dialogues, *b* does not appear) with the *a* persona of the first eclogue. The *tu* addressed in "Ecloga II" may be read simultaneously, in Petrarchan tradition, as the beloved and as poetry itself. Subtitled "La vita silenziosa" [The silent life], the second eclogue seems to situate itself in a moment when the response of poetry is not heard. Most of its verbs are in the future tense. One of these predicts the intervention of Urania, muse of astronomy, in a hopeful image of sky-originating truth: *Talvolta Urania il vero / come armato frutto ci spezzerà davanti* [Urania now and then will break truth open before us like armoured fruit] (vv. 52–53).

The third eclogue, subtitled "La vendemmia" [The vine-harvest], designates autumn as a time of blueness, of "skyness," in fact, considering the multiple semantic fields indicated by the Italian *azzuro*. In this eclogue, we read about another future in line 18: *riavrò anche il supremo il superfluo l'azzuro* [I shall have again even the supreme the superfluous the azure]. Further on, in lines 20–26, we find *basta /*

THE SEEING "io" AND THE BEAUTY OF POETIC VISION

cosí poco alla precaria anima . . . per essere: raggio / che s'acqueta d'un cielo ove cadere [so little / is enough for the precarious soul . . . to be: a ray / that grows calm when it finds a sky to fall in].

The space challenged by the advent of the rocket is the very space of that which is both supremely and superfluously essential to the *anima*. "Ecloga III: La vendemmia" further identifies *tu* as poetry as it moves to the past tense in verses 27–30:

> In autunno era il tempo
> del grande guadagno,
> molto anelata vendemmia, quando
> esistevi, poesia: pura.
>
> ❐
>
> [In autumn was the time
> of the great gain,
> the much-awaited vine harvest, when
> you, poetry, used to exist: pure.]

But we shall pause next at a text in which *a*'s interlocutor is not *b*, or poetry, at all, but rather a monster whose main characteristic is a singular organ of visual perception.

The second eclogue in dialogue brings a monstrous modality to the pastoral scene, for the shepherd here is the one-eyed Polyphemus. The season is spring, birth moment in the annual *rursus*, and *a* depicts himself as no more than a phenomenological bubble in a modern, scientific twist on both the linguistic *io-non-io* of *Vocativo* and the mythic Οὔτις ("no man") of Homer. The subtitle alliteratively announces this spherical triumvirate as well as the text's dominant image, the sphere: "Ecloga IV: *Polifemo, Bolla fenomica, primavera*" [Eclogue IV: *Polyphemus, phenomenological bubble, springtime*]. The recurring appearance in the poem of the spherical shape as *occhio* encourages our reading to associate the other spherical images with that of the organ of visual perception. The structural similarity of this eclogue's images thus suggests the notion that perception (the eye) is closely related to being (the phenomenological bubble). Specifically, this essential notion of perception is represented here in two versions of the subjective gaze, that of *a* and that of Polyphemus. To the extent that this poem may be read as the association of perception with being, we see in the figure of the monster the destruction of one singularity of perception—and, hence, a threat to perception-associated being in general—by a missile-inflicted blinding: Polyphemus' wounded eye is analogous to the rocket-pierced *cielo* of the first eclogue.

Simultaneous with this metaphysical assumption of the subjective gaze, there occurs an accession to the material reality of the signifier per se: that is, as only minimally or vestigially referential, as maximally syllabic. Stefano Agosti uses a horizon metaphor to describe this when he writes:

> La situazione delle *Ecloghe* raggiunge il punto limite quando il linguaggio finisce per coprire l'intero orizzonte dell'esperienza, diventando esso stesso oggetto del dire: per cui *langue* e sillabazione individuale, vale a dire i materiali e i contenuti interiorizzati, assumono il medesimo statuto indifferenziato di "significanti." Esempio massimo, e senz'altro macroscopico in quanto l'operazione qui riferita si estende alla totalità del componimento, è l' "Ecloga IV: *Polifemo, Bolla fenomica, Primavera*" . . . la quale già prefigura anche per identità di soluzioni locali (cfr., ad esempio, i versi: "Ancora un poco è giusto / ch'io stia al gioco, stia al fiato, / all'afflato / di lutea passibile cera," *ib.*) le successive prove della *Beltà*.[16]

◻

> [The situation of the *Eclogues* reaches its peak when language finally covers the entire horizon of experience and itself becomes the object of speech: hence *langue* and individual syllabification, that is, internalized material and content, take on the same undifferentiated status of "signifiers." The most obvious example, one which is doubtless macroscopic in as much as the operation related here extends to the entire composition, is the "Eclogue IV: *Poliphemus, Phenomenological Bubble, Springtime*" . . . a poem which already prefigures even in the similarity of its individual solutions (cf., for example, the lines: "For a while it's still right / that I play the game, make the effort, / feel inspired, / by vulnerable luteous wax," *ib.*) the later attempts in *La beltà*.]

Agosti finds a second example of the signifier's increased materiality in the poem he calls "Variante" (but which, in the IX *Ecloghe*, is entitled "13 Settembre 1959 [Variante]")[17] in an inexact indication of the second anniversary of the placing in orbit of the first man-made satellite):

> L'esempio limite è invece dato dalla "Variante" . . . —che non per nulla esce tutta da quel verso dell'Imperatore Adriano posto in epigrafe alla IV ecloga: *"Animula vagula blandula,"* citazione di citazione, o sorta di *topos* citazionale (cfr. Pound, Eliot, ecc.)—ove i termini del *pastiche* (o del "gioco") sono trascesi proprio per l'eccesso della manipolazione della materia verbale: i significanti, in turbinosa emancipazione, costituiscono essi stessi il testo, il quale si dà come spessore materico fono-semantico senza supporto di senso continuo. Il movimento circolare (la composizione si vuole ripetuta indefinitamente) sottolinea l'istanza non progressiva—non logica—del "discorso." Siamo oramai alle soglie della

situazione linguistica della *Beltà*, verso cui assicurano il transito quegli "Appunti per un'Ecloga" . . . posti come epilogo al volume.[18]

◘

[The key example is given, instead, by "Variant" . . . —which, not surprisingly, comes entirely from the verse of the Emperor Hadrian set in epigraph to the fourth eclogue: "*Animula vagula blandula,*" the quote of a quote, or a kind of citational *topos* (cf. Pound, Eliot, etc.,)—where the terms of the *pastiche* (of the "game") are transcended simply by the excessive manipulation of the verbal material. In a flurry of emancipation, the signifiers themselves constitute the text, which in turn appears as a materical phono-semantic thickness without the support of continuous meaning. The circular movement (the poem may be repeated indefinitely) underlines the nonprogressive—nonlogical—instance of its "discourse." We are already on the verge of the linguistic situation of *La beltà*, toward which those "Notes for an Eclogue" that appear as an epilogue to the book assure passage.]

The epigraph of the fourth eclogue emblematizes the signifier as a plastic entity, so to speak: here, fascination with assonance and diminutive suffix may be found in the curious personification of soul, and *animula* thus perhaps signals a precedence of the appearance of the signifier per se over its referent. The appearance lends itself to manipulation, and, when the signifier undergoes an apparent change, a new nonexistent referent may result.

In any case, *a* enters speech with caution here, as a word with both common and aulic associations is spoken in quotation, the effect of which is to specify that its utterance does not originate in *a* himself. Here, the beginning of speech is the word of another, a momentary borrowing.

The first line group is the address of *uomo*, identified as *termine vago* (not only "vague," but also "desirous," according to the etymology of the Italian), literally in line five and implicitly, as well, in the series of appositions identifying *uomo* as *fiato* and *bruma* as *impropria luce* and, finally, as an almost unimaginable *salto che il piede spezza sopra il mondo*. The ephemerality climaxes in this leap (which, paradoxically, also recalls the apex of technology we saw earlier) as *uomo a cui non rispondo* associates the *io-non-io* of *Vocativo* not only with the *a* persona and the technological trajectory of the eclogues, but also with Odysseus, who calls himself ὄυτις ("no man") in the Homeric Polyphemus story:

> Persone: *a, Polifemo*
>
> *a*—"Dolce" fiato che muovi
>   le nascite dal guscio, il coma, il muto;

THE SEEING "io" AND THE BEAUTY OF POETIC VISION

```
            "dolce" bruma che covi
            il ritorno del patto convenuto;
5           uomo, termine vago,
            impropria luce, uomo a cui non rispondo,
            salto che il piede spezza sopra il mondo.¹⁹
```

◘

[Characters: *a*, *Polyphemus*

```
        a—"Sweet" breath that moves
            the births from the shell, the coma, the mute;
            "sweet" mist that broods over
            the return of the agreed-upon pact;
5           man, you vague term,
            improper light, man I don't resemble,
            foot-crushing leap over the world.]
```

We may note that even in this first line group there appears a series of spherical images: the birthing *guscio*, the *ritorno* (another *rursus*), and, finally, the *mondo* as locus. We may read in this series a passage from origin through a kind of repetition or return to a universalization: a passage held fast by the sphere.

There are still more spheres in the second line group:

```
            Godono i prati acqua silenzio e viole;
            da fiale laghi, nevi si versano.
10          Occhio, pullus nel guscio: ho veduto
            nell'errare del mondo errante il sole.²⁰
```

◘

```
            [The fields take delight in quiet water and violets;
            lakes, snows pour themselves from phials.
10          Eye, pullus in its shell: I have seen
            the sun wandering in the wandering of the world.]
```

In this landscape where water is silent (lacking the compromises and possibilities, perhaps, of its own language), a superimposition of medical phials onto the landscape as sites of origin for lakes and snows gives a medico-somatic parameter—one not bound by considerations of realism—to the landscape.

Following this surreal image is the poem's central identification of perception with being: *Occhio, pullus nel guscio*. The embryonic *pullus* encircled by the *guscio* is placed in apposition to the sphere that determines visual perception and is followed by the first recounting verbality of the text, *ho veduto*. The persona has seen other spheres: the world, the sun. But here we come upon an anti-Copernican inversion: the sun has been perceived to be moving, *errante*, because it has been perceived from within the movement of the world, *nell'errare del mondo*. The scientific error arises from the site of subjective perception located in the world, but this site, the *occhio*, is in turn a nascent or prenascent being, *pullus*. Scientific correctness of observation is thus shown to have little to do with the essential identity determined by even scientifically incorrect perception. On the contrary, the very error of perception is simultaneously the germinal form of being.

In the next line group, the world receives an appositive definition identical to that given to man in the first line group, *termine vago*, and is further identified as a generic springtime of faint, embryonic psyche. The *termine vago* which is man is thus revealed as analogue for the *termine vago*, which is world:

> Mondo, termine vago, primavera
> che mi chiami nel tuo psicoide fioco.²¹

> [World, vague term, springtime
> who calls me into your faint embryonic psyche.]

The line group continues with *a*'s statement of position, both moral and descriptively locative; it is just, he says, that he remain in the *gioco* (or *fiato* or *afflato*). We note the association of the ludic with the essential, or *passibile cera*, the somatic wax, in which both the *io* and the *mondo primavera* exist, *are*, in ludic mode:

>   Ancora un poco è giusto
> 15 ch'io stia al gioco, stia al fiato,
>   all'afflato,
>   di lutea passibile cera,
>   io, e mondo primavera.²²

>   [For a while it's still right
> 15 that I play the game, make the effort,
>   feel inspired,
>   by vulnerable luteous wax,
>   I, and springtime world.]

THE SEEING "io" AND THE BEAUTY OF POETIC VISION

Next *a* describes himself in a present arrival, *vengo*, when he appears both straight and bent. Here, the Odysseus story seems to pick up again (if we assume that the second line group's considerations of perception and being, as well as those of the world as a *termine vago* in the third line group, are a departure from the earlier hint at Homeric nomenclature in *uomo a cui non rispondo* of line six). The *a*, like Odysseus in the cave of Polyphemus, is straight like Odysseus upon entering the cave and bent like Odysseus upon leaving it, mantled in sheepskin. The correspondence of *a* with the Homeric hero is further suggested by the image of mantling wool in line 23. But, just as an atoll is superimposed on a mountain in Zanzotto's first book, the Odysseus-related images here are superimposed upon the spherical image dominant throughout this eclogue, rendered here as *germe* in line 21. The result is no less surreal than the *salto* of the first line group:

```
        E vengo dritto, obliquo,
20      vengo gibboso, liscio;
        come germe che abbonda
        di dente ammicco e striscio
        e premo alle lane onde ammanta
        il dí le sue fetali clorofille.²³
```

```
        [And I come straight, oblique,
20      I come hunchbacked, smooth;
        like an embryo that's full
        of teeth I wink and slither
        and press against the wool coverlets whence day
        mantles its fetal chlorophylls.]
```

We remark, also, the apparently contradictory synesthesia contained not only in the image of the dentated embryo but also in the snake-like *striscio* and the mammalian *lane* with which the day cloaks its *fetali clorofille*. There is a confusion of life forms here that takes cohesion only in the shared, if misplaced (in the vegetal realm) notion of embryonic—and implicitly spherical—unity.

The line group continues:

```
25      M'adergo, prillo, come a musicale
        sferza la trottola. Poi che qui tutto è "musica."
        Non uomo, dico, ma bolla fenomenica.
        Ah, domenica è sempre domenica.²⁴
```

25   [I rise up, I whirl, like a top
     to a musical whip. Since everything here is "music."
     Not man, I say, but phenomenological bubble.
     Ah, Sunday is always Sunday.]

The direct embryonic simile we saw earlier in line 21 recurs here with the different second term; embryonic analogy passes to mechanical—the dimunitive mechanical, however, of a toy somehow prompted to circular movement by music. Yet these risings and whirlings are hardly selectively determined, since, *a* tells us, *qui tutto è "musica."* Here we encounter once again the eloquence of punctuation. The quotation marks tell us, in spite of *a*'s all-embracing statement, that the *"musica,"* like the *"dolce"* with which his utterance began, is someone else's, not original, and somehow inauthentic. It remains a perceived phenomenon, one remarked as such, as does man who is no more than a phenomenological bubble, an embryo matured by eventuality to nothing more than a larger sphere than the one in which he was germinated. And the line group ends with the tautology of a television title. Music as a quotation: not a poetry contest, but a technological imposition of nonessential speech.[25]

The following line group opens with three declarative sentences which successively describe the influence of stimuli (such as *"musica,"* perhaps) on the phenomenological bubbles, represent the shape of hope and need as a sphere, and, finally, announce *a*'s recantation of traditional letters—letters, it would seem, that depend on any shape other than the spherical structure that seems to determine the being of *non uomo*:

          Le bolle fenomeniche alle mille
30   stimolazioni variano s'incupano
          scintillano. Sferica
          è anche la speranza, anche la sete.
          Abiuro dalle lettere consuete.[26]

                    ▢

          [The phenomenological bubbles vary,
30   grow dark, sparkle to a thousand
          stimulations. Spherical
          also is hope, also thirst.
          I abjure customary letters.]

After this abjuration of letters, a literal sphere invokes the emblematic season of germination, specified here by still more spheres, minimalized as bacteria and fleas' eggs, a season which is also that of drunkenness (altered perception?) and theological as well as secular mystery: the vocative's desire is another *"musica"*:

35
        O primavera di cocchi e di lendini,
        primavera di líquor, dei, suspense,
        "vorrei trovare
        parole nuove":[27]

35
        [Oh springtime of cocci and nits,
        springtime of liquors, gods, suspense,
        "If I could find
        some new words":]

Minimal border movements appear as adversatives to *a*'s desire, however, and the adversatives pass to ludic imagery of players and game, with a hint of inevitability suggested by the etymology, still persistent in Italian, that causes the players to arise out of the game, to take their being quite literally from it, as *gioco* gives rise to *giocatori*. (Such etymological motivation is weakened in English since Shakespeare's time, and even then "players" and "play" suggest a seriousness of representational pretense rather than the ludic gravity of these minimal Zanzottan spheres. We can see how such quotidian Italian words as *gioco* and *giocatori* present difficulties to the English translator.)

        ma il petalo e la frangia, ma l'erba e il lembo muove,
        muovono al gioco i giocatori.[28]

        [but the petal and the fringe, but the grass and the
                                            ledge move,
        the players move into the game.]

The line continues, suggesting a further minimal specification of *giocatori* as *monadi* and leading to the first direct address by *a* of this eclogue's interlocutor, himself specifically indicated by his most evident spherical part. *a* speaks to the monster's eye:

                              Monadi
40   radianti, folle, bolle a corimbi e tu

> tondo comunque, a tutta volta, estremo
> occhio di Polifemo.²⁹

◻

>   [Radiant
> 40   monads, crazy, corymb bubbles and you're
> round anyway, a total vaulting, Polyphemus'
> last eye.]

The one-eyed monster, the *caso limite* metaphor, the emblematic sphere to which the spherical reduction of being, of perception and consequently of utterance in *a*'s discourse turns, offers only negation—and this from a deictically indicated site of its own blighting, its non-sight as site, negation, then, and an oath that, though announced, never arrives:

>   *Po.*—No, qui non si dissoda, qui non si cambia testo,
>   qui si ricade, qui
> 45 frigge nel cavo fondo della vista
>   il renitente trapano, la trista
>   macchina, il giro viziosissimo.
>   E qui su questo,
>   assestandomi, giuro:
> 50 io Polifemo sferico monocolo
>   ebbro del vino d'Ismaro primavera,
>   io donde cola, crapula, la vita
>   (oh: vino d'Ismaro; oh: vita; oh: primavera!).³⁰

◻

> [*Po.*—No, here one doesn't till, here one doesn't
>   ⌊change text,
>   here one falls again, here
> 45 the reluctant trepan, the mean
>   machine, the most vicious twist
>   sizzles in sight's deep cavity.
>   And, settling down here,
>   on this, I swear:
> 50 I, spherical monocular Polyphemus,
>   drunk on the wine of springtime Ismarus,
>   I from whom life drips, guzzles
>   (oh, Ismarus wine! oh, life! oh, springtime!).]

The pointed stake with which Odysseus blinded Polyphemus is inextricably imbedded in the monster's eye. The fact that this *renitente trapano* is appositively designated as *la trista / macchina, il giro viziosissimo* superimposes the Homeric piercing episode upon that of the rocket-satellite in the first Zanzottan eclogue. Polyphemus' eye is the monstrous analogue of the skies that are pierced by the other *trista macchina*, that of man's modern technology, the skies that suffer the insulting presumption of the man-made satellite's moon-miming orbit. The significance added by the metaphor of Polyphemus lies in the effect: such piercing *blinds*. The monstrous singularity of perception (*io Polifemo sferico monocolo*) is destroyed by the penetration of a missile thrown by man, of "no man." Odysseus wanted to evade the monster's perception; his survival depended upon blinding Polyphemus' eye. *a* wants to find *"parole nuove"*; he addresses his desire to the unique perceptive orb of the monster. But the blinding that saved Homer's hero negates *a*'s desire: there is no undoing, no new text, nothing in the blinded singular orb to which *a* speaks but another fall. And the monstrous shepherd, drunk with spring (the parody of a shepherd who, in Virgil's eclogues, would have been comely and praised wine and spring in flights of poetry—the *"parole nuove"* of a bygone era) here swears an oath that never arrives; and that of which he might have sung lingers vestigially in parenthetical exclamation.

Odysseus saved himself, his being, by blinding Polyphemus; the historical advent of technology into the metaphysical *cielo* of poetic—and essential—perception does not save *a* but only reduces him to an embryonic inevitability, a phenomenon lacking its own words of desire. The sweet perception of being as *Animula vagula blandula* has been transformed to a mere phenomenological effect, just as the poetry—or music—of Latin has been transformed to the secondary *"musica"* of modern Italian.

We shall not depart from *a*'s dilemma in "Ecloga IV" without mentioning two other poems that seem to delineate it, particularly with regard to the notion of falling again (v. 44, *qui si ricade*) and the indicated oath (v. 49, *giuro*).

In "Riflesso" [Reflection/Reflex], the third poem after "Ecloga IV" and the second in a section entitled "Intermezzo" (with panic, D'Annunzian overtones), the *io* which other texts identify as persona *a* addresses a *tu*, identified elsewhere as persona *b*, or poetry itself. In this text of both reflection and conditioned reflex, the persona using the first person identifies as *semantico silenzio* that which poetry, *tu*, asked of him:

> con ire di fanciullo o con disfatte
> pause d'adulto,

THE SEEING "io" AND THE BEAUTY OF POETIC VISION

15   che tu volessi, tu, da me, perché,
            universa impresenza,
            unicità e miriade,
            chiesi;
            tu, da me, perché,
20   semantico silenzio.³¹

◘

            [with boyish anger or the undone
            pauses of adulthood,
15   that you wanted, you, from me,
            universal impresence,
            unicity and myriad,
            because I asked;
            you wanted them from me, because,
20   semantic silence.]

This *semantico silenzio* may be read either as the absence of significant utterance or as a silence which, in its very lack of utterance, is significant. Neither reading is inappropriate, but the reference of the dependent clause beginning in line 15 to *ire di fanciullo* and *disfatte pause di adulto* perhaps implies a precedence of the second reading we suggest.

We next read that this request for *semantico silenzio* is accompanied by (or is identical to) a request for an unspeakable eloquence of materiality and somatic reality which determine the essence of the speaking persona (*ch'io fossi*, v. 27):

            E queste nubi e questi
            spessi monti e i linguati
            rivi e il sassoso sonno
            e l'insonnia e i sospiri
25   e il prato come spuma come iride,
            solo questo da me, per me,
            ch'io fossi
            tu mi chiedevi.³²

◘

            [And these clouds and these
            thick mountains and the tongued
            streams and the stony sleep
            and the insomnia and the sighs
25   and the field like foam like iris-sky,
            you were asking

219

only this from me, for me,
so that I might be.]

The vocative that next follows identifies poetry as *nome, tenebra,* and, not the least significantly, as *alapa*. The sacred blow of poetry first encountered in *Dietro il paesaggio* thus persists in Latin here, in a future fall of everything (*tutto . . . ricadrà,* vv. 35–36) upon the *fatiscente / anima* (a modern rendition of *animula vagula blandula,* one might imagine) and the *bocca inetta,* promising with downward plunge a future proximity to an *eco*. Then, at least, in a reflection of poetry, *a* will find a site (for perception, for being):

                O nome
      mai saputo abbastanza mai perduto
30   abbastanza, tenebra
      che s'innamora, alapa
      che disintegra e aggrega, tu, nell'ora
      che tutto sulla fatiscente
      anima
35   tutto sulla bocca inetta
      ricadrà e sarò prossimo all'eco:
      allora almeno.[33]

◻

              [Oh name
     never known enough, never lost
30 enough, shadow
     that falls in love, alapa
     that disintegrates and aggregates, you, in the hour
     when everything will fall back on the crumbling
     soul
35 everything on the inept mouth
     and I shall be close to the echo:
     then at least.]

The oath never spoken by the monstrous shepherd is superseded by the illocution of an oath made by the persona in "Con quel cuore che basta" [With the heart that suffices], the text that follows "Riflesso." "Con quel cuore che basta" establishes that *tu* is a maternal figure and thus associates the *tu* of poetry in the *IX Eclogues* with the *tu* of the mother and the *nome sepolto* in *Vocativo*. The oath itself states clearly the essential rapport between *io* and poetry, specifically, poetry as determined by perception: the *cielo* of *Vocativo*, here identified as Urania, muse of astronomy:

                  Ma ora
        ora anche il vero amore
        tarda talvolta a farmi vivo.
15   Si lasci che io dica "io."
        Quanto è difficile: io.
        Ora: "io-sono" è questa emorragia...
        . . . .
        Ti prego, fammi un segno, lasciati
20   scorgere: tu tenera come onda,
        rutila pescagione, rete, foce,
        solco di mare, succo.
        Perché posso giurarlo, posso
        a fatica scavarlo, ma scavarlo
25   da me, questo che oggi non vuole
        dirsi: con te, io ero.
        . . . .
        Energia divenivo,
        statura anima attenzione
30   degna di misurarsi ai cieli.
        Notti di resine, di corpi felici.
        Cieli vigna abbondante, non munta, profumo.
        Bevevo alla tua coppa, Urania.[34]

◻

                [But now,
        now even true love
        is sometimes slow to bring me to life.
15   Let me say "I."
        How hard it is: I.
        Now: "I-am" is this hemorrhage...
        . . . .
        I beg you, give me a sign, let me catch
20   a glimpse of you: you, tender like the wave,
        the rutile catch, the net, the river-mouth,
        the sea's furrow, its juice.
        Because I can swear it, I can
        dig it up if I try, but dig it up
25   by myself, this which today does not want

THE SEEING "io" AND THE BEAUTY OF POETIC VISION

> to say itself: with you, I was.
> . . . .
>
> I was becoming energy,
> stature, soul, attention
> 30   worthy of comparison with the skies.
> Nights of resins, of happy bodies.
> Abundant unmilked vine, skies, perfume.
> I drank from your cup, Urania.]

The close association of perception and being is maintained in the two first person verbs of the following line group: *vedevo* and *ero*. Polyphemus, deprived of his vision, can make no such declaration. Unblinded, *a* could attest to his being as long as he could see the stars:

> Corpi sommi. Vi vedevo scorrere
> 35   veloci oltre il campo del vedere.
> Scorrevi mare, notte, fresca mirra.
> Posso giurarlo: io ero.
> Senza nulla disperdere, nulla
> offuscare, nulla ferire. Senza
> 40   piú, ma con solo quel cuore che basta.
>
> Beveva il mare; suggeva ai tuoi seni.[35]

☐

> [Highest bodies. I saw you quickly flow away
> 35   beyond the field of sight.
> You were flowing, sea, night, fresh myrrh.
> I can swear it: I was.
> Without wasting anything, clouding
> anything, wounding anything. Without
> 40   more, but with only the heart that suffices.
>
> The sea was drinking; it was sucking at your breasts.]

We may summarize briefly the issues of perception, essence, and poetry which have been raised so far. We suggested that the spherical metaphors in the *IX Ecloghe* work in the book as a whole to delineate a space in which speaking is grounded. This intra-orbital space is represented variously as the world, the eye, and the germinal unit of being in the texts we have read. Our suggestion that the spherical metaphor also refers to utterance arises from the instances in Zanzotto's texts where the phenomena of perception and being are shown, by means of the same generic metaphor, to be situationally analogous to the phenomenon of speech. The most evident of these instances is perhaps found in the fourth eclogue, where man is identified as *bolla fenomenica, termine vago,* and *germe.* The essential *termine vago* desires *"parole nuove"* much in the same way the *io* of *Vocativo* yearns to find a *nome sepolto*. The desire is essential; in both cases, language determines being.

What Zanzotto's eclogues would seem to specify in this metaphysical structure is that language determines being by first determining perception and, further, that the most essential perception is available through the *errare* of poetic language. If in previous ages such an *errare* might be placed in a metaphoric *cielo* as the site of origin and authenticity, our age paradoxically suffers an alienation from this essential poetic *cielo* precisely because our prideful technology has invaded the skies. This invasion is basically a travesty of former proprieties of perception: the satellite "sees"—records, measures—the space of mystery from which human "seeing" previously derived its notions of significance. The anonymous technological invention of the rocket thus also blinds, just as the missile thrown by "no-man" blinds the mythic vision of Polyphemus the shepherd-poet, once sky-like in its unique, omnivisant sphere.

It is evident that the metaphoric structure is complex, especially when perception is situated both within the space circumscribed by an orbit and on the surface of the greater, sky-bound sphere, the *cielo*. But as we pass now to those four texts which address being, perception, and poetry most directly, we would perhaps do well to recall something not mentioned literally in the fourth eclogue's "visual" play on the *Odyssey* episode: Homer himself was blind.

    Persone: *a, b*

    b—In attonita mistificazione
        immaginare cose senza voce
        noi senza noi? Ma io guardo il mio volto,
        la mano brucio nel sole, nell'acqua,
5   non sognerò l'informe;
        stagione aperta, programma,
        elemento che oscilla
        e si modula, "lingua"
        chiedo di poter dire. . . .

10   *a*—Se un odiato dettame talvolta mi toglie
        ai dolci paesaggi, se

THE SEEING "io" AND THE BEAUTY OF POETIC VISION

```
         (pacata la terra
         e precaria accogliendomi ogni giorno
         risorgente da puri sonni)
15       se il ricostruito
         vero talvolta
         vado obliando nell'abietta necrosi
         che noi siamo a noi stessi,
         pure, improvviso afferro
20       il rivolgimento, l'accordo;
         vinco tremori, raggiro
         ostacoli esili e inumani,
         e amore
         tutto il mio amore
25       è me, profondo e spesso
         me, ed in quel ciclo tutto
         con innovato candore vige, palpita.
         Vedi: il canale di linfe beato,
         curvo ai tramonti, azzurro;
30       vedi: gli arbusti, il sole, il greto,
         vedi: gli operai, le api, i fumi,
         tutto il mosaico onde ci componiamo,
         tessere inerti noi stessi ma impegno
         che il crudamente segregato unisce,
35       ecco la lieve vita
         che ti si soffia nella mente,
         ecco la fola
         che tuo intimo seno fa del mondo
         e ti soffolce fulva, fedele, calda.
40       Foglie a mille avvolgeranno i tuoi giorni,
         tu stessa, amara, ti vedrai nello smalto
         del canale attenuarti
         con la luna
         pallida coppa
45       inclinata sull'aureo settembre;
         ecco già quel che fosti
         e quel che sarai si confondono
         nel taglio della luna e del canale,
         ma io ti sorreggo io ti colgo con questo
50       mormorio piú depresso del nulla,
         e non so se tu sia
         tutta in questa carenza d'un silenzio
         appena appena smosso, già ricadente:
```

THE SEEING "io" AND THE BEAUTY OF POETIC VISION

```
           ma della lena
55         ch'è di noi, ch'è da noi,
           del grande sogno
           che ostentatamente testimonio
           (ore e paesi
           e te, su tutto, te fra questi segni
60         assurta, stella-nova
           in faccia al sole ai boschi alle insidiose
           tardità) so che a te paragono
           e ritesso e riporto ogni linea
           amando e parlando in un atto
65         come perché tu sia. Ché dire, emergere,
           (anche se sogno
           è questo stesso sillogismo)
           speechi di sé risplendono: sovrana
           convenzione.
70         E tu fatica e prega e emergi
           con me per chi di fatiche alimenta
           queste sere, addolcisce di riposi,
           con me parla dei sanguinei
           giardini di settembre
75         volti al naufragio,
           delle strade che chiudono, dei cieli
           cui già mirano le ombre,
           di quest'eco in disparte, che accoglie
           in una fiamma tranquilla, odorata
80         come un giaciglio, la nostra sostanza.
           Perché la luce non ha che la luce
           a esplicarla, nel suo
           attimo.[36]
```

◻

[Characters: *a, b*

```
           b—Imagine in astonished
              mystification things without voice,
              we without we? But I look at my face,
              burn my hand in the sun, in the water,
5             I shall not dream the formless;
              open season, program,
              element that oscillates
              and modulates, I ask
              to be able to say "language." . . .
```

THE SEEING "io" AND THE BEAUTY OF POETIC VISION

```
             a—If a despised dictate takes me at times
               from the sweet landscapes, if
               (the placated and precarious
               earth receiving me each day
               as I arise from pure sleeps)
     15        if the reconstructed
               truth I tend
               at times to forget in the abject necrosis
               we are to ourselves,
               nonetheless I suddenly grasp
     20        the upheaval, the accord;
               I conquer tremors, I dodge
               subtle and inhuman obstacles,
               and love,
               all my love,
     25        is me, deep and dense
               me, and in that cycle everything
               flourishes, palpitates, with renewed candour.
               Look: the canal blessed with lymph-streams
               curved in the sunsets, azure;
     30        look: the bushes, the sun, the gravelly shore,
               look: the workers, the bees, the fumes,
               the whole mosaic whence we compose ourselves,
               ourselves inert tesserae but the undertaking
               that unites the harshly segregated,
     35        here is the gentle life
               that breathes within your mind,
               here is the fairy tale
               that makes the world your inmost breast
               and fulvous, faithful, warm, supports you.
     40        A thousand leaves will wrap round your days,
               and, bitter, you will see yourself fade
               in the canal's enamel
               with the moon,
               pale body,
     45        bent over golden September;
               here already what you were
               and what you will be merge
               in the blade of the moon and the canal,
               but I support you, I grasp you with this
     50        murmur lower than nothing,
               and I do not know if all of you is here
```

```
              in this scarcity of a
              scarcely scarcely shifted, again already falling, silence:
              but from the breathing
    55        which is ours, which comes from us,
              of the great dream
              that I obstinately witness
              (hours and towns
              and you, above all, you, risen
    60        among these signs, nova-star
              facing the sun, the woods, the insidious
              latenesses) I know that to you I compare
              and reweave and bring back each line,
              loving and speaking in one act
    65        as if thence you may be. For speaking, emerging,
              (even if this very syllogism
              is a dream)
              shine forth as mirrors of themselves: sovereign
              convention.
    70        And you, please toil and pray and emerge
              with me for those who nourish these evenings
              with toil, who sweeten them with rest;
              speak with me of the bloody
              September gardens
    75        turned towards wreckage,
              of the enclosing streets, of the skies
              the shadows already aim for,
              of this echo in an aside that gathers our substance
              in a tranquil flame, smelling
    80        like a sleep-mat.
              For light has only light
              to explain it, in its
              instant.]
```

In this, the seventh of Zanzotto's eclogues, subtitled *"Sul primato della poesia"* [On the primacy of poetry], poetry's primacy is argued not by persona *b*, the personification of poetry, but rather by persona *a*, the one seeking *"parole nuove"* in the fourth eclogue. Here, poetry itself is the persona searching for a *"lingua"* as a code or *programma* which will be malleable enough to adapt itself to the oneiric form of things (*non sognerò l'informe*). The language poetry desires here is materialistic in the sense that it determines an intimate perception of form. Poetry cannot imagine *cose senza voce*; without the words, the

THE SEEING "io" AND THE BEAUTY OF POETIC VISION

things would disappear. Their being, and that of *noi*, depends on a *"lingua"* which poetry seems, in her confusion, not to possess. *Noi senza noi* would create an essential lack.

But the reassuring response of *a* delineates a Petrarchan *rursus* in line 10 whose obstinacy is that of poetry itself, associated under aulic aegis in the lines that follow with the affect of love; *amore* in lines 23–25 is the essence of subjective being, an *intelletto d'amore* both modern and timeless in Italian poetry.

Next, the task of uniting the tesselated units of the perceptible which in turn determine our own being (lines 32–34) is seen as vital, as the vitality of poetry, as the persistence of an essential amorous affect which, though an error or fable (or *errare*), is also desire (*fola* suggests both) and has the capacity to place the world itself on intimate terms with the perception provided by poetry—the intimate terms of a nurturing.

In verse 40 and following, we see the revelatory association of poetry and the moon, the pale sphere mimicked in our time by man's crass technology. Both poetry and the moon would seem to be on an irreversible wane, but still another Petrarchan adversative appears in line 49 to introduce a singular subjective support. This is the upholding force of one who does not even know whether his depressed murmur sustains a poetic entirety now paradoxically perceptible mostly in silence, because of a lack of code.

But the syntax does not end with the colon marking a new fall in line 53; it continues with an adversative anaphora that introduces the analogy of poetry and being, an analogy testified to by the breath and dream of which the *noi* is composed. This analogical comparison is also (v. 63) a return, a *rursus*, of linearity—*ogni linea*: not only the trajectories found elsewhere in Zanzotto's texts (the low blow of Apollonic inspiration, the deictic directionality of the vocative, the desacralizing advent of technology) but also, perhaps, an etymological suggestion (*linea—lineamenti*) of perceptible somatic essence.

It is love and utterance, perceptible together in the act of poetry, that in turn allow for the perception of poetic—and other—being: *amando e parlando in un atto / come perché tu sia* (vv. 64–65). If our age has it that such essential perception is only hypothetical (the *come* of line 65), *a* nonetheless defends such hypothesis as a causal, though oneiric, syllogism, a *sovrana convenzione* (vv. 65–69). Speech and emergence, utterance and essence, are declared to reflect each other: without the one, the other would be imperceptible. In a radical Zanzottan reworking of the Dantesque *amor mi spira*, this mirroring renders being perceptible.

The convention, *programma*, or code that provides for this mirroring is the convention that simultaneously endows the perceived with essence. This is further evident in lines 70 and following. After showing that the dialogue to which *a* exhorts *b* will be engaged as a generalized act of love, the *caritas* in exchange for the humble charities of those who perhaps look to the poet for a speech lost to themselves (the *buona gente senza piú dialetto* of *Vocativo*, for example), Zanzotto's text arrives at a series of requests in which *a* asks *b* to speak to him of certain things. The last of these is an echo that gathers in *la nostra sostanza* (v. 80). This echo has all the force of its mythical, name-endowing appearance; an utterance of love, the echo—always a *rursus* of subjective utterance—*names* the one to whom it returns. The *rursus* of linguistic convention renders being perceptible by naming it: the *eco*, because it is perceptible, is more essential than the *nome sepolto*, the imperceptible origin. In the instant of perception, *la luce . . . nel suo attimo* (vv. 81–83), source is not of the essence, as the tautological light of the poem's last lines tells us.

If we are surprised to find *a*, the would-be poet persona, gently informing *b*, the poetry persona, of the primacy of poetry, we may recall a similar moment in an emblematic predecessor of Zanzotto. And if we do think of Leopardi at this point, our musings are not discouraged by the sequence in the *IX Ecloghe* that places "Sylvia" just after the seventh eclogue. In Leopardi's *Canti*, the poem immediately preceding "À Silvia" [To Sylvia] is not an eclogue but the hammering Metastasian strophes of "Il risorgimento" [The resurgence]. Nonetheless, the insistent rhythmic returns of Leopardi's text are the vehicle of another return, the return of the poet to poetry, and they contain the realization that even the poet's most desperate lament—that for the desire, now gone, to end his own life—is itself testimony to the vital affect which is perceived as both love and poetry. We might offer the following as an encapsulated comparison of Zanzotto's seventh eclogue, "*Sul primato della poesia*," with Leopardi's "Il risorgimento."

If what Zanzotto's text calls a syllogism were to be stated in classically logical form, it might go something like this : (1) the affect of love determines the subject's perception of his own being; (2) participation in language determines the subject's perception of his own being; (3) language and love determine the perception of subjective being by mirroring it. In this structure, the perception of subjective being is analogous to that of lyric poetry, which is also determined by a redundant coincidence of affect (love) and effect (language), whether under Dante's aegis (*amor mi spira*) or Petrarch's (*Laura/lauro*) or Leopardi's. The eclogue thus obviates in a syllogism (one which our age, perhaps, has repressed, since it is oneiric, the text tells us, a "reasoning" dependent on a waylaying of reason available perhaps only in dream, as in *a*'s earlier desire to ". . . *trovare parole nuove.*" Even if words are always quotations, always other's words, they have held, nonetheless, the key to this perception all along. The appositive rapport of *dire* and *emergere* is the motivation, in Zanzotto's poem, for *amando e parlando in un atto / come perché tu sia*—or a restatement of that simultaneity—where the *tu* is not only poetry in a metaphysical sense but also subjective being.

In somewhat similar, though nonsyllogistic, nononeiric fashion, the reemergence which is both poetic and subjectively essential in Leopardi's "Il risorgimento" occurs with a recognition of affective causality: *Pur di quel pianto origine / era l'antico affetto.*[37]

(A note on a woodland Silvia.)

The essential precedence of perceptible over original being established in "Ecloga VII: *Sul primato della poesia*" is of central importance in the subsequent "Sylvia," where we read of a past conviction of finality which is undermined by subjective recognition of the lack of beginning in verses one through four:

> Finita, ieri, il mio cuore ti disse.
> E ancora inizio non avevi
> e ancora mai nell'inizio non sei
> e sempre sei l'annuncio dell'inizio.[38]

> [My heart, yesterday, said you were finished.
> And yet you had no beginning,
> and yet you are never in the beginning
> and are always the announcement of the beginning.]

Later in the poem, present subjective utterance clearly states in verbal apposition the consubstantial reciprocation of utterance and being: *Io / io vi richiamo, io sono* [I / I call you back again, I am] (vv. 14–15). Verse 22 gives the reason why the earlier conviction of an ending was misled: an ending would imply a beginning, but, as this verse states, *Non ha inizio l'amore* [love does not have a beginning].

Significantly enough, this declaration is followed by a citation, a borrowing in the manner of the earlier *"vorrei trovare parole nuove," "musica,"* and *"lingua."* The borrowing here is not of a popular song but rather of the second line of Leopardi's moonstruck invocation, "Alla luna": *"Or volge l'anno, sovra questo colle"* ["now turns the year, upon this hill"]. This sky-related quotation of the poet who, before

Zanzotto himself, most exemplifies the lament for the passing of an age of poetic inspiration with the advent of modern "truths" is itself an indication of *rursus*, of anniversaries allowing for no origin but only constant, commemorative return, in an echo, itself, of the shade of Petrarch found also in the sylvan equivalent of love in the final line group of "Sylvia." The woman, the beloved, *Silvia*, in a *Laura / lauro* consubstantiation, is called *Sylvia* by Zanzotto; her presence is perceived as *bosco*, the very landscape of signification in Zanzotto's first book. *Sylvia, Silvia,* and *Laura* are all, finally, Daphne—Daphne revealed not only as the essence of utterance but also as the utterance of essence:

25	E fronde cupe cupo nel fondo del bosco, dell'unico bosco, del bosco eterno mi fanno mi vivono mi stormiscono in mille diversi cupi cori.[39]

◻

25	[And dark fronds in the dark depths of the wood, of the only wood, of the eternal wood make me, live me, rustle me in a thousand diverse dark choruses.]

The metaphysical assimilation of affect and utterance in a dyadic unity determinant of perception and therefore of being has a discernible history in Italian literature, as we have signalled by our references to Dante, Petrarch, and Leopardi. We would begin a reading of "Ecloga VIII: *Passaggio per l'informità, La voce e la sua ombra, Non temere*" [Eclogue VIII: passage through formlessness, the voice and its shadow, fear not] by noting that the two images preceding the final reassurance of the subtitle depend to some either partial or synesthetic extent on the notion of visual perception. *Informità* might be perceived audially and tactilely as well as visually, although any such specific sensory limitations would most likely not do justice to the essential metaphysics at stake in the text. For our present musing, however, we would consider it in its visual parameter, encouraged in this by the images of visual perception that are seeded throughout the *IX Ecloghe*. *La voce e la sua ombra* also insists on a visual perception to modify, in a realistic impossibility rendered representable via synesthetic hendyadis, the voice one might otherwise expect to be accompanied by resonance.

Visual imagery aside, however, formlessness and synethesia may serve in themselves as emblematic notions in the eighth eclogue, where *a* and *b*, though still identifiable as striver-after-poetry and poetry personified, blend their roles as they state their perceptions of what is and what will be. If we have read persona *b* (poetry) as the informed, the knowing, the source-realm (or *cielo*) for persona *a*'s—or the *io*'s—being, we find here a moving reversal of roles, a reversal which finds *a* as Virgil to *b*'s Dante. Such a reversal is but an apparent one, however, for in the metaphysics of being established up to this point, tautological *rursus* denies precedence: affect and utterance together may determine perception and therefore being, but perception and being reciprocally or tautologically also determine affect and utterance. In this logic reduced to circularity, what matters is not explanation of origin, or even of linear causality; such considerations are outside the sphere the tautology describes. What matters instead is reciprocation, return, mirroring. Thus the poet may guide the poetic as he is also guided by it. Guiding is the key. And with all due respect for the traditional cliché about poetic vision, what Zanzotto's eighth eclogue seems to present so tenderly may be read as a case, in the very most desirable sense and with Homer in mind, of the blind leading the blind.

Our marginal musings would return for a moment to the characterizations of the fourth eclogue, to a recycled Odysseus, the monster-shepherd Polyphemus, and, implicitly, also the blind Homer, and we would superimpose a little rhapsody here on the text we are about to read. (As rhapsody, it is defenseless, and offered as an inessential preface.)

We recall that Polyphemus, once capable of unique vision, is blinded by a pointed missile. We recall, also, that Polyphemus is a shepherd whose appearance in an eclogue implies that he is also a poet. Thus, Polyphemus and Homer have both poetry and blindness in common. We might infer, although we would not insist that it is logical to do so, that poetic vision is associated with, even dependent upon, blindness to the apparent. If Odysseus manages to escape from the cave of Polyphemus, this is due not only to his ruse—a fraudulent one to the extent that he represents himself as a sheep, but also to Polyphemus' inability to detect the ruse. Polyphemus' blindness makes it impossible for him to detect the fraudulence of the sign. He is able only to determine the departure of apparent sheep; he is condemned to accept as literal the appearance of what he cannot see. And so he loses Odysseus to further pursuits of glory and adventure and remains, as Zanzotto's fourth eclogue ends, alone with his song of Ismaran wine.

THE SEEING "io" AND THE BEAUTY OF POETIC VISION

The figure of Homer lying behind the figures of Zanzotto's text might suggest that poetic vision is really a blindness to the fraudulence of signs which, because they are fraudulent, are capable of being arbitrarily manipulated over a potentially endless chain of signifieds. The message might be that poetry depends on a blindness which has to accept the trickery of the perceptible with the imposed innocence of one unable to determine what is honestly and what is fraudulently represented. It might even imply that blindness to the potential fraudulence of the evident permits a deeper vision; the *Odyssey* itself is testimony, in part, to a vision of the evidence of fraud and the cost of its final defeat in human events.

To speculate further, when *a* said to *b* in the poem we are about to read, *starò perché tutto l'occhio offrii* [I shall remain, for I offered my whole eye], this may be not so much a declaration of total and willful giving over of subjectivity *to* the act of perception as a declaration of willing sacrifice *of* subjective perception in the blind recognition that perception of the apparent itself will not make for endurance or being as much as will a perception not dependent on the apparent. The metaphysics that would posit perception, affect, utterance, and being in a sustaining tautology is thus undermined by an apparent sacrifice of one of its elements. Simultaneously, it passes out of tautology into, literally, a void in which logic—linear or circular—loses direction and all that matters is guidance, a void in whose vacuum only one thing obtains, like light throughout paradise in Dante: *estrema bellezza*. Here, Zanzotto's new poetics recall their beginnings *dietro il paesaggio* in a *guidare* which is the prize of the poet's blindness. This is the eighth eclogue:

    Persone: *a, b*

    b—Soffia oro settembre nelle lente
       giornate, nel
       sole largamente speso, libero.
       Ora dei fumi
5   e dei fati d'un tempo piú non resta
       traccia sul mondo e mai remoto
       piú da quest'oggi d'anime e d'intenti
       giunti a frutto, di filtri e
       d'elitre lampeggiante,
10   mai piú remoto fu il timore.
       Mai dalla terra
       piú distratta è la morte e se pur stanche
       labbra e stanchi occhi si chiudono

```
            forse in qualche paese
15          —che non è qui, non qui tra i nostri passi—
            è solo per avere
            una calma piú alta ma contigua
            a questa che ci adempie e che ci affama.

         a—Eppure scarse e sorde—e non sono
20          che mesi—, scene
            cui m'affido ora tepide eloquenti,
            io vi vedevo e nelle vostre
            glaciali stanze il pianto
            versavo (ogni essere
25          ogni segno ogni senso attraversato
            da una corrente di menzogna: pseudo:
            non sogno, falsità).
            E voi ricordo, chimici
            nomi, angeli, fomenti,
30          a sostentarmi a indurmi
            oltre me stesso ai greti
            affannati del sonno. E oltre il sonno la spada
            infallibile, l'alba, il novissimo
            incredibile sangue mio di ogni alba,
35          il mio sangue ad aprirmi al peggio, all'alba,
            fortissima nell'odio.
            E anche la tua mano,
            brezza, latte, levamen,
            anche la mano tua sento posarsi
40          dolce e tuttavia piena
            sulla mia fronte, come
            se destandomi, infante, ecco il vomito
            mi lacerava, e un'altra mano
            infinitamente digitata
45          m'aiutava premendo sulla fronte.
            Sento la mano tua e il mio morto
            sudore, jazz antichi
            frondeggiano, fa notte
            su grammofoni antichi
50          metallici,
            nulla mi giova, lo so, a nulla giovo,
            inficiarmi si tenta, trasgredirmi.

         b—E ora tutto questo non è piú
            che una nota di guasto in fianco al pomo
55          altissimo, vermiglio,
```

     e ora tutto questo non è piú
     non piú dell'indolente
     forma già umana
     che tanto
60   s'impiccioli sotto le zolle vivide
     tanto se ne umiliò
     che né umana né forma
     né—benché scarsa—
     sostanza piú si crede.
65   E ora tutto questo non è piú
     non piú di quanto cova
     forse nel profondo della valle
     e, benché sia meriggio, ingombro in sé
     giace, e nei suoi misteri
70   muscosi. Ma tu
     non cadrai, tu fiorirai per sempre
     del tuo vero. Esitando e vagando
     inabile, cedendo
     facendoti
75   sanie informale, nigredo, liquame,
     fimo implorante, fimo
     muto, vincesti.

   a—Ma io starò, perché tutto l'occhio offrii:
     a ciò che arde ogni frode
80   perché tutto volle arso nella frode.
     Ora potrò, cibo, lasciarmi cogliere.
     Ora avrò l'invenzione, il movimento,
     Ora avrò anche te e l'unico
     amore, ora che piú non conta nemmeno l'amore,
85   ti sveglierò
     ti guiderò nel sole,
     ora che piú non conta nemmeno il sole,
     perché tutto conosce
     maestramente l'arte dell'esistere.
90   Ora mi sarà inutile
     dirti e dire, poi che tutto dice
     di te, per me. Ti guiderò nel vuoto
     sempre piú vuoto e cerulo
     che settembre apre
95   intorno ai cuori, estrema
     bellezza cui la prossima
     condanna nulla lede, anzi l'avvia

felice e fonda come
un fiume che piú non afferra
100   non cura se non il suo stesso fluire.⁴⁰

◻

[Characters: *a, b*

b—September blows gold in the slow
days, in the
widely spent, free sun.
Now no trace remains on the world
5   of the fumes
and the fates of long ago, and never more remote
from this today of souls and intentions
come to fruition, of philtres and
flashing elytra,
10   never more remote was fear.
Never is death
more distracted from the earth, and even if tired
lips and tired eyes perhaps
close in some town
15   —that isn't here, not here where we walk—
it's only to have
a higher calm, but one contiguous
to this one that fulfills us and starves us.

a—And yet scarce, deaf scenes—and it's
20   only been months—, scenes
now tepid, eloquent, to which I entrust myself,
I saw you, and in your
icy rooms I poured out
my cry (each being,
25   each sign, each sense traversed
by a current of lies: fake:
not dream, falsity).
And I remember you, chemical
names, angels, fomentations,
30   maintaining me, leading me
beyond myself to the toilsome
riverbeds of sleep. And beyond sleep the infallible
sword, the dawn, my newest
incredible blood of each dawn,
35   my blood opening me to the worst, at dawn,
dawn filled with hatred.

　　　　　And your hand too,
　　　　　breeze, milk, levament,
　　　　　I feel your hand, too, resting
40　　　　sweet and full all the same
　　　　　on my brow, as
　　　　　if, waking up as an infant, here came the vomiting
　　　　　to lacerate me, and another
　　　　　endlessly fingered hand
45　　　　helped me by holding my brow.
　　　　　I feel your hand and my dead
　　　　　sweat, old jazz tunes
　　　　　bear leaves, night falls
　　　　　on old metallic
50　　　　record players,
　　　　　nothing is good for me, I know, and I'm not good
　　　　　　　　　　　　　　　　　　　　ᒪfor anything
　　　　　they try to impugn, to transgress me.

　　　　b—And now all this is nothing more
　　　　　than a sour note in the side of the
55　　　　highest vermilion apple,
　　　　　and now all this is nothing more
　　　　　nothing more than the once-human
　　　　　indolent form
　　　　　that grew so small
60　　　　beneath the thriving sod,
　　　　　that humbled itself so much
　　　　　that it no longer believed itself to be
　　　　　either human or form
　　　　　or—even scarce—substance.
65　　　　And now all this is nothing more
　　　　　nothing more than what broods
　　　　　perhaps in the depth of the valley
　　　　　and, even though it's noon, lies
　　　　　laden in itself, and in its mossy
70　　　　mysteries. But you
　　　　　will not fall, you will always bloom
　　　　　with your truth. Hesitating and wandering
　　　　　unable, giving up
　　　　　making of yourself
75　　　　formless sanies, nigredo, sewage,
　　　　　imploring dung, mute
　　　　　dung, you won.

	a—But I shall remain, for I offered my whole eye
	to that which burns every fraud
80	because it risked burning everything with fraud.
	Now food, I'll be able to let myself be gathered.
	Now I'll have invention, movement,
	I'll even have you and the only
	love, now that not even love matters anymore,
85	I'll wake you up
	I'll lead you in the sun,
	now that not even the sun matters anymore,
	since everything masterfully
	knows the art of existing.
90	Now speaking you and speaking
	will be useless to me, since everything speaks
	of you, for me. I shall lead you in the void
	ever more empty and blue
	that September opens
95	around our hearts, last
	beauty which the next
	condemnation does not harm but rather starts up
	happy and deep like
	a river that no longer grasps
100	nor cares for anything but its own flowing.]

The voice of poetry opens this eclogue in the golden September light we shall find again at the poem's close. The *rursus* from September to September is also a quotidian passage, one signalled in a circle of hours from evening to noon to a final effacement of the sun which leaves the second September constantly opening onto a cerulean void. This *rursus*, however, is not so much a progression toward a void as a course from implicit void to explicit void, for what *b*'s opening stanza describes is the terrestrial orb voided of ancient inhabitants, fear, and even death.

This implicit void is presented in contrast to a present internal fullness of intent: *quest'oggi d'anime e d'intenti / giunti a frutto* (vv. 7–8). In the sky above this contradictory landscape, the sun is largely spent, as we learn in the first three lines, where evening is offered as the dying-down of a fire. *b*'s opening discourse presents a kind of generalized weakening: *nel / sole largamente speso* (vv. 2–3), *più non resta /traccia* (vv. 5–6), *mai remoto / più* (vv. 6–7), *mai più remoto* (v. 10), *Mai. . . più distratta* (vv. 11–12). As the sun is spent, so disappear some of the perceptible entities of imagination (*dei fumi / e dei fati d'un tempo.* vv. 4–5), affect (*il timore*, v. 10), and closure (*la morte*, v. 12); these fade away with Apollo's light as if they had once depended on it in order to be perceptible themselves. That light, however, is now *largamente speso*.

But it is also *libero* (v. 3). The spending of source light liberates that light in a one-word signal of a shift, perhaps, from signifying specificity to signifying generality, a shift, perhaps, from the identifiably apparent to the indefinitely luminous. The *mors in Arcadia* which *b* admits only in a supposition (*se pur stanche / labbra e stanchi occhi si chiudono / forse in qualche paese*, vv. 12–14) manifests itself as closure of the organs of visual perception and verbal utterance, the redundant essentials of an earlier tautology. This is a death in which perception and utterance seem to wear out like the sunlight. It is, perhaps, an apparent death of sign-bound being. But it is not the death of poetry, for poetry, which is *b*, describes it, imagines it as elsewhere: *che non è qui, non qui tra i nostri passi* (v. 15). This distant death will not obstruct the path upon which poetry and the poet are together bound. It is, *b* goes on to say, a miming of the calm that obtains now that the spent sun is free: *è solo per avere / una calma piú alta ma contigua / a questa che ci adempie e che ci affama* (vv. 16–18). The hypothetical closing of mouth and eyes is a higher calm than the deictic *questa*, but it is nonetheless contiguous to the present calm. *Questa* would thus seem to be a calm dependent neither on utterance nor on perception, a calm that the death of utterance and perception may take as model. It is a calm of both fullness and hunger, of both satisfaction and desire, a cycle rendered simultaneous. Most importantly, perhaps, it is a calm shared by *b* and *a*.

The fading light of evening is a time *di filtri e / d'elitre lampeggiante* (vv. 8–9); in the freed luminosity, some things sparkle very small. Apparent twilight formlessness provides a setting for forms which might be overlooked in the bright light of day. A new perception not dependent on daylight becomes possible. The nonreflectant luminosity of things themselves is now minimally manifest.

But the poet objects to the fading of the light. *Eppure* (v. 19) breaks in, as *a* insists on the tepid eloquence of the scenes that have given narratable form to his life. He addresses them in good faith, *scene / cui m'affido ora* (vv. 20–21), as he begins an autobiography of sight and sound based on the visualizing recall of *io vi vedevo* (v. 22) and the perceptible architecture of poetic utterance, *nelle vostre / glaciali stanze* (vv. 22–23), chambers for the cry of subjective anguish, *il pianto / versavo* (vv. 23–24).

The scenes of life viewed in the rooms of poetry: this is the structure of *a*'s autobiography. But this chambering of experience is undermined as soon as it is recalled by the revelatory interruption of a parenthesis. Just as mention of sneeze or orgasm interrupts discourse in Zanzotto's later texts to provide involuntary reminders of the soma, so does this parenthesis interrupt and reveal the remembered *scene*, the building blocks of *a*'s autobiography, as being something less than essential, much less true than a dream: (*ogni essere / ogni segno ogni senso attraversato / da una corrente di menzogna: pseudo: / non sogno, falsità*) (vv. 24–27). Being and signification are traversed by lies and *a* knows it in spite of himself.

a's discourse persists nonetheless beyond its own interruption through the scene of an insomniac night ridden with chemical angels to a murderous dawn. We have seen this dawn before in the invocation to the vampire's seductive promise of liberation from morning—the *Dai mattini orribili tu liberami* of "Impossibilità della parola" in *Vocativo*. It would seem that the poet is not yet free from the horrid rooms of dawn; but here, at least, the iterated *alba* leads to solace.

Even in this sequence of scenes, the *stanze* of a life, solace arrives as the presence of poetry immediately synchronized to the pageant of the past, a solace of alleviation and mitigation: *levamen* (v. 38). The touch of poetry is here no lowly swipe but a *posarsi* as sweet as that of Laura's limbs or Recanati's moon on the landscape of *mia fronte* (vv. 39–41). The *scena* evoked to describe this touch shows the poet as a child and poetry's hand as maternal. The imperfect temporality of the remembered scene in the simile beginning in verse 41 gives way to present sensation in verse 46, *Sento la mano tua*, which itself reiterates the *la mano tua sento posarsi* of verse 39, an iteration of maternal presence and touch as the evening present returns with outdated, mechanically reproduced music.

This oscillation of past and present culminates in what *a* earlier called *"musica"* ("Ecloga IV"): the persistence in the present of the past songs of others; the notion that song—poetry—is always past and always other, a maternal alterity reduced to a recorded quotation. The *stanze* enclosing the *scene* of present perception are closed within metallic machines. This modern alienation of mechanical reproduction where once there were singing contests seems to cancel the efficacy of poetry's soothing, motherly touch, and no transgression or impugning of the self allows *a* to get beyond this autobiography's closing on a sour note of reciprocal inefficacy: *nulla mi giova, lo so , a nulla giovo* (v. 51).

Poetry responds not with an adversative but with an additive. The present is not a concentration of the past but an addition to it. The continuity expressed in *E ora* is the beginning of a new music, and all that precedes, *tutto questo*, perseveres deictically as nothing more than a wrong note, a small, circular mistake that now is subsumed by Apollo's fruitful orb (vv. 53–55).

Anaphora reinforces the additive as verse 56 introduces a redefinition of *tutto questo* that appositively designates the *nota di guasto* as the once-human form that indolently reduced itself to such a degree that it has almost lost all notion of itself as either human or form (vv. 56–64): a kind of *uomo-non-uomo,* we might imagine.

What we might easily read as *b*'s biography of *a* in these lines if we recall the subjective struggles with language and being in earlier texts passes with the next instance of anaphora to a realm rendered in landscape terms. In verses 65–70, *tutto questo* receives a nonspecific nominal definition, one dependent for figuration on verbs alone: *non è piú / non piú di quanto cova . . . e . . . giace.* The hypothetical place of this posturing is perhaps analogous to the *fondo del mio viaggio* of "Arse il motore." In this deep site, the mysteries of *quanto cova . . . e . . . giace* persist in verdant dampness even at midday, the moment of no perceptible shadow signs. *Tutto questo,* *a*'s perceived entrapment of his being in scenes of stanzaic narration, is declared by poetry herself to be nothing more than a situation of self-enfolding that, after a blow of inspiration, perhaps, does not risk rising on its own even at the sole moment when to do so would not entail the possibility of any misleading signification or fraud.

b's only adversative appears in line 70 to declare that *a* is not *tutto questo,* that there is a truth to *a* which will effect an essential flowering and provide a sure foothold. By his very hesitations and wanderings, by his surrender and his rendering of himself as the basest of base matter, *a*, poetry declares, has been victorious. This enigmatic victory may be clearer if we see it in a larger context as the penetration by the poet of the *situs* to which Apollo's blow long ago consigned him; *a* has ceded his being to the decaying matter of the site of poetic inspiration and so, himself, will one day flourish.

Poetry's promising prophecy is met with a poet's adversative in verse 78. What *b* has described as a ceding to the site is stated by *a* as a ceding of sight, *perché tutto l'occhio offrii* (v. 78). The grounding of the poet's being in the humus where decay leads to flowering is revealed as a simultaneous renunciation of perception of the apparent. *a*'s victory is an ability to endure (*Ma io starò,* v. 78) gained by this renunciation. And the renunciation itself is more than self-denial; its function is an offering of perception to some realm of implicitly sacred volition in which all fraud is annihilated (vv. 79–80). The poet will endure because he has relinquished his self-bound perception to a will that reveals the fraudulence of the apparent.

The present emerges in verse 81 from this causal rapport of aorist and projected temporalities as a time of role reversal and paradox. Designating himself as *cibo*, *a* declares that he will now be able to allow himself to be gathered in (v. 81). No longer will the poet seek nurturing from mother poetry; he will now make of himself the nourishment for poetry. Simultaneously, he will gain *invenzione, movimento, te* (poetry itself), and *l'unico amore*. *a*'s prophesied possession of the singular affect is shown in verse 84 as the paradoxical result of the lost value of that affect. What no longer counts is what the poet will gain. Blinded, he can no longer count on what he saw as *amore*. Blinded, however, he can have it. By relinquishing his capacity to count on signs, perhaps, he can now avoid the fraud of the apparent. This blindness, we shall soon see, will make him a very good driver.

For it is as poetry's guide that *a* now blindly sees himself. He will awaken poetry and conduct it *nel sole*, now that the sun, source of both inspiration and signification, as is love, also no longer counts (vv. 86–87). The metaphoric, orbic specificity of that upon which utterance and essence were earlier seen to depend passes with the relinquishing of sight to a universal cognitive mastery: *perché tutto conosce / maestramente l'arte dell'esistere* (vv. 88–89).

This universalization is one not only of cognition but also of signification, as it exempts the poet from the imperative of subjective utterance (vv. 91–92). Now that he realizes that *tutto dice / di te, per me* (vv. 91–92), the poet is perhaps also freed from his mistaken perception of himself as bonded within language, just as Apollo's luminosity is freed at twilight: a free light and a free speech. Poetry is all around, *a* seems to say; it needs not a mouthpiece but a guide.

Ever since Apollo's blow laid the driver low in Dietro il paesaggio, he has been trying against the insurmountable odds of linguistic determination to be a "poet," to say that which would somehow escape or circumvent the potential falsity or arbitrariness of the sign. Now, poetry herself has gently taught him that, by leaving an apparent, impossible imperative of authenticity behind, he can give up passing his notion of being from determined room to determined room in the apparent architecture of poetry. In his blindness, *a* can enter a landscape where the abyss is not a threat but a supreme beauty. The poet will be a driver once again, over openings where the imminent end of *estrema bellezza* is also its paradoxical beginning, end and beginning obviated in a flow like that of a river where origin and authenticity are moot.

In this passage through that which has no form, the poet will recognize his voice as a shadow of the voice of poetry which is all around. Fear is gone, and poetry continues. If much of our reading has played on the semantic fields of *guidare*, it is only to suggest a comparable flow of metaphor from the first book to this one. And, as the eighth eclogue's century of lines rounds out, we may wonder if Apollo's early blow wasn't a request for a lift all along.

In the eighth eclogue, *a* has relinquished his view of things and is rewarded by the revelation that, even independently of his apparent perception, all things signify. The utterance dependent upon subjectivity is freed, as is the subject dependent upon utterance. For the space of one poem, at least, the tautology of being and language is opened onto a void of beauty. But, in the following eclogue, even this is problematized. The difficulty for the poet is no longer one of subjective identity but rather identity of the word per se. If poetry is to continue, its words will necessarily be the words of the lie, the *menzogna*, which is the individual utterance, the always falsifying reduction of that *tutto* which anyway signifies for itself.

"Ecloga IX: *Scolastica*" [Eclogue IX: *Scholastics*] is the last eclogue of the book and the final dialogue between *a* and *b* alone. Numerical presumption of completion is deferred to the Virgilian model. But, as if in homage, this modern mimesis that falters before completion of a decade offers in penultimate position, here a play on endings and beginnings, a literal questioning and answering in which poetry is a subtle teacher and the issue, on both sides of the conversation, is one of pedagogy.

The voice of poetry opens the dialogue with images of spaces, a river, and autumn reminiscent of the closing lines of "Ecloga VIII":

    Persone: *a, b*

    b—Per spazi, per gradini
       come spazi cadenti
       verso i miei piedi dal diffuso
       sonno delle foschie, come di sogni
5   popolato (ed è sale di libere
       uve, industrie animali,
       programmata efficienza, vittorie),
       fiume sempre in dialogato transito
       fiume tra poco amazonico,
10   ora qui ai seni del Montello
       verso me vieni leggiero convinto,
       né ti rapisce l'orizzonte,
       ma a gioire d'autunnali tregue
       tra gialle effusioni di foglie

15   tra dorsi disposti all'oblio
       sfumi con le ore, torni con le ore,
       amico indifferente
       ristoro e distrazione
       nell'inizio decisa.[41]

◻

       [Characters: *a*, *b*

       b—Through spaces, up stairs
       falling like spaces
       towards my feet from the diffuse
       sleep of the mists, as if it were populated
5   by dreams (and such sleep is the salt of free
       grapes, animal industries,
       programmed efficiency, victories),
       river in continual dialogated transit,
       river soon Amazonian,
10   now here in the Montello's breast
       you come towards me lightly, with conviction,
       nor does the horizon carry you off,
       but for the taking of pleasure in autumnal truces
       among yellow effusions of leaves,
15   among slopes tending toward oblivion,
       you fade with the hours, you return with the hours,
       indifferent friend,
       refreshment and distraction
       decided in the beginning.]

Here is the sleep of mists populated as if by dreams, the *sogni* which, in the previous eclogue, stood in opposition to *falsità*. The implicit truth of this sleep, moreover, is revealed parenthetically as something like the salt of earthly industry, another signal, perhaps, of universalized signification, in verses 5–7.

In *a*'s presence (with *a* as her guide through these spaces, we might imagine), *b* addresses the river which, in the final simile of the previous eclogue, is offered as a symbol of a continuity and process which does not rely on notions of origin or terminus but rather equates those notions, thereby rendering them moot. The *fiume* is a dialogated passage, one effected by communicative exchange (v. 8) which, though it shall soon attain vast proportions (v. 9), comes toward *b* in the maternal specificity of Montello's wood (v. 10) as not much more than a determined stream (v. 11).

As if in response to the notion of signification beyond in *Dietro il paesaggio,* or in a recollection of the landscape artistry of Leopardi's "Infinito," *b* declares that the horizon will not capture this flow (v. 12). Instead, the *fiume* fades and returns with a *rursus* of hours as *amico indifferente / ristoro e distrazione / nell'inizio decisa* (vv. 17–19). The notion of this process, this flow of meaning that laps round the feet of poetry as a distraction decided long ago, is perhaps analogous to the notion of poetic vision as a blindness to the apparent. Distraction, a turning away from apparent purposefulness, is here the dyadic complement to poetry's *ristoro,* the appositive definition of poetry's *amico,* indifferent, perhaps, because distracted, *amico,* perhaps, because indifferent to apparent purpose of determination (*e non della ventura*). The significance which asserts itself in a waylaying of intention rather than in a trajectory of purposefulness is the kind of meaning poetry here seems to mean.

Like an attentive pupil, *a* responds to all this with an interrogative assumption. His sense of a linear propriety with beginnings and endings is confused. Perhaps he has not quite understood. Perhaps understanding is not quite the point:

20   *a*—È questa, in tanto ingiusta posizione,
            l'ora, l'inizio?[42]

        ◻

        [*a*—Is this, in such an unfair position,
           the hour, the beginning?]

a's address to poetry, whose close association with the metaphor of the river suggests an expanding identity not simply as poetry but also as language, next shows a concern for the objects of a pedagogy incumbent, in turn, upon himself:

           Domani
       per i mille sentieri nei mattini già freddi,
       sarà brina formiche e bambini:
       e nella scuola che vive
25   di quanto sa bearla l'infinita corrente,
       nella scuola povera e nuova
       tra candore di fogli,
       nel Montello, cesto muscoso, boccio
       di funghi multicolori, di prati,
30   di querce clamorose

per uccelli e per venti,
povera e nuova tu stessa, starai.⁴³

◻

[Tomorrow
on a thousand pathways in the already cold mornings
there will be hoarfrost, ants and children;
and in the school that lives
25 on what the endless current knows how to bless it with,
in the school poor and new
among leaf whiteness,
in the Montello, mossy basket, bud
of multicolored mushrooms, of fields,
30 of oak trees clamoring
with birds and breezes,
you will be poor and new yourself.]

The verb of endurance, *stare*, with which *a* declared his situation after sight in "Ecloga VIII," here appears as the durability of poetry (and language) in the schoolhouse *che vive / di quanto sa bearla l'infinita corrente* (vv. 24–25). Whatever blessing the endless flow may impart to this sweet school is enough to sustain it in life: its life is thus poetry; its life depends on a beatitude of language.

With the early-morning images of children's warm awakenings before him, *a* begins to worry about how *b* (poetry, language) will respond:

Ma che dirai a quelle anime di brina,
di arnia, a quel festante grappolo
35 che intorno al tuo cuore s'ingloba, e stordisce
di curiose energie la pur schiusa
aula che dà sul mai stabile greto?
Sorgono i bimbi da lane e stupori
d'autunno, scendono
40 dalla casa cui l'ape e la dalia
fanno lustro sempre piú dimesso,
e il sole aiuta il pane e la pioggia
aiuta il bere. Tutto
gioca con loro, o pioggia o sole
45 o ramo o nano o vetro,
e per loro il gran fiume
d'azzurro si ravviva i capelli leggiadri.⁴⁴

◻

[But what will you say to those hoarfrost souls,
those beehive souls, that merrymaking bunch
35   that gathers round your heart and stuns
with curious energies the classroom
that was left open anyway and looks out onto the
                                    ⌞never stable riverbank?
The children rise from wool coverlets and autumn
stupors, they descend
40   from the house that the bee and the dahlia
polish to an ever simpler shine,
and the sun helps the bread and the rain
helps drinking. Everything
plays with them, both rain and sun
45   and branch and dwarf and glass,
and for them the big azure
river shakes out its shining hair.]

a's very lexicon posits a closeness between these children and poetry. In the eighth eclogue, he said to *b*, *tutto dice di te* (vv. 91–92); here he says, *Tutto / gioca con loro* (vv. 43–44). All things speak of poetry; all things play with children, even the river of poetic meaning, here perhaps become, in the metaphor's suggestion, also the blue sky and the breeze.

The ludic contact of the young with the world is also a contact, innocent and natural, with poetry and language. What words, *a* asks, will *b* find with which to articulate a response when such articulation would implicitly intrude upon the unsophisticated oneness of the space both poetry and children share, the *tutto*? The image of the open schoolroom and the unstable outside world in verses 35–37 may imply some urgency. What reductive words can prepare these innocents for the *mai stabile greto* that awaits them?

a answers his own question with a statement of linguistic bankruptcy:

            Vengono i bimbi, ma nessuna parola
49   troveranno, nessun segno del vero.[45]

            ◻

            [The children come but will not find
            any word, any sign of the true.]

a is suggesting once again the familiar notion of linguistic inauthenticity which seemed to have been superseded in the previous eclogue.

THE SEEING "io" AND THE BEAUTY OF POETIC VISION

His appositive identification of *parola* as *segno del vero* hearkens back to the unattainable *nome sepolto* of *Vocativo*. Without this *parola*, the signification which is already in all things will become a lie as it passes through the instance of *parola*-bereft language, even that of poetry, *in noi*:

50
        Mentiremo. Mentirà il mondo in noi,
        anche in te, pura.[46]

◻

        [We shall lie. The world will lie in us,
        even in you, pure one.]

Yet *a* offers a hypothesis of mutual support between the virginal writings of the children and pure poetic language in what may be read as an implicit equation of such virginity with the supportive blindness of the preceding eclogue:

                Forse
        per te di tenui note
        si costelleranno odorati quaderni;
        a domande, a pastelli, a scritture
55   vergini, verginalmente
        darai forza.[47]

◻

                [Perhaps
        for you pencil-smelly notebooks
        will be studded with tenuous notes;
        to questions, crayons, virginal
55   writings, virginally
        you will give strength.]

Such innocent support scratched out on schoolroom artifacts would perhaps need the guidance of a teacher to render it readable beyond childhood. No teacher will appear, however, the next lines tell us, implying that the dyad of necessity and falsity will persist in an untutored world:

        Necessità e finzione:
        ché nulla, nulla dal profondo autunno,
        dall'alto cielo verrà, nessun maestro;

THE SEEING "io" AND THE BEAUTY OF POETIC VISION

60 nessun giusto rito
    comincerà domani sulla terra.⁴⁸

◻

[Necessity and pretending:
for nothing, nothing will come from deep autumn,
no teacher, nothing from highest sky;
no just ritual
will begin tomorrow on the earth.]

Poetry (language) responds with another hypothesis of its own pedagogical effect, a valuation of the illumination of a question over the surety of a response. But *a* proposes that poetry's pedagogy is due to poetry's ability to generate an answer within itself. The smallest unit to which poetry may be reduced, the minimal unit of signification, becomes a god, a world of language; it affirms itself. Feeling that this—the question that is its own answer—is what he lacks, *a* resorts to scripture, approximation of the *logos* he seems to attribute to poetry, in his request for *una risposta*:

b—Io forse insegno a tollerare, a chiedere
    ciò che illumina
    piú nel chiederlo che nella risposta.

a—Tu forse insegni perché una risposta
65 hai generato in te. Sei poco,
    un suono solo, una vocale, un nài,
    un sí; da fare grande
    come l'iddio, un mondo tutto
    di microcristalline
70 affermative sillabe.
    Oh, una sola risposta: e tutto
    insegnerò, sed tantum dic verbo.⁴⁹

◻

[b—Perhaps I teach to tolerate, to ask for
    that which enlightens
    more in the asking than in the answer.

a—Perhaps you teach because you have generated
65 an answer within yourself. You are little,
    a single sound, a vowel, a nay,

THE SEEING "io" AND THE BEAUTY OF POETIC VISION

>   a yes; to make as big
>   as god, a whole world
>   of microcrystalline
>   affirmative syllables.
>   Oh, one answer only: and I shall teach
>   everything, sed tantum dic verbo.]

The words of another, of the centurion to Christ as reported in Matthew, 8:8, are signs of a great faith in the word. *b* responds to this faithful quotation with a promise of audial perception:

>   *b*—Riudrai le voci del profondo autunno,
>   del magistero, del pozzo profondo,
> 75   se sapesti udirle nel primo
>   giorno, se sapesti che primo
>   è ogni giorno.⁵⁰

>   [*b*—You shall hear again the voices of deep autumn,
>   of teaching, of the deep well,
> 75   since you knew how to hear them on the first
>   day, since you knew that every day
>   is first.]

The acceptance of each day as the first, as something other than an apparent repetition, the acceptance of the individual manifestation as the authentic one is the key to hearing these deep, instructive, ripe voices. Thus the dawn, the moment that apparently challenges the private truths of dream and sleep, is revealed in a reversal of its former vampiristic negation as that which will turn *nostra menzogna* into truth:

>   Non essere stanco
>   di durare tra le albe, esse faranno
>   verità della nostra menzogna.⁵¹

>   [Do not tire
>   of enduring in the dawns; they will make
>   truth of our lie.]

Poetry encourages the poet to endure beyond these moments when he feels truth taken from him by the necessity and falsity of inauthentic signification. She continues with a paternal simile to teach

THE SEEING "io" AND THE BEAUTY OF POETIC VISION

a that each sign has value. Even assailed, the sign maintains what might be called its own appropriateness; as sign, it carves out its own sector of meaning, and it rids itself of the superfluous and the vain in each individual manifestation. The father knew this, taught it; and the father sustains and supports from a depth beyond death:

<pre>
80   Come a lui che insegnava
      agli operai quanto sia nitido
      il segno sul foglio ed il taglio nel legno;
      vale ogni segno, ogni taglio, estinzione
      del troppo e del vano, ombra aggredita.
85   A lui, tuo padre. Senti che da sotto
      di tutto se stesso ti regge; sentine tutto il respiro:
      non è, nemmeno nella morte,
      ancora non è faticoso.⁵²
</pre>

◻

<pre>
80   [Like the man who used to teach
      the workers the clarity of
      the sign on the paper and the cut in the wood;
      every sign, every cut has its worth, as extinction
      of the excessive and the vain, as a shadow assailed.
85   For him, your father. Feel how he supports you
      from beneath all his being; feel all his breathing:
      even in death, it is not,
      it is still not, strained.]
</pre>

(In an aside, we might suggest that the image of the father works here as a sign itself of the logos that is less a legal stricture than a basal possibility of signification. Hölderlin's shadow falls across these lines, for the notion of a supportive heritage of meaning that might be implied by this paternity is also found in his "Bread and Wine," where the poet expresses it in a trajectory not unfamiliar in Zanzotto:

> Father! Clear light! and long resounding it travels, the
> ⌊ancient
> Sign handed down, and far, striking, creating, rings
> ⌊out.
> So do the Heavenly enter, shaking the deepest
> ⌊foundation.
> Only so from the gloom down to mankind comes their
> ⌊Day.⁵³

The image of sustenance through a heritage of generational stratification places *a* above his father and, implicitly, below those to whom he in turn may be father. It is perhaps from this implied *enterrement* of the poet in a humus of even meaningful signs that *a* next cries out for distinction. The irony of his desire is that such distinction quite literally depends on that from which it would differentiate itself, a sign: *segnami* (v. 90), the very letter of what he himself said he would do *sed tantum dic verbo*. The letter of the Italian verb *insegnare* reveals teaching as a marking, a transference and individual manifestation of inherited sign:

>   *a*—Oh dalle mille sovrapposizioni
> 90   distinguimi ancora, segnami, non
>   lasciarmi andare in mille onde incomposte
>   ineroiche, non sono
>   trecciuto fiume e nemmeno ruscello
>   in cui almeno la talpa confidi.[54]

◻

>   [*a*—Oh distinguish me again from the thousand
>   superimpositions, mark me, don't
> 90   let me go in a thousand disorderly unheroic
>   waves, I am not
>   a richly-braided river nor even the rivulet
>   in which at least the mole confides.]

a's cry to be signed is a cry for exemption from a plurality of formlessness which lacks even the positive moral distinction traditionally available to a narrative's protagonist (vv. 90–92). His negative self-definition may be read as an attempt to dissociate himself from any ontological participation in the formlessness he calls *mille onde*. But the strength of the metaphor persists: the waves from which *a* would distance himself when he claims to be neither river nor stream are still the undulations of the *fiume* running through this eclogue and the previous one as the continuity of poetic (linguistic) significance beyond tautology and into beauty. And, in verse 94, the notion that there may be something in the necessary falsity of this river of language that, nonetheless, also opens the way for the truth of a poetic vision would seem to belie itself in *a*'s discourse. His insistent denial of any identification with the river may be to some degree a case of protesting too much; it closes, in fact, with a note of nostalgia: the *ruscello* that he says he is not is one *in cui almeno la talpa confidi*. The small river is a recepticle for the minimal blind faith of a minimal animal; the rippling stream is a place of the essential confidence of the small beast who, like *a* in a more confident moment, and like Homer, is blind.

In any case, these waves which in their thousands join the metaphor of the *humus* of inherited sign values to the metaphor of the river of universal signification (the *mille sovrapposizioni* of verse 89 and the *mille onde* of verse 91) hold an unwelcome appeal for *a*:

95   Eppure tra questa che seppi menzogna,
        nella vita, rabbioso m'attardo.⁵⁵

◻

95   [And yet surrounded by what I knew to be a lie,
        in life, angrily I linger.]

It is difficult to talk about what comes next in this eclogue because one has the sense of trampling down fields of flowers through which a light and expert foot has earlier gently made its way, causing no harm, clearing a path through great beauty. We hazard to do so by beginning with the lines just preceding.

The Petrarchan signal of a turning point in verse 95 perhaps signals more than a passage in the syntax present here; perhaps it signals a turning point, a minimally represented conversion, in the greater syntax of all we have read of Zanzotto until now. The *eppure* is an additive adversative, so to speak; it offers persistence and endurance without denying what precedes it, even though what precedes it is denial. The subjective disappointments of the past—the landscape surface that resisted reading, the vocative illocution rendered deictic isolation by an echo, the tautology of being and utterance somehow apparently undone by blindness and a river—are not cast away in a negation but retained, *eppure,* as an index, *questa,* that the relative clause defines as *menzogna.* To call something a lie is not to negate it, and anyway, here the lie is clausally relative. Moreover, calling it a lie here depends on past knowledge, *seppi,* the assurance of *sapere* in the remote past.

Even if all that precedes this turning point is *menzogna,* it is also vital. The comma at the end of verse 95 indicates that the prepositional phrase, *nella vita,* is not intended to delimit the lie only to part of life. The text is an entity of falsehood; it is all that precedes. And *nella vita* is revealed by commas as the *locus* of angry lingering, the site where *rabbioso m'attardo.* The key to the turning point of *eppure'*s endurance perhaps lies in this tesselated syntax that shows the coincidence of the place of the lie and the place of life: *m'attardo tra questa che seppi* *menzogna, m'attardo nella vita*. And it is perhaps this coincidence of vitality and falsity that provokes the rage.

Here is where *a*'s lesson begins, then. He has made a statement which he seems to feel needs a clarification, for what follows is just that. Our recognition that the clarification is given to *b* and to us in the guise of a benevolent pedagogical tactic reveals that somehow *a* has come into the role of teacher which he earlier said would be possible for him only if poetry (language) would give him an answer, *sed tantum dic verbo*. And the fact that this tactic is a simile, the first used by *a* in this lengthy text, may be a hint. The much sought after *verbo* may avail itself to *a* to whatever extent *a* is able to refrain from burdening it with the responsibility of purposeful, direct, authentic meaning. If *a* can receive it instead and use it in the truthful subtlety of indication that can arise even from a lie, if *a* can consider the *verbo*, that is, as itself a kind of trope, then the word might respond.

The essential verb in verse 97 appears after the familiar word of both gathering and offering, *ecco*. What follows is a gift, a gift of definition made possible only by the mediation of *come se*, as if that which cannot be said with any assurance of authenticity will be made clear by a distraction of direct trajectories. *a* does not say what is; he says what "it" is like. And the *come se* series pulls our reading further and further into realms of recognition, from the familiarity of the minimal landscape through circular configurations and the *andare* that began in the eclogue before—or in all the books before—to a second term in which being and utterance are joined in a quotational troping of the very pronoun whose utterance for so long has symbolized the paradoxical separation and union of being and language. This joining, *a* tells us, is the gift of poetry:

```
           Ecco, è come se verso la brughiera
           che è eletta dalla lepre
           e che il pioppo circonda e vuole a
100        ombroso letto ai riposi
           della sua corona che perisce
           nei giorni, è come se
           in questo andare che non ha ancora
           senso, ma già rifiuta la paura
105        rifiuta il silenzio—ah, individuata
           e subito confusa legge, bruto
           plasma, densissima lingua—
           io sia colui che "io"
           "io" dire, almeno, può, nel vuoto,
110        può, nell'immenso scotoma,
```

> "io," piú che la pietra, la foglia, il cielo, "io":
> e, in questo, essere indizio, dono,
> dono tuo, agli altri donato.[56]
>
> ◻

	[That's it, it's as if, headed for the brush
	that the hare chooses
	and the poplar surrounds and wants for its
100	shadowy bed for the resting
	of its crown that perishes
	in the daytimes, it's as if
	in this going that does not yet have
	meaning but already refuses fear
105	refuses silence—ah, law personalized
	and immediately confused, brute
	plasma, thickest tongue—
	it's as if I were he who "I"
110	"I" can, at least, say, in the void,
	can, in the immense scotoma,
	"I," more than the rock, the leaf, the sky, "I":
	and, in this, be token, gift,
	your gift, given to others.]

The circular images of *circonda* in verse 99 and *corona* in verse 101 might be more easily overlooked had we not been sensitized to them by orbicular figurations in previous texts. And if those earlier spheres suggested *rursus*, the eye, and even part of the first person pronoun, the progression here from the image of the circular poppy's quotidian cycle to the notion of *vuoto* as *scotoma* and, finally, to the *io* who says "*io*" may be read as a condensation of the semantic fields fecundated by this metaphor from its early appearance as artificial satellite until now.

By agreeing to call himself "*io*," by recognizing that language is in some sense always a quotation—of itself, of the world it would signify, of the *tutto* of self and universe that already signifies without intervention—this would-be poet perhaps also accepts that the inauthenticity of language at least allows for a miming, a troping, of the *parola*, the *nome sepolto*, whose existence is conceivable only this way, through the distraction of the trope. The artificial satellite is a feeble imitation of Diana's moon, its perception but a mocking limitation of man's imagination. But its beeps, faint though they be in all their reductive insufficiency, perhaps at least convey to earth something of the unspeakable grandeur of the *cielo*. Bound by imitation, representation, quotation, *l'altra mano dell'uomo* is the only one he has left, but it is a hand that can write. *Sed tantum dic.*

a accepts the vision to which his age condemns him. Just as Zanzotto's *IX Ecloghe* titularly defer completion to Virgil, so does *a*, in the ninth of Zanzotto's eclogues, defer blindness to Homer. The perfection of poetic vision had a language spoken even by the gods, but the authentic blindness of that vision is left to the mythic master. *a*, who would be but an apprentice, has not been blinded so beatifically; but his willingness to relinquish his perception of the apparent, his sight and his site, has left him at least with an awareness of his own *scotoma*, the blind spot at the intersection of image reception. And this *immenso scotoma* is within him as well as around him. The tesselated apposition of the syntax here joins this essential blind spot to the *vuoto* which, since the former eclogue, is recognized as *estrema bellezza*. And, just as the *scotoma* of intersecting perceptions is the fulcrum on which retinal reception depends, so is this blinded word, the *"io,"* pronoun subject with blinders on, the hinge upon which hangs both the beauty and its conveyance. Perhaps the *scotoma* may be read as a trope of Homeric blindness. The gift of poetry is that trope of insight, that blind spot paradoxically miming poetic vision, that distraction of perception which, in spite of everything, *eppure*, allows words to convey the unutterable—even *"io."*

And, though trapped in the defensive security of inherited signification, the stratified *humus* that renders every sign a quotation as it recognizes value in every sign, the *"io"* is still elemental, germinal, a promise, a risk:

	Primo elemento di una
115	proposizione, morula
	imprecisa, persa ancora
	in bui uteri, promessa.
	Primo elemento, stacco
	d'invischiato volo, soffio
120	sugli occhi—anche dei bimbi—rischio
	di chi fu piaga e piaga
	è ancora, ma piú
	scopre nel suo tremare
	l'ostinazione, la brace,
125	l'ala di mosca superstite; e guarda,
	tondo, torpido scrigno di sguardi,[57]

THE SEEING "io" AND THE BEAUTY OF POETIC VISION

115   [First element of a
proposition, imprecise
morula, still lost
in dark uteri, a promise.
First element, start
of an ensnared flight, breath
120   on the eyes—even of the children—risk
of he who was a wound and wound
is still, but who discovers
in his trembling more
the persistence, the embers,
125   the wing of the fly that survived; and gazes,
a round, torpid cask of glances,]

The subject's quotational troping is a first element, a venturing, a breath on the eyes even of children in an image that gives essence to perception and stretches the *rursus* of former tautology into a new trajectory of intent, wounded, distracted by pain. This risky intent, bolstered by the blind spot, is one, finally, of perception. The *io* who says "*io*" *nell'immenso scotoma* intends "*io*" as the venturing of one who discovers in his own trembling the minute endurance of an *ala di mosca superstite* and keeps on looking, *e guarda*, even if his gaze is an orbicular cumulation of other gazes, a *scringno di sguardi*, even if his signs are an inheritance without origin, even if his knowledge of *questa* as *menzogna* is past and

anche se ancora non sa
né amore né insegnamento.[58]

[even if he still knows
neither love nor teaching.]

A skeletal eclogue stands as afterword to the nine. In a hesitancy of conclusion, "Epilogo: *Appunti per un'Ecloga*" appears as the penultimate text of Zanzotto's fourth book. As *appunti*, these verses project a future text which will be essentially unlike those that precede. In this epilogue, in fact, we see that poetry's identity has multiplied, as *c*, *d*, and *e* join *b* as respondents to *a*'s discourse. The new, diverse, lettered personifications of poetry have no literal lines to speak, however. Their presence in this one-sided conversation is indicated in stage direction parentheses and italicized signals of some of the signifying systems *a* now recognizes as valid.

THE SEEING "io" AND THE BEAUTY OF POETIC VISION

If the heritage of this modern day (small case) poet, the gift given to him that he may give it in turn, is the realization that *vale ogni segno*, as *b* told him in the ninth eclogue, then future poetry will be written in any system that signs, *segna*. In this network of expanded value might be found the response to the cry, *insegnami*, for if the universe of signs can somehow indicate that which is beyond sign, *dietro*, it will also indicate even the subject resistant to sign, the subject who has now taken the threat of reductive linguistic determination in hand, in his left hand, in quotes, in tropes.

The conversation begins with *b*:

>   Persone: *a, b, c, d, e*
>
>   *b*—(*materia, macchie, pseudo-braille*)[59]
>
>
>
>   [Characters: *a, b, c, d, e*
>
>   *b*—(*matter, spots, pseudo-braille*)]

The elements of *b*'s discourse in the eclogue of the future are nonphonetic, aleatoric, avowedly fake, especially the dot figurations that give literacy to the blind. Poetry (language) will have an implicitly tactile parameter; it will not be constrained to its traditional letter but will expand to include unlettered signs. We may find in this indication a forecast (paradoxical, perhaps, considering the implications of *pseudo-braille*) of the cartoons that later come to populate Zanzotto's texts. In any case, this parenthetical indication signals that which is not yet written but which is already at work in the text, the germinal hints of a new rapport of subjectivity and language.

The following line marks the beginning of *a*'s nonparenthetical discourse, a monologue, interrupted by other parentheses of future poetry, that may be read as a kind of minimally narrative recapitulation of how *a* came to find himself in the company of these interruptive, still silent interlocutors:

>   *a*—L'anancasma che si chiama vita:
>   macchie, macchine, muscoli, ceneri,
>   spasmi, fu il corso di quella partita
> 5   in cui perdesti te stesso e il tuo stesso perderti[60]
>
>
>
>   [*a*—The anancasm we call life:
>   spots, machines, muscles, ashes,

THE SEEING "io" AND THE BEAUTY OF POETIC VISION

<blockquote>

5
spasms, that was how the game went
where you lost yourself and your self-loss itself]

</blockquote>

The *vita* appositively designated as *menzogna* in the last eclogue is here recognized as the nominal indication of a repetitive gesture, an involuntary, obsessive tick, *anancasma*. This image of corporeal *rursus* goes beyond physiology to include, in addition to the flesh of *muscoli*, the spots we might associate with writing, *macchie* (and whose aleatoric implications might also bespeak something of the arbitrariness of the sign in general), the mechanical devices of modernity, *macchine* (a literal outgrowth, we might note, of the *macchie* that precedes), the substance that remains when form disappears, *ceneri*, and the involuntary insistent *spasmi* which metaphorically somatize the interruptions elsewhere represented literally by parentheses: life as an involuntary obsession, as the sum of one interruption after another, *anancasma*.

But *a* goes on to define this vital obsession also as the path taken by *b*, the lot that poetry (language) chose for itself, *il corso* being perhaps a reminder of the path over and into beauty's void in the eighth eclogue. It is a *corso* upon which poetry (language) got lost, says *a*, but upon which it also lost the sense of loss itself, *il tuo stesso perderti*. Lost in the obsessive, interruptive course of life, poetry (language) loses even the notion of being lost.

The next line belongs to a new interlocutor, one we have imagined to be another manifestation of poetry (language), an alphabetical spinoff, so to speak, of *b*:

<blockquote>

c—(codici vari per tutti i suoni)[61]

◻

[c—(various codes for all sounds)]

</blockquote>

Future utterances of this third persona are indicated as codes of sonorities; here, phonetic as well as musical notation is implied, networks of signs which will never themselves be sounds but which will indicate the absence of the sounds they stand for and thus present them for reading, reproduction, reception.

Like all the other lettered personae but *a*, *c* has only one parenthetical line, and *a* resumes his (interrupted) monologue with a continuing definition of the *corso* of poetry (language) which is also the *anancasma* of life:

<blockquote>

a—Non tesi, terra, energia, spirito
nemmeno, non carme civile o intimo.

</blockquote>

>   In chiave di fuoco o di tenebre.
> 10 Ma retina o reticolo,
>   ma poi trama ed omento: convenzione
>   prima in cui tutto si rifa ragione.⁶²

☐

> [a—Not thesis, earth, energy, spirit
>   even, not civil poem or intimate one.
>   In the key of fire or shadows.
> 10 But retina or network,
>   but then plot and omentum: first
>   convention in which everything becomes reason again.]

The negative passes to the positive as the images of poetry (language) pass from those of rhetorical intent, external materiality, spirituality, and traditional forms readable, perhaps, as light's origin or shadowy indications of origin elsewhere to those of vision and viscerality. The surface that perceives, *retina*, is placed in dyadic interchangeability with the cellular network of the soma, *reticolo*. The assonant, alliterative dyad of sight and cellular web subsequently reveals itself (*ma poi*) as weft or plot (*trama*) on the one hand, and as visceral connective (*omento*) on the other. This anatomy of perception and being is defined by *a* over the drama of a colon as the primary convention whereby *tutto* becomes *ragione*.

Indications of rhythmic technicalities, the traditional heartbeats of poetic heritage, appear next with persona *d*:

> d—(*Catena di dattili, spondei etc.*)⁶³

☐

> [d—(*Chain of dactyls, spondees, etc.*)]

The recognition of the value of all signs does not exclude the signs that were already valued prior to that recognition. If anything, one might find in *d*'s indications a heightened sensitivity to the significance of that which, though made manifest through the letter, remains nonliteral, the privileging rhythms that have historically signalled their *situs* as that of poetry.

a continues with a vocative of indefinable entities of stellar victory, an incitement, an induction of *tu*, poetry (language), to a space beyond silence and starlight: an ecstatic, space-age metaphysics of language:

>   *a*—O quale e quanto in quella viva stella
> 15   pur vinse, quale e quanto si sospinse
>   oltre le soglie della sua stessa luce;
>   al di là del silenzio quale e quanto t'induce!⁶⁴

◻

>   [*a*—Oh, such a one and so much a one won anyway
> 15   in that live star, such and so much a one propelled
>   himself
>   past thresholds of his own light;
>   beyond silence such a one and so much a one leads you!]

The conventionality (or *menzogna*) of poetry (language) has been recognized and accepted by this apprentice, who already knows how to handle "*io*." Here, he addresses the *quale e quanto* of that which somehow guides this convention beyond itself. The lack of definition provided literally in the linguistic convention of these pronouns tropes what cannot be defined.

The final interruption occurs at this point:

>   *e*—(*simboli matematici etc.*)⁶⁵

◻

>   [*e*—(*mathematical symbols, etc.*)]

Even the mysteries of signs which signify without passing through Babelian-determined phonemes are shown here to be part of poetry's language. Where *vale ogni segno*, those signs which recognize no borders are of an importance at least equal to the importance of those indicated by *b*, *c*, and *d*; they will appear in later books, from *Pasque* on.

a's last lines begin with a gerundive integration of his own position on the edge of the impossible:

>   *a*—Integrando, sul limite, sospinti
> 20   solo minimamente sopra il suolo
>   dell'impossibile, impossibilmente
>   qui, e pure qui a dire l'impossibile
>   e il possibile. E reversibilmente
>   . . . .
> 25   Avverbio in "mente," lattea sicurezza⁶⁶

◻

THE SEEING "io" AND THE BEAUTY OF POETIC VISION

> [*a*—Integrating, at the edge, propelled
> 20   only minimally above the floor
>   of the impossible, impossibly
>   here, and yet here to say the impossible
>   and the possible. And reversibly
>   . . . .
> 25   Adverb in "ly" (as in "mentally"); milky security]

He describes not his liminal position alone, but also that of the other, *b* (poetry, language), or the others (*c, d, e,* now also poetry, language), in the pluralization of *sospinti*. In this syntax, verbal temporality demurs to the gerund, the participle and the infinitive in a timeless moment of Janus-door passage—*sul limite, minimamente sopra il suolo,* endings that are also beginnings. Over and over again, *a* insists on the *impossibile,* even as it literally contains the *possibile,* and on presence *qui, e pure qui. Eppure,* once again, signalling a presence or perhaps a presentation, a rendering present, a re-presentation of the impossible and the possible in *dire.*

And, as the *impossibile* becomes an adverb in verse 21, it, itself, loses nominal passivity on a suffix-threshold of the verbal, the active. This verbalization is the presencing of the *impossible, impossibilimente / qui.*

The third adverb implicates *l'impossibile / e il possibile reversibilmente* within each other. It may also indicate a reversibility of the intentionality of *e pure qui a dire* where the *dire* might imply the presence, *qui.* But the syntax begun by the addition of this adverb, *E reversibilmente,* is missing, unwritten, though not unindicated, as the eloquence of the dotted line, minimal satellites as testimony of something not *qui,* a *pseudo-braille* of illegibility, writes itself between *reversibilmente* and *Avverbio in "mente."*

More than any other single line, perhaps, *a*'s final *versus* in the book of eclogues, the last verse in this text where the future begins, may reveal the part—the role—of speech in the story we have been tracing. The role of language, its unrolling within and around the subject, is perhaps condensed in the grammatical term, *Avverbio in "mente."* The *mente* may be read as the mind, the flow of consciousness and the unconscious that gives site to the *qui* in which poetry effects the reversibility of the impossible and the possible. And the *mente* may be read as suffix, as the sign of a distraction from the nominal or descriptive, presumptions of logos authenticity, to the verbal, signal of process. A sign dependent for meaning on its own deictic effect on another sign, this *mente* suffix incorporates a metaphor, a troping of the nominal or adjectival by the marginally verbal, a rendering modal of that which otherwise names or describes. It implies connection and similarity across the internal constructs of language. It is, perhaps, like a quotation, the troping of language by itself. For our apprentice poet, it is apposite to an innocent, infantile security whose milkiness speaks partially of whole galaxies, *lattea sicurezza*: the intellect of poetry as a troping of both the most intimate and the universal. *Minimamente, impossibilmente, reversibilmente,* "*mente*," "*io*": sidera feriam vertice.

There is an irony in beginnings and endings. We now end where we initially said it would be easier to begin: in the middle. And even this midpoint does not hold, for *IX Ecloghe* is but the fourth of the twelve books of Zanzotto's poetry which have so far been published.[67] But our early eagerness to begin in the middle now reveals itself as an avidity for those texts of Zanzotto that are most well-known, from *La beltà* on, a greedy impatience to tread in realms where certain recognitions—and equally certain debates—could be counted on. Our own text now ends with all the uncertainties of beginnings. These are what we have traced. What we would call the linguistic apprenticeship in *Dietro il paesaggio, Elegia e altri versi, Vocativo,* and *IX Ecloghe* seems to draw to a close with the tropic recognitions of the last eclogues, on the threshold of a *beltà* still to come.

Suddenly, it is as difficult to stop writing as it was earlier to begin. One has the feeling of leaving a dear place and a dear friend: the poems themselves and all the projections they allow in their story of *a*, of "*io*," of the Apollo-struck guy in the car. But, just as we found a *sostegno* for our own beginnings in Zanzotto's words themselves, so do we now lean for support on such words for an ending. And, since the "Epilogo" is not the final text of the *IX Ecloghe*, there still remains one for us to quote. The value of *ogni segno* extends the notion of *segno* to that of *langue* itself as Zanzotto passes from the Italian of the poetry contest to an azure of French in "Bleu." Here already is the *azzurro*, shining in the beauty of Gallic alterity, which will be one of the emblems of *La beltà*. Here, too, is the *razzo* of the lyric poets' lament, now a *fusée* to pierce transparencies. And one might imagine the landscape of this linguistic crossing to be already the Hölderlinian peaks, the *saldamente costrutte Alpi,* of that same *beltà*.[68] And as the notes of "Nel blu dipinto di blu" fade away on a radio somewhere, we depart in an ether of value and valediction.

> Bleui ébloui
> je m'éveille et je ris

de cet orage sans rancune
qui voile d'ailes terre et lune.

5   Et j'entends le choeur
des abeilles surprises
des grillons des fleurs
qui de pluie s'irisent,

    et sur le toit, fusée
10   qui tout espace transperce,
le drapeau de l'été
miroite aux averses.[69]

◻

[Blued dazzled
I wake up and laugh
at this rancorless storm
that veils earth and moon with its wings.

5   And I hear the choir
of surprised bees
of crickets of flowers
grown iridescent in the rain,

    and on the roof, a rocket
10   that pierces all of space,
the summer flag
shimmers in the cloudbursts.]

Notes

INTRODUCTION

1. Paolo Valesio, "The Beautiful Lie: Heroic Individuality and Fascism," in *Reconstructing Individualism: Autonomy, Individuality, and the Self in Western Thought*, ed. T. Heller, M. Sosna, and D. Wellbery (Stanford: Stanford University Press, 1986), 166.
2. Giacomo Leopardi, *Zibaldone di pensieri* (Milan: Mondadori, 1973). Entries for discussions of *parola* appear in the *indice analitico*, 1567; for discussions of *termine*, 1606.
3. *La beltà* (Milan: Mondadori, 1968), 15–16.
4. Ibid., 104–105.
5. *Gli sguardi i fatti e senhal* (Pieve di Soligo: Tipografia Bernardi, 1969), 2.
6. *A che valse?* (Milan: Scheiwiller, Strenna per gli amici, 1970), 18.
7. Ibid., 23.
8. Jacques Lacan, "The Subversion of the Subject and the Dialectic of Desire in the Freudian Unconsciousness," in *Écrits: A Selection*, trans. Alan Sheridan (New York: Norton, 1977), 292–324.
9. *Pasque* (Milan: Mondadori, 1973), 62.
10. *Dietro il paesaggio* (Milan: Mondadori, 1951), 36.
11. *Il galateo in bosco* (Milan: Mondadori, 1978), 111.
12. Walter Benjamin, "The Task of the Translator: An Introduction to the Translation of Baudelaire's *Tableaux parisiens*," in *Illuminations* (New York: Harcourt, Brace and World, 1955), 71.
13. *Il galateo in bosco*, 74.
14. *Fosfeni* (Milan: Mondadori, 1983), 63–64.
15. *Idioma* (Milan: Mondadori, 1986), 22.
16. Ibid., 108–109.

ONE: A FIRST ROUND KNOCKOUT

1. Andrea Zanzotto, "Arse il motore," in *Dietro il paesaggio* (Milan: Mondadori, 1951), 11.
2. In a conversation held in Pieve di Soligo during the summer of 1987, Zanzotto recounted to me that he imagined this vehicle as a bus. His recollection of the images he had in mind when he initially wrote "Arse il

motore" in 1941 or so led to the following narration, which I reproduce approximately:

It is mid-spring, when sudden snows can come, when the snow stays on the ground for a few days and then disappears. It's a notion of going towards the night and of losing, therefore, a sense of the landscape. As to *ruote e carri*, these are the wheels and carts you catch glimpses of in courtyards or at the railroad station. The *abbandono del mondo* is an expressionistic deformation of the coming of evening, while the *clessidre* and so forth are in homage to a certain kind of cubism, to Picasso, to surrealism. The *viaggai solo* refers to one of the passengers on the bus who experiences a progressive feeling of being abandoned by other people.

3. Francesco De Sanctis, *Storia della letteratura italiana* (Milan: Feltrinelli, 1967), 760ff.
4. Friedrich Hölderlin, *Oeuvres* (Paris: Pleiade, 1967), Letter #240, "A Casimir Ulrich Böhlendorff," 1009.
5. *Dietro il paesaggio*, 55.
6. This is as apt a moment as any to mention the excellent translations of Zanzotto's work done by Ruth Feldman and Brian Swann. This pair of translators, whose work has been consistently of the greatest importance by making available in English the work of contemporary poets in the Romance languages, has provided the largest selection of Zanzotto's poetry available in English to date in their volume, *Selected Poetry of Andrea Zanzotto* (Princeton: Princeton University Press, 1975). Another translator of Zanzotto is Lawrence R. Smith, whose *The New Italian Poetry: 1945 to the Present* (Berkeley, Los Angeles, London: University of California Press, 1981) contains seven of Zanzotto's poems. These anthology selections end with *Pasque*. Translations of some more recent poems are available in the 1980 volume of the series *Altro Polo: A Volume of Italian Studies*, entitled *Italian Poetry Today: A Critical Anthology*, edited by Raffaele Perrotta (Sydney: The Frederick May Foundation for Italian Studies, University of Sydney, 1980) and in *Circhi e Cene / Circuses and Suppers* (Verona: Plain Wrapper Press, 1978), where the translations are my own.
7. Giuseppe Ungaretti, "Piccolo discorso sopra *Dietro il paesaggio* di Andrea Zanzotto" [1954], in *Vita d'un uomo: saggi e interventi*, ed. Mario Diacono and Luciano Rebay (Milan: Mondadori, 1974), 694–695.
8. Amedeo Giacomini, "Da *Dietro il paesaggio* alle *IX Ecloghe*: l'io grammaticale nella poesia di Andrea Zanzotto," in *Studi novecenteschi* 4, nos. 8/9 (July-November 1974):187 n. 1.
9. Our brief discussion of Zanzotto's reading of Ungaretti and Montale should take note of a symmetry of reciprocity. It is not only Ungaretti who reads Zanzotto, but Montale, as well, though his publication about the Pievan poet concentrates on a later book, *La beltà*, and thus is not germane to our present study. See Montale's "La poesia di Zanzotto," in *Corriere della sera*, 1 June 1968. We would further note, moreover, that, while the influence of the "hermetics," especially Ungaretti and Montale, on Zanzotto may be discerned more or less easily in Zanzotto's early stylistics, the Pievan poet's thematics of subjectivity differ markedly from those of the hermetics. Instead, Zanzotto seems to pick up an historical thread left dangling after Pascoli. For an elaboration of this "genealogy,"

see my "Occasioni di metafora: Il soggetto della decapitazione: Carducci, Pascoli e Zanzotto sulla linea," *Hellas*. nos. 8/9 (December 1985).

10. As noted by Giorgio Bàrberi-Squarotti in "Zanzotto o gli schemi dell'astrazione," in *Poesia e narrativa del secondo Novecento*, 4th ed. (Milan: Mursia, 1978), 170.
11. See my "Interview with Andrea Zanzotto (Pieve di Soligo: July 25, 1978)," in *Stanford Italian Review* 4, no. 2 (Fall 1984):253–265.
12. This is the topic of "La morte meditata: A Key to Ungaretti's Metaphysics," a paper submitted by this writer in partial fulfillment of the requirements for the Master of Arts degree in Italian, Department of Italian, Columbia University, New York City, 1972.
13. These ideas were discussed in the July 1978 interview, cited above (#11). Also see "Petrarca e i poeti d'oggi," from the radio program, "Piccolo Pianeta Letterario," RAI, May 10, 1974 (with Maria Corti, Vittorio Sereni, Antonio Porta, and Zanzotto), and published in *L'Approdo letterario* 66 (June 1974). See also "Petrarca fra il palazzo e la cameretta," preface to Francesco Petrarca, *Rime*, ed. Guido Bezzola (Milan: Rizzoli, 1976), 5–16.
14. Ibid., preface to Petrarca, *Rime*.
15. Ibid.
16. Zanzotto, "Primavera di Santa Augusta," in *Dietro il paesaggio*, 13–14.
17. Zanzotto, "Elegia pasquale," in *Dietro il paesaggio*, 22–23.
18. Zanzotto, "La Pasqua a Pieve di Soligo," in *Pasque*, 57–65 and n., 96.
19. Émile Benveniste, "Le langage et l'expérience humaine," in *Problèmes de linguistique générale*, Vol. I (Paris: Gallimard, 1966), especially 74ff.
20. The vanity of the personified landscape or that of a landscape-oriented time of day appears in other poems of *Dietro il paesaggio* and is often associated with mirrorings, as in "Indizi e luna," where we read, "La verde sera al suo specchio s'adorna").
21. Marziano Guglielminetti, "La ricostruzione della sintassi poetica," in *Studi novecenteschi*, 4, nos. 8/9 (July-November 1974):167–173. Guglielminetti highlights Zanzotto's recourse to rhetoric in all the books up until *La beltà* not only to demonstrate part of Zanzotto's stylistic self-differentiation from hermetic practice but also to establish the early 1940s texts collected and published as *A che valse?* in 1971—texts which contain many of the rhetorical devices we have noted in *Dietro il paesaggio*—as the appropriate beginning of Zanzotto's opus. Given the dates of the *A che valse?* poems, it is difficult to dispute this chronological coincidence or perhaps even precedence. Our choice here, however, is to treat as "beginnings" the chosen point of public departure, the first published book, which excludes the texts known twenty years later as *A che valse?* (but not because they did not yet exist). We do so for reasons of exposition that should become clear in the course of our discussion.
22. Guglielminetti, "La ricostruzione," 170.
23. Friedrich Hölderlin, "Die Heimath" [Home]. See Friedrich Hölderlin, *Poems and Fragments,* trans. Michael Hamburger (London: Routledge and Kegan Paul, 1966), 143.
24. Zanzotto, "Nel mio paese," vv. 12–18, in *Dietro il paesaggio*, 57.

25. Ibid. vv. 1–4.
26. Zanzotto, "Al di là," vv. 1–8, in *Dietro il paesaggio*, 59.
27. Ibid., vv. 19–24.
28. Zanzotto, "Là cercando," vv. 1–16, in *Dietro il paesaggio*, 60.
29. Zanzotto, "L'Acqua di dolle," in *Dietro il paesaggio*, 62.
30. Zanzotto, "Quanta notte," vv. 30–32, in *Dietro il paesaggio*, 43.
31. Nicolas J. Perella, *Midday in Italian Literature: Variations on an Archetypal Theme* (Princeton: Princeton University Press, 1979), 273 n. 20.
32. Zanzotto, "Atollo," in *Dietro il paesaggio*, 34–35.
33. The *occhialuto uomo* [eyeglassed man] is a figure of the modern, alienated man familiar to readers of Aldo Palazzeschi's *Perelà, uomo di fumo* (Florence: Vallecchi, 1954), where he serves as a moniker for the novel's protagonist.
34. Zanzotto, "Con dolce curiosità," in *Dietro il paesaggio*, 65–66.
35. Zanzotto, "Declivio su Lorna," in *Dietro il paesaggio*, 67–68.
36. Zanzotto, "Lorna," in *Dietro il paesaggio*, 69–71.

TWO: AFTER THE FALL

1. Zanzotto, "L'amore infermo del giorno," in *Dietro il paesaggio*, 75–76.
2. Especially evocative of Fellini-esque imagery for this reader is "Là sul ponte" (in *Dietro il paesaggio*, 77):

>   Là sul ponte di san Fedele
>   dove la sera abbonda
>   di freddo fieno
>   e dove la pioggia raccoglie
> 5   tutte le sue vele madide
>   c'è da ieri una fanciulla bionda
>   che ha un nome come una corona
>   e che ha perduto per sempre
>   una mano per salutare una rosa.
>
> 10 Sulle rive oscure del fieno
>   c'è una nave di pioggia
>   abbandonata dalla notte
>
>   Dalle stretture delle sorgenti
>   là si libera talvolta
> 15 la dalia abbigliata di rosso
>   e illumina la crisalide
>   intricata del sole.
>
>   Là un animale azzurro
>   deperisce nella sua tana
> 20 e l'estate legata dalla neve
>   non conosce altro frutto che se stessa.

	[There on the bridge of San Fedele
	where the evening abounds
	with cold hay
	and where the rain gathers
5	all its damp veils
	a blond girl has been since yesterday
	who has a name like a crown
	and has lost one of her hands forever
	for having greeted a rose.
10	On the dark banks of the hay
	there is a ship of rain
	abandoned by the night
	From the narrows of the fountains
	there now and then the red-adorned
15	dahlia frees itself
	and illuminates the sun's
	intricate chrysalis.
	There an azure animal
	pines away in its den
20	and the snow-bound summer
	knows no fruit other than itself.]

3. Zanzotto, "Salva," in *Dietro il paesaggio*, 79.
4. Zanzotto, "La fredda tromba," in *Dietro il paesaggio*, 81.
5. Zanzotto, "In basso," vv. 5–7, in *Dietro il paesaggio*, 82.
6. Zanzotto, "Perché siamo," vv. 28–47, in *Dietro il paesaggio*, 85.
7. Luigi Milone, "Per una storia del linguaggio poetico di Andrea Zanzotto," *Studi novecenteschi* 4, nos. 8/9 (July-Nov. 1974): 209ff.
8. Ibid.
9. Zanzotto, "Dietro il paesaggio," vv. 20–24, in *Dietro il paesaggio*, 89.
10. Milone, "Per una storia," 209–210.
11. Zanzotto, "Dietro il paesaggio."
12. The books are Lorenzo Bianchi's *Versioni da Friedrich Hölderlin* (Bologna: Zanichelli, 1925) and Vincenzo Errante's *La lirica di Hoelderlin*, I, *Saggio biografico critico: riduzione in versi italiani* and II, *Commento* (Florence: Sansoni, 1943).
13. Friedrich Hölderlin, "Patmos, Fragments of the Later Version," in *Poems and Fragments*, 479.
14. Hölderlin, "The Poet's Vocation," stanzas 5–7 in *Poems and Fragments*, 173–175.
15. Hölderlin "Rousseau," vv. 30–32, in *Poems and Fragments*, 130.
16. Interview, July 25, 1978.
17. Zanzotto, "Nella valle," in *Dietro il paesaggio*, 90–91.
18. Carlo Marcona, *Storia dei Papi*, I (Milan: Edizioni Librerie Italiane, 1961):132.
19. Thanks to Professor Nicolas J. Perella for noting the contribution of magianism in general to the semantics of the text at this point.

20. Jacques Lacan, "La chose freudienne," in *Écrits I* (Paris: Seuil, 1966), 242.
21. See Lacan, "The mirror stage as formative of the function of the I as revealed in psychoanalytic experience," in *Écrits: A Selection*, 1–7.
22. Sigmund Freud, "Das Unheimliche," in *Imago*, 5 (1919). Now as "The Uncanny" in Freud, *On Creativity and the Unconscious*, ed. Benjamin Nelson. (New York: Harper and Row, 1958), 122–161.
23. Ibid., 144.
24. Lacan, "Le séminaire sur *La lettre volée*," in *Écrits I*, 19–75.

THREE: GATHERINGS OF POETRY AND MUSHROOMS

1. See, for example, the articles on Zanzotto in *Studi novecenteschi* 4, nos. 8/9 (July-November 1974); Giorgio Bàrberi-Squarotti, *Poesia e narrativa del secondo novecento*, 170–177, and Stefano Agosti, Introduction to *Andrea Zanzotto Poesie* (Milan: Mondadori, 1973), 9–27, as well as the critical anthology included in the same book, 28–32.
2. Personal communication. Interview of July 1978 conducted in Pieve di Soligo and published in the *Stanford Italian Review*, 4, no. 2 (Fall 1984):253–265.
3. Stefano Agosti, ed., *Andrea Zanzotto Poesie*.
4. Amedeo Giacomini, "Da *Dietro il paesaggio* alle *IX Ecloghe*," and Luigi Milone, "Per una storia."
5. Personal communication, August 1976, in Pieve di Soligo. What follows is a reconstruction based on my recollection of one of my conversations with Zanzotto.
6. Personal communication, July 1978. *Il galateo in bosco* appeared in 1978, *Fosfeni*, 1983, and *Idioma*, in 1986.
7. For a more detailed discussion of the innovative aspects of the turning points of thought in Petrarch's sonnets, see "The Petrarchan Sonnet: The Turn of the Thought," submitted by this writer in partial fulfillment of the requirements for the Master of Arts degree in Italian, Department of Italian, Columbia University, New York, 1972.
8. Zanzotto, *Elegia e altri versi* (Milan: Edizioni della Meridiana, 1954), 24.
9. Ibid., 11.
10. Ibid., 13, v. 14.
11. Ibid., 14.
12. Ibid., 15.
13. These are the initial lines of sections III, IV, and V, respectively, of "Ore calanti," in *Elegia e altri versi*, 17–19.
14. "Martire, Primavera," in Zanzotto, *Elegia e altri versi*, 22–23.
15. "Elegia," in Zanzotto, *Elegia e altri versi*, 27.
16. Ibid.
17. Ibid.
18. Ibid., 28.
19. Ibid., 28–29.

20. Ibid., 29–30.
21. See our discussion of "Elegia pasquale," chap. I.
22. Milone, "Per una storia," 209.
23. Interview of July 1978. See note #2 above.

FOUR: ZANZOTTO'S *GRAMMATICALISMO*: Positions and Performance

1. Michel David, *La psicoanalisi nella cultura italiana* (Milan: Mursia, 1967), 585.
2. Stefano Agosti, *Andrea Zanzotto Poesie*, 13. As regards the "pre-Lacanianism" associated by David with *Vocativo*, Zanzotto himself has said in *L'effetto Lacan* [the Lacan effect] (Rome: Lerici, 1979):

> Forse è vero, come ha detto Michel David, che in me si era sviluppato un certo inconsapevole lacanismo. *Vocativo* è un titolo senza dubbio riconducibile a qualcosa di lacaniano; forse lo è meno l'insieme del libro (1948–1956).

◻

> [Perhaps it is true, as Michel David has said, that a kind of unaware Lacanism had developed in me. *Vocative* is doubtlessly a title that can remind us of something Lacanian; perhaps this is less the case of the book in its entirety (1948–1956).]

If an author's reaction to criticism be suspect, we need not remain with Zanzotto's response. Zanzotto, in fact, continues with a description not only of his own suspicions at the time of *Vocativo* but also of his difficulties in dealing with those suspicions—difficulties which, we may note both from their nature and from the syntax and rhetoric he uses to describe them in the same 1979 text, are perhaps his constant companions *al lungo andare*.

> Il trasformarsi di ogni discorso, anzi di "tutto" in mero significante, anzi in lettera; il sospetto che l'io fosse una produzione grammaticalizzata dell'immaginario, un punto di fuga e non di realtà . . . Ma si poteva veramente affermare, dire, enunciare tutto questo? Non ne sarebbe rimasta la bocca irreparabilmente muta? Non ne sarebbero andati in corto circuito i relais cerebrali? Da nessun luogo mi giungevano allora effetti di verità che non fossero distruttivi, mentre in me si accumulavano, come per dare all'io una specie di superconsistenza ferrea, strati sempre più maledetti di angoscia.

◻

> [The transformation of every discourse, even of "everything" into a mere signifier, or rather a letter; the suspicion that the I was a grammaticalized production of the imaginary, a point of escape and not of reality . . . But could all this really be affirmed, said, enunciated? Wouldn't one's cerebral *relais* be short-circuited? At that time, no ef-

fects of truth reached me—from anywhere—that weren't destructive, while within me were accumulating, as if to give my I a kind of iron superconsistency, ever more damnable layers of anguish.]

3. Agosti, *Andrea Zanzotto Poesie*, 13–14.
4. Ibid., 15–16.
5. Luigi Milone, "Per una storia," 214–215.
6. Zanzotto, "Epifania," in *Vocativo* (Milan: Mondadori, 1957), 11. (Later in a second, amplified, 1981 edition, 13, where v. 8 reads, *echi, gemme, correnti,* but otherwise no changes occur.)
7. Zanzotto, *Vocativo*, 7.
8. Zanzotto, "Piccola elegia," in *Vocativo*, 13.
9. Ibid.
10. Ibid.
11. Ibid.
12. Ibid.
13. Zanzotto, "Altrui e mia I," in *Vocativo*, 17.
14. Ibid.
15. Ibid., 17–18.
16. Giuseppe Ungaretti, *Vita d'un uomo: tutte le poesie* (Milan: Mondadori, 1970), 181.
17. Ibid.
18. Zanzotto, "Altrui e mia I," 18.
19. Ibid.
20. Ibid.
21. Zanzotto, "Altrui e mia II," in *Vocativo*, 19.
22. Zanzotto, "Elegia del venerdí I," in *Vocativo*, 21–22.
23. Zanzotto, "Elegia del venerdí II," in *Vocativo*, 23.
24. Zanzotto, "Esperimento I," in *Vocativo*, 25–26.
25. Zanzotto, "Esperimento II," in *Vocativo*, 27.
26. Ibid.
27. Ibid.
28. Ibid.
29. Zanzotto, "Prima persona," in *Vocativo*, 51.
30. Ibid.
31. Ibid., 51–52.
32. Ibid., 52.
33. Zanzotto, "Esistere psichicamente," in *Vocativo*, 66.
34. Émile Benveniste, *Problèmes de linguistique générale* I (Paris: Gallimard, 1966), 258–266.
35. Ibid., 259.
36. Ibid., 259.
37. Ibid., 259–260.
38. Zanzotto, "Impossibilità della parola," in *Vocativo*, 67–69.

39. Zanzotto, "Caso vocativo I," in *Vocativo*, 28.
40. Zanzotto, "Caso vocativo II," in *Vocativo*, 29.
41. Ibid., 29–30.
42. See Austin, J. L., *How To Do Things With Words* (Cambridge: Harvard University Press, 1962), 99. Our discussion here follows, to some extent, the explanation given by C. Kerbrat-Orecchioni, in "Note sur les concepts d' 'illocutoire' et de 'performatif'," in *Linguistique et Sémiologie: L'Illocutoire* (Lyon: Imprimerie de l'Université Lyon II), 74ff.
43. Ibid.
44. Here we are following somewhat the discussion of speech acts in Oswald Ducrot and Tzvetan Todorov, *Encyclopedic Dictionary of the Sciences of Language* trans. Catherine Porter (Baltimore: Johns Hopkins University Press, 1979), 343.
45. Ibid., 342.
46. See Benveniste, "De la subjectivité dans le langage," in *Journal de psychologie* 55(1958):257–265; later reprinted as Chapter 21 of his *Problèmes de linguistique générale* I.
47. Ibid., chapters 22 and 23.
48. Ducrot and Todorov, *Encyclopedic Dictionary*, 344.
49. For this and what follows, see Austin, *How To Do Things With Words*, 99ff., and especially 147.
50. Ducrot and Todorov, *Encyclopedic Dictionary*, 344, paraphrasing John Searle in *Speech Acts: An Essay in the Philosophy of Language* (London: Cambridge University Press, 1969).
51. See, for example, Orecchioni, "Note sur les concepts d' 'Illocutoire' et de 'Performatif'," 77.
52. I owe much of what follows to conversations with Dr. Joëlle Bensmaia, Professor of Philosophy, Centre Nationale des Récherches Scientifiques, Paris.
53. Zanzotto, "Colle di Giano II" [Janus Hill, II], in *Vocativo*, 72, vv. 25–26.
54. Zanzotto, "Esperimento II," in *Vocativo*, 27, v. 13.
55. Zanzotto, "Caso vocativo II," in *Vocativo*, 29, v. 11.
56. John Searle, *Speech Acts*, 57.
57. *O miei mozzi trastulli / pensieri in cui mi credo e vedo, / ingordo vocativo / decerebrato anelito*. In "Caso vocativo I," vv. 1–4.
58. Zanzotto, *Vocativo*, 85.
59. Zanzotto, "Campèa I," in *Vocativo*, 63.
60. Ibid.
61. Ibid.
62. Ibid., 63–64.
63. Ibid., 64.
64. Zanzotto, "Campèa II," in *Vocativo*, 65.
65. Ibid.
66. Ibid.
67. Zanzotto, "Colle di Giano I," in *Vocativo*, 70.

68. Ibid.
69. Zanzotto, "Colle di Giano II," in *Vocativo*, 71.
70. Ibid., 71–72.
71. Zanzotto, "Colle di Giano III," in *Vocativo*, 73.
72. Ibid.
73. Zanzotto, "Dal cielo," in *Vocativo*, 75.
74. Ibid., 75–76.
75. Ibid., 76–77.
76. Ibid., 77.
77. Zanzotto, "Bucolica," in *Vocativo*, 78.
78. Ibid.
79. Ibid.
80. Zanzotto, "Fuisse I," in *Vocativo*, 80–81.
81. Zanzotto, "Fuisse II," in *Vocativo*, 82–83.
82. Zanzotto, *Vocativo* (1981), 87–97. Zanzotto's prefactory remark to the Appendix is as follows:

> Questi frammenti, scelti fra altri perché connessi più nettamente con alcune delle poesie di *Vocativo*, sono inediti e risalgono al periodo 1953–55. L'ultimo componimento, apparso anni dopo sulla rivista "La Situazione" (maggio 1958), è del 1955.

◻

> [These fragments, chosen from among others because they are more clearly connected to several of the *Vocativo* poems, are unpublished and date from the period 1953–55. The final composition, which appeared years later in the magazine *La Situazione* (May 1958), is from 1955].

83. Ibid., 77–79.
84. Zanzotto, "Amo e sono infelice?," in *Vocativo* (1981), 89.
85. Ibid., 89–90.
86. Zanzotto, "Da un eterno esilio," in *Vocativo* (1981), 91.
87. Zanzotto, "Molle clivo, dove traluce a raso," in *Vocativo* (1981), 92.
88. Zanzotto, "Per il mite dicembre ove l'erba," in *Vocativo* (1981), 93.
89. *Vocativo* (1981), 94–95.
90. Ibid.
91. "Per la morte della madre di L.G.," in *Vocativo*, 96.
92. Ibid.
93. Ibid.
94. Ibid.
95. Ibid., 97.
96. Ibid.

FIVE: THE SEEING "io"

1. See Heidegger, Martin, "What Are Poets For?" and "Language," in *Poetry, Language, Thought,* trans. Albert Hofstadter (New York: Harper & Row, 1971).
2. Zanzotto, "Un libro di Ecloghe," in *IX Ecloghe* (Milan: Mondadori, 1962), 7–8.
3. This statement as well as the discourse on Virgil as emblem of a choice of poetry over history which follows were imparted to me by Zanzotto in an interview in Pieve di Soligo on July 25, 1978. See *Stanford Italian Review,* 4 no. 2, (Fall 1984):253–265.
4. Zanzotto, "Ecloga I: *I lamenti dei poeti lirici,*" in *IX Ecloghe,* 9.
5. In his Introduction to *Andrea Zanzotto Poesie,* Stefano Agosti cites verses 10–14 of this poem as an illustration of what he calls a *divaricazione* [straddling] between the "remote, inauthentic body of language" and the "active cells of an originary syllabification that the poet causes to circulate within that body." On p. 113, Agosti says,

> Ma si dà anche un'altra e capitale conseguenza di quell'equiparazione di tutti gli stati del verbo, equiparazione che vede implicati, come si è detto, i punti estremi della divaricazione, configurabili, rispettivamente, nel corpo remoto e inautentico della lingua e nelle cellule attive d'una originaria sillabazione che il poeta fa circolare dentro di esso. La conseguenza è una duplice irradiazione di senso lungo le catene del discorso: quella del "silenzio" che circonda e percorre gli enunciati asseverativi ("semantico silenzio," dice il poeta, cfr. a p. 126), e quella del "mormorio" che promana da una materia inerte e tacita. Ecco, a puro titolo di esempio, i testi di questa divaricazione-imbricazione: scorrimento *in re* del senso entro l'opaco e il non-significante, e del silenzio entro la realtà semanticamente più attiva proprio perché più fonda e irriducibile, p. 113:
>
>> Significati allungano le dita,
>> sensi le antenne filiformi.
>> Sillabe labbra causole
>> unisono con l'ima terra.
>> Perfettissimo pianto, perfettissimo.
>
> È dall'*Ecloga I.*

◻

[But another, capital consequence of that equalizing of all states of the verb turns up, a consequence of that equalizing that considers, as we have said, the extreme points of the straddling capable respectively of figuration in the remote, inauthentic body of language and in the active cells of an originary syllabification that the poet causes to circulate within that body. The consequence is a double radiation of meaning along the chains of the discourse: that of the "silence" which surrounds and goes before the affirmative enunciateds (the poet calls it a "semantic silence," see p. 126), and that of the "murmuring" that precedes from inert, tacit matter. Here, then, as examples, are the texts of this straddling-imbrication: an *in re* flowing of the meaning within the opaque and the nonsignifying, and of the silence within a reality which is semantically more active precisely because it is deeper and irreducible. On p. 113:

> Signifieds lengthen their fingers,
> meanings, their filiform antennas.
> Syllables lips clausulas
> in unison with the vilest earth.
> Most perfect cry, most perfect.]

6. Zanzotto, "Ecloga I," in *IX Ecloghe*, 9.
7. Ibid.
8. Ibid., 9–10.
9. Ibid., 10.
10. Ibid.
11. Ibid., 10–11.
12. Ibid., 11.
13. Ibid.
14. Ibid.
15. Ibid.
16. Agosti, Introduction to *Andrea Zanzotto Poesie*, 19.
17. Here is the text of the poem to which Agosti refers (*IX Ecloghe*, 12–13):

13 SETTEMBRE 1959 (VARIANTE)

Luna puella pallidula,
Luna flora eremitica,
Luna unica selenita,
distonia vita traviata,
5   atonia vita evitata,
mataia, matta morula,
vampirisma, paralisi,
glabro latte, polarizzato zucchero,
peste innocente, patrona inclemente,
10 protovergine, alfa privativo,
degravitante sughero,
pomo e potenza della polvere,
phiala e coscienza delle tenebre,
geyser, fase, cariocinesi,
15 Luna neve nevissima novissima,
Luna glacies-glaciei
Luna medulla cordis mei,
Vertigine
per secanti e tangenti fugitiva

20   La mole della mia fatica
     già da me sgombri
     la mia sostanza sgombri
     a me cresci a me vieni a te vengo
     . . . .
     . . . .
     (Luna puella pallidula)
     . . . .

            ◻
     [September 13, 1959 (Variation)]

     Luna puella pallidula,
     Luna hermitical flora,
     Luna sole selenite,
     Distonia misled life,
     mataia, mad morula,
     vampirism, paralysis,
     glabrous milk, polarized sugar,
     innocent plague, inclement patron saint,
     protovirgin, privative alpha,
     degravitizing cork,
     apple and potency of the dust,
     phyal and consciousness of the shadow,
     geyser, phase, cariocinesis,
     Luna snow snowest newest,
     Luna glacies-glaciei
     Luna medulla cordis mei,
     Vertigo
     along secants and tangents fleeing

     From me you already remove
     the mass of my struggle
     you remove my substance
     you grow towards me you come to me I come to you
     . . . .
     . . . .
     (Luna puella pallidula)
     . . . .]

18. Agosti, Stefano, Introduction, *Andrea Zanzotto Poesie*, 19.
19. Zanzotto, "Ecloga IV: *Polifemo, Bolla fenomenica, Primavera*," in *IX Ecloghe*, 24.
20. Ibid.
21. Ibid.
22. Ibid., 24–25.
23. Ibid., 25.
24. Ibid.
25. Zanzotto informed me, during our 1978 discussions, that both line 28, which does not appear in quotation marks, and lines 36 and 37, which

do, are verses of popular songs heard on Italian radio and television broadcasts during the time the poem was being written. Line 28 quotes the title of a popular television program, "Domenica è sempre domenica," which referred to soccer; and so another circular reference appears, one apparently more ludic than, say, Poliphemus' eye.

26. Zanzotto, "Ecloga IV: *Polifemo, Bolla fenomenica, Primavera,*" in *IX Ecloghe*, 25.
27. Ibid.
28. Ibid.
29. Ibid., 25–26.
30. Ibid., 26.
31. Zanzotto, "Riflesso," in *IX Ecloghe*, 33–34.
32. Ibid., 34.
33. Ibid.
34. Zanzotto, "Con quel cuore che basta," in *IX Ecloghe*, 35–36.
35. Ibid., 36.
36. Zanzotto, "Ecloga VII: *Sul primato della poesia,*" in *IX Ecloghe*, 63–66.
37. Leopardi, Giacomo, "Il risorgimento," in *Canti* (Turin: Einaudi, 1962), 161–167, vv. 25–26.
38. Zanzotto, "Sylva," in *IX Ecloghe*, 67.
39. Ibid., 68.
40. Zanzotto, "Ecloga VIII: *Pasaggio per l'informità, La voce e la sua ombra, Non temere,*" in *IX Ecloghe*, 69–73.
41. Zanzotto, "Ecloga IX: *Scolastica,*" in *IX Ecloghe*, 75–76.
42. Ibid., 76.
43. Ibid.
44. Ibid., 76–77.
45. Ibid., 77.
46. Ibid.
47. Ibid.
48. Ibid.
49. Ibid., 77–78.
50. Ibid.
51. Ibid.
52. Ibid.
53. Hölderlin, Friedrich, "Bread and Wine" ("Brod und Wein") in *Poems and Fragments*, 247. (Note that the dialect spelling, *brod*, for *brot*, is Hölderlin's; for example, see Hölderlin, *Sämtliche Werke* [Stuttgart: W. Kohlhammer Verlag, J. G. Cottasche Buchhandlung Nachfolger, 1951], 591ff.) The original of these lines is as follows:

> Vater! heiter! und hallt, so weit es gehet, das uralt
> Zeichen, von Eltern geerbt, treffend und schaffend hinab.
> Denn so kehren die Himmlischen ein, tiefschütternd gelangt so
> Aus den Schatten herab unter die Menschen ihr Tag.

54. Zanzotto, "Ecloga IX: *Scolastica*," in *IX Ecloghe*, 78–79.
55. Ibid., 79.
56. Ibid.
57. Ibid., 79–80.
58. Ibid., 80., vv. 127–128.
59. Zanzotto, "Epilogo: *Appunti per un'Ecloga*," in *IX Ecloghe*, 82.
60. Ibid.
61. Ibid.
62. Ibid.
63. Ibid.
64. Ibid., 82–83.
65. Ibid., 83.
66. Ibid.
67. Subsequent to *IX Ecloghe*, Zanzotto's poetry volumes are (as mentioned in the introduction) *La beltà, Gli sguardi i fatti e senhal, A che valse? (versi 1938–1942), Pasque, Filò* (Venice: Edizioni del Ruzante, 1976), *Il galateo in bosco, Mistieroi* (Milan: Mondadori, 1982), *Fosfeni*, and *Idioma*.
68. See "L'elegia in petèl," in Zanzotto, *La beltà*, 67–69.
69. Zanzotto, "*Bleu*," in *IX Ecloghe*, 84.

Bibliography

ZANZOTTO AS POET AND NARRATOR
(in chronological order)

Dietro il paesaggio. Milan: Mondadori, 1951.
Elegia e altri versi. Milan: Edizioni della Meridiana, 1954.
Vocativo. Milan: Mondadori, 1957.
IX Ecloghe. Milan: Mondadori, 1962.
Sull'altopiano (racconti e prose 1942–1954). Vincenza: Neri Pozza Editore, 1964.
Premesse all'abitazione. In *Le Sette piaghe d'Italia.* 139–166. Milan: Nuova Accademia, 1964.
La beltà. Milan: Mondadori, 1968.
Gli sguardi i fatti e senhal. Pieve di Soligo: Tipografia V. Bernardi, 1969.
A che valse? (versi 1938–1942). Milan: Scheiwiller, Strenna per gli amici, 1970.
Pasque. Milan: Mondadori, 1973.
Filò. Venice: Edizioni de Ruzante, 1976.
Il galateo in bosco. Milan: Mondadori, 1978.
poesie 1938–1972. Ed. Stefano Agosti. 2d ed. Milan: Mondadori, 1980.
Filò e altre poesie. Rome: Lato Side, 1981.
Mistieròi. Milan: Mondadori, 1982.
Fosfeni. Milan: Mondadori, 1983.
Idioma. Milan: Mondadori, 1986.

TRANSLATIONS

Selected Poetry of Andrea Zanzotto. Ed. and trans. Ruth Feldman and Brian Swann. Princeton: Princeton University Press, 1975.
"Cinq sonnets." Trans. Gérard Genot. *Po&sie 6.* Paris: Librairie Classique Eugène Belin, 1978.
Circhi e cene / Circuses and Suppers. Trans. Beverly Allen. Verona: Plain Wrapper Press, 1978.
Italian Poetry Today: A Critical Anthology. Ed. Raffaele Perotta. In *Altro Polo: A Volume of Italian Studies.* Sydney: The Frederick May Foundation for Italian Studies, University of Sydney, 1980.

The New Italian Poetry: 1945 to the Present. Trans. Lawrence R. Smith. Berkeley, Los Angeles, London: University of California Press, 1981.

Le Galaté au Bois. Intro. and ed. Philippe di Meo. St. Nazaire: Arcane 17, 1986.

ZANZOTTO AS CRITIC (in chronological order)

"L'inno nel fango" [on Eugenio Montale]. *La fiera letteraria* 12 July 1953.
"Il comprensibile amore di Gasparina." *La fiera letteraria* 24 Oct. 1954.
"Il maestro universitario" [on Diego Valeri]. *La fiera letteraria* 3 March 1957.
"L'ultimo Valeri." *Comunità* no. 50 (June 1957).
"Solmi e la S.F." [on *Levania e altre poesie*]. *Aut aut* no. 40 (July 1957).
"L'ultimo Luzi" [review of *Onore del Vero*]. *Comunità* no. 59 (Apr. 1958).
"Poesie femminile." *Comunità* no. 62 (Aug.-Sept. 1958).
"I settant'anni di Ungaretti." *Comunità* no. 63 (Oct. 1958).
"Un neo-tenter de vivre." *La situazione* no. 14 (Apr. 1960).
"Michaux, il buon combattente." *Il caffè*, anno 8 (June 1960).
"Giuseppe Berto tra *Il cielo è rosso* e *Il brigante*." *La provincia di Treviso* no. 2 (Mar.-Apr. 1962).
"I 'Novissimi'." *Comunità* no. 99 (May 1962).
"Antonio Canova, Ugo Foscolo e il fantasma classico." *La provincia di Treviso* no. 6 (Nov.-Dec. 1962).
"Eluard dopo dieci anni." *Questo e altro* no. 3 (Mar. 1963).
"Ricordo di Paul Eluard." *Terzo Programma* no. 1 (1963):233–249.
"A faccia a faccia" [notes on Carlo Bo's essay, "Eredità di Leopardi"]. *Questo e altro* no. 4 (Oct. 1963).
"Fantasia vecchia e nuova" [on an article by Vittorini in *Il Giorno* 28 Oct. 1964]. *L'Approdo letterario* no. 29 (1964):91–93.
"Noventa tra i moderni." *Comunità* no. 130 (June-July 1965). Rpt. in *I metodi attuali della critica in Italia*. Eds. M. Corti and C. Segre. Turin: ERI, 1970.
Postface to Michel Leiris, *Età d'uomo*. Milan: Mondadori, 1966.
"L'altra faccia della luna" [on Piero Jahier]. *Paragone* no. 194 (1966):93–99.
"Sur Pierre Revedy." *Entretiens sur les lettres et les arts* no. 20 (1966).
"Sviluppo di una situazione montaliana. (Escatologia-scatologia)." *Omaggio a Montale*. Ed. Silvio Ramat. Milan: Mondadori, 1966.
"Alcune prospettive sulla poesia, oggi." *L'Approdo letterario* no. 35 (1966):102–106.
"Michaux: un impegno nelle origini." *Avanti* 27 Nov. 1966.
Interview in re: Sereni. *Paragone* no. 204 (1967):90–112.
"Riflessioni sulla poesia." *Uomini e libri* no. 23 (1969):46–48.
"Dal paesaggio ai dialetti: il Veneto che se ne va." *Corriere della sera* 21 Apr. 1970.
"Ungaretti: la presenza delle varianti, il mito dell'autobiografia." *Paragone* no. 254 (Apr. 1971).

"Il pensiero perverso" [on Ottiero Ottieri]. *Avanti!* 6 June 1971.
"In margine a *Satura*." *Nuovi Argomenti* nos. 23/24 (1971):213–220.
"Giuseppe Ungaretti." *Dizionario critico della letteratura italiana*. Vol. III. Turin: UTET, 1973.
Preface to Guido Piovene, *Le stelle fredde*. Milan: Club degli editori, 1973.
"Infanzie, poesie, scuoletta (appunti)." *Strumenti critici* no. 20 (Feb. 1973).
"Gli scrittori e il Manzoni." *Italianistica* no. 1 (Jan.-Apr. 1973).
"La trincea e la fabbrica" [on B. Brugnaro]. *Il giorno* 21 Nov. 1973.
"I cento metri" [on Giovanni Comisso]. *Il mondo* 31 Jan. 1974.
"Parole-figure di un pittore" [on V. Guidi]. *Il giorno* 1 May 1974.
"Guidi poeta." *Il giorno* 1 May 1974.
"Petrarca e i poeti d'oggi." Interview with Maria Corti, Vittorio Sereni, Andrea Zanzotto, Antonio Porta. *L'Approdo letterario* no. 66 (1974):93–100.
"Voci al fondo della paura" [review of *Vi scrivo da un carcere in Grecia* by Alessandro Panagulis]. *Corriere della sera* 7 July 1974.
"Al poeta non piace la scienza" [on Leonardo Sinisgalli, *L'ellisse*]. *Corriere della sera* 4 Aug. 1974.
"Donne vino e canto" [on Carolus Cergoly, *Inter pocula, Poesie segrete triestine*]. *Corriere della sera* 1 Sept. 1974.
"Parole, comportamenti, gruppi (appunti)." *Studi novecenteschi* 4 nos. 8 /9 (July-Nov. 1974):349–355. Dedicato a Zanzotto.
"Realtà vince il sogno" [on Carlo Betocchi, *Prime e ultimissime*]. *Corriere della sera* 5 Jan. 1975.
"Le lune sognate nei versi di Solmi." *Corriere della sera* 13 Jan. 1975.
"I bambini terribili" [on W. Busch, *Max e Moritz ovvero Pippo e Peppo* and Sergio Tofano, *Qui cominicia la sventura del Signor Bonaventura*]. *Il mondo* 16 Jan. 1975.
"Vita domestica" [Rev. of M. Picci, *Ritratto di famiglia*]. *Corriere della sera* 3 Mar. 1975.
"Un dio che divora gli artisti" [on A. Alvarez]. *Corriere della sera* 9 Mar. 1975.
"I nodi della mente sciolti dalla poesia" [on R. D. Laing]. *Corriere della sera* 10 June 1975.
"Rime per l'io fantasma" [on Antonio Porta]. *Corriere della sera* 10 Aug. 1975.
Preface to Joseph Conrad, *Il compagno segreto*. Milan: Rizzoli, 1976.
"Nella calle del vento" [on Diego Valeri]. *Corriere della sera* 14 Mar. 1976.
"Uno sguardo dalla periferia: intervista con Andrea Zanzotto." *L'Approdo* no. 1206 (May 8, 1976).
"Per una pedagogia." *Omaggio a Pasolini. Nuovi Argomenti* no. 49 (1976):47–51.
"Poesia?" *Il Verri* 1 (1976):110–113.
"Petrarca fra il palazzo e la cameretta." Preface to Francesco Petrarca, *Rime*. Ed. Guido Bezzola. Milan: Rizzoli, 1976.
Text for *Essere Venezia* by Fulvio Roiter. Udine: Magnus, 1976.
"Una stanza piena di libri." In *Francesco Petrarca nel VI centenario della morte*. 79–85. Riccardo Bacchelli et. al. Bologna: Boni, 1976.
"Alcuni sottofondi e implicazioni della S.F." *Il Contesto* (Jan. 1977).

BIBLIOGRAPHY

"Dialetto e tradizione linguistica orale." *Libera stampa* (Lugano) 12 Feb. 1977.

"L'uomo impiegatizio" [on Giovanni Guidici]. *Corriere della sera* 28 Apr. 1977.

"Autoritratto." *L'Approdo* no. 1392 (May 12, 1977).

"Poesia che ascolta le onde" [on Biagio Marin]. *Corriere della sera* 5 June 1977.

"Così parlò il sapiente." *Tuttolibri* 2 July 1977.

"Penna e le spine dell'eros" [on Sandro Penna]. *Corriere della sera* 11 Sept. 1977.

Interview with Antonio Tabucchi on Pessoa. *Quaderni portoghesi* Vol. 1, no. 2 (1977):185–194.

"Pedagogia." *Pasolini: cronaca giudiziaria, persecuzione, morte.* Milano: Garzanti, 1977. Later as "Pedagogy" in *Pier Paolo Pasolini: The Poetics of Heresy,* trans. and ed. Beverly Allen. 30–41. Saratoga: ANMA Libri, 1982.

"Da 'Botta e risposta' a 'Satura'." *Eugenio Montale.* Milano: Rizzoli, 1977.

"Rizoma" [on Gilles Deleuze and Félix Guattari]. *Libera stampa* (Lugano) 4 Mar. 1978.

"La carta s'increspa: sta sorridendo." *L'Espresso* 10 Dec. 1978.

"Perché mi piace il dottor Vampiro." *L'Espresso* 14 Oct. 1979.

"Fiutò un bubbone chiamato Italia" [on Belli, Manzoni, Leopardi]. *Il Messaggero* 17 Nov. 1979.

"Nei paraggi di Lacan." In *L'effetto Lacan.* Rome/Cosenza: Lerici, 1979.

"Lottando col Super-io" [on Luca Canali]. *Il Messaggero* 5 Mar. 1980.

"A proposito di una conversazione con Montale." *Nuova antologia* (Apr.-May 1980).

"Il percorso della poesia." *Rinascita* 20 June 1980.

"Da quella neve lontana il fuoco di Rigoni Stern." *Nuova rivista europea,* no. 18 (July-Sept. 1980).

"Una prodigiosa potenza creativa" [on Leo Tolstoy]. *Gazzetino* 19 Sept. 1980.

"Fiches Leiris." *Il Verri* no. 18 (1980):92–101.

Introduction to Franco Fortini, *Una obbedienza. 18 poesie 1969–1979.* Genoa: San Marco dei Guistiniani, 1980.

"Pasolini poeta." In *Pasolini, Poesie e pagine ritrovate,* ed. Andrea Zanzotto and Nico Naldini. Rome: Lato Side, 1980.

"Pier Paolo Pasolini." *Poesia italiana del Novecento.* Vol. II. Milan: Garzanti, 1980.

"Ipotesi intorno alla 'Città delle donne'." In Federico Fellini, *La città delle donne.* Milan: Garzanti, 1980.

"Alcune premesse ad una rilettura di Buzzati." *Nuova rivista europea* no. 23 (May-July 1981).

"Vade retro, fame antica. Ti esorcizzo col digiuno" [on Fulvio Tomizza]. *Il Piccolo* 26 Nov. 1981.

"Testimonianza." In *Atti del convegno su Giuseppe Ungheretti,* ed. Carlo Bo. 733–743. Urbino: 4 Venti, 1981.

"Ugo Foscolo, oggi." In *Per Ugo Foscolo,* eds. Enzo Mandruzzato and Andrea Zanzotto. Abano Terme: Francisci, 1981.

Preface to R. Pascutto, *L'acqua, la piera, la tera*. Treviso: Matteo, 1981.
"Su 'Teorema'." In *Per rileggere Pasolini. Materiali*. Bellinzona: Salvioni, 1982.
Introduction to *Cento Haikù*. Milan: Longanesi, 1982.
"Pedagogy." In *Pier Paolo Pasolini: The Poetics of Heresy*, trans. Beverly Allen. Saratoga: ANMA Libri, 1982.
"Stramba crociera per inseguire la 'Voce' del nostro mondo guazzabuglio." *Corriere della sera* 26 Feb. 1983.
"Il diario senza fine dell'ultimo Montale." *Corriere della sera* 11 Sept. 1983.
"Pasolini nel nostro tempo." In *P.P. Pasolini. L'opera e il suo tempo*. Padua: CLUEP, 1983.
"Poche rose fra le spine del Gruppo 63." *Tuttolibri* 12 Nov. 1983.
"Le gallinette di Saba e la carsicità della poesia." *Nuova rivista europea*, no. 45 (Feb. 1984).
"Poesia di Turoldo." *Il Gazzettino* 22 July 1984.
"L'avventura della poesia" [on Pier Paolo Pasolini]. *Rinascita* 29 Dec. 1984.
"Pasolini, l'Academiuta di lenga furlana." In Nico Naldini, *Nei campi del Friuli*. Milan: Scheiwiller, 1984.

ZANZOTTO AS TRANSLATOR

H. de Balzac. *Il medico di campagna*. Milan: Garzanti, 1977.
H. de Balzac. *La ricerca dell'assoluto*. Milan: Garzanti, 1975.
Georges Bataille. *La letteratura e il male*. Milan: Rizzoli, 1973.
———. *Nietzsche, il culmine e il possibile*. Milan: Rizzoli, 1970. Original title, *Sur Nietzsche*, 1945.
Paul Eluard. *Poems*. In "Ricordo di Paul Eluard." *Terzo programma* 1 (1963).
Michel Leiris. *Età d'uomo*. Milan: Mondadori, 1966; 1980 edition with postface by Andrea Zanzotto.

ARTICLES

Agosti, Stefano. "Zanzotto o la conquista del dire." *Sigma* no. 21 (March 1969).
———. *Introduzione alla poesia di Zanzotto*. In Andrea Zanzotto, *Poesie 1938–1972*. Milan: Mondadori, 1973.
———. "Discorso, parola analitica, linguaggio poetico." In *Psicoanalisi e istituzioni*, ed. Franco Fornari. Florence: Felice Le Monnier, 1976.
———. "Diglossia e poesia: l'esperimento di *Filò* di A. Zanzotto." *Il piccolo Hans* no. 15 (July-Sept. 1977):57–76.
Allen, Beverly. Ed. Special poetry issue *Stanford Italian Review* Vol. 4, no. 2 (Fall 1984).

———. "Zanzotto's *grammaticalismo*: Positions and Performance." *Stanford Italian Review* Vol. 4, no. 2 (Fall 1984):209–244.

———. "Interview with Andrea Zanzotto (Pieve di Soligo: July 25, 1978)." *Stanford Italian Review* Vol. 4, no. 2 (Fall 1984):253–265.

———. "Witnessing Winterlight: Difficulty in Zanzotto's '*Vocabilità, fotoni*'." Unpublished.

———. "Occasioni di metafora: Il soggetto della decapitazione: Carducci, Pascoli e Zanzotto sulla linea." *Hellas* nos. 8/9 (Dec. 1985):89–99.

———. "Nietzsche's Italian Decline: The Poets." *Stanford Italian Review* Vol. 6, nos. 1–2 (1987).

Balduino, Armando. "Scheda bibliografica per Zanzotto critico." *Studi novecenteschi* 4 nos. 8/9 (July-Nov. 1974):341–347.

———. "Zanzotto e l'ottica della contraddizione (impressioni e divagazioni su *Pasque*)." *Studi novecenteschi* 4 nos. 8/9 (July-Nov. 1974):281–313.

Bandini, Fernando. "A Zanzotto." *Dizionario critico della letteratura italiana*. Vol. III. Turin: UTET, 1973.

———. "Scheda per *Sull'altopiano*." *Studi novecenteschi* 4 nos. 8/9 (July-Nov. 1974):175–183.

Bataille, Georges. "Le sacré." *Cahiers d'art*. nos. 1–4 (1939):47–50. Now in *Oeuvres complètes*, I:559–563. Paris: Gallimard, 1970.

Benjamin, Walter. "The Task of the Translator: An Introduction to the Translation of Baudelaire's *Tableaux parisiens*." In *Illuminations*. New York: Harcourt, Brace and World, 1955, 71 ss.

Cambon, Glauco. Foreword to *Selected Poetry of Andrea Zanzotto*, trans. and eds. Ruth Feldman and Brian Swann. Princeton: Princeton University Press, 1975.

Cendrars, Blaise. "Les Pâques à New York." *Poésies complètes*. I:10–33. Paris: Editions Denöel, 1947.

Conti Bertini, Lucia. "Andrea Zanzotto." In *Dieci poeti italiani contemporanei*. 197–225. Florence: CLUSF, 1981.

Cristini, G. "Pasque di Andrea Zanzotto." *Il Ragguaglio librario*, no. 6 (June 1974):213.

Cucchi, Maurizio. "La beltà presa a coltellate?" *Studi novecenteschi* 4 nos. 8/9 (July-Nov. 1974):251–271.

Felman, Shoshana. "Turning the Screw of Interpretation." In "Literature and Psychoanalysis: The Question of Reading: Otherwise." *Yale French Studies* nos. 55/56 (1977):94–207.

Freud, Sigmund. "The 'Uncanny'." Trans. Alix Strachey. In *On Creativity and the Unconscious: Papers On the Psychology of Art, Literature, Love, Religion*. 122–161. New York: Harper Colophon Books, 1958. First published in *Imago* 5 (1919).

Giacomini, Amedeo. "Da *Dietro il paesaggio* alle *IX Ecloghe*: l'io grammaticale nella poesia di Andrea Zanzotto." *Studi novecenteschi* 4 nos. 8/9 (July-Nov. 1974):185–205.

Grosser, Hermann. "Contributo all'analisi di due raccolte zanzottiane." *Acme* no. 32 (1979):225–267.

Guglielminetti, Marziano. "La ricostruzione della sintassi poetica." *Studi novecenteschi* 4 nos. 8/9 (July-Nov. 1974):167–173.
Harrison, Robert Pogue. "The Italian Silence." *Critical Inquiry* 13 no. 1 (Autumn 1986):81–99.
Jakobson, Roman and Morris Halle. "The Metaphoric and Metonymic Poles." In *Fundamentals of Language*. The Hague: Mouton, 1956:76–82.
Kerbrat-Orecchioni, C. "Note sur les concepts d' 'illocutoire' et de 'performatif'." In *Linguistique et sémiologie: l'illocutoire*. Lyon: Imprimerie de l'Université Lyon II:1977. 74ff.
Marchi, Marco. "E co ò vist la gran testa." *Paragone* no. 340 (1978):97–109.
Martinet, André. "Plurilinguisme et interférence." *La linguistique, guide alphabétique*. Milan: Rizzoli, 1972.
Milone, Luigi. "Per una storia del linguaggio poetico di Andrea Zanzotto." *Studi novecenteschi* 4 nos. 8/9 (July-Nov. 1974):207–235.
Montale, Eugenio. "La poesia di Zanzotto." *Corriere della sera* 1 June 1968.
Nuvoli, Giuliana. "Una dialettica della disperazione in prestito." *Studi novecenteschi* 4 nos. 8/9 (July-Nov. 1974):237–250.
Papa, Marco. "Il dialetto e la ginestra: leopardismo dell'ultimo Zanzotto: appunti." *Rassegna della letteratura italiana* no. 82 (1978):496–504.
Quinsat, Gilles. "Aux limites (sur A. Zanzotto)." In *Ecrit en marge*. 221–236. Seyssel: Ed. du Champ Villon, 1987.
Risset, Jacqueline. "Sovraesistenze." *Studi novecenteschi* 4 nos. 8/9 (July-Nov. 1974):329–332.
Rizzo, Gino. "Zanzotto, 'fabbro del parlar materno'." In *Selected Poetry of Andrea Zanzotto*, trans. and eds. Ruth Feldman and Brian Swann. Princeton: Princeton University Press, 1975.
Siti, Walter. "Per Zanzotto: Possibili prefazi." *Nuovi Argomenti* no. 32 (Mar.-Apr. 1973):127–142.
———. "Le Pasque di Zanzotto." *Rinascita* no. 15 (12 Apr. 1974).
Tellini, Gino. "La 'subnarcosi' di Zanzotto." *Studi novecenteschi* 4 nos. 8/9 (July-Nov. 1974):315–328.
Troisio, Luciano. "La Luna e i senhals." *Studi novecenteschi* 4 nos. 8/9 (July-Nov. 1974):273–280.
Ungaretti, Guiseppe. "Piccolo discorso sopra *Dietro il paesaggio* di Andrea Zanzotto." In *Vita d'un uomo: saggi e interventi*, eds. Mario Diacono and Luciano Rebay. 693–699. Milan: Mondadori, 1974.
Valesio, Paolo. "The Beautiful Lie: Heroic Individuality and Fascism." In *Reconstructing Individualism: Autonomy, Individuality, and the Self in Western Thought*. Ed. T. Heller, M. Sosna, and D. Wellberg. Stanford: Stanford University Press, 1986.
Van Bever, P. "La beltà di Zanzotto." In *Storia linguistica dell'Italia del Novecento*. Rome: Bulzoni, 1973.
Varese, Claudio. "Solo gli isolati comunicano." *Studi novecenteschi* 4 nos. 8/9 (July-Nov. 1974):333–340.
Zagarrio, G. "Poesia fra editoria e anti." In *Il Ponte* anno 26, no. 3 (Mar. 1970): 378–393, 733–746.

BOOKS

Agostino, Stefano. *Il testo poetico: teoria e pratiche d'analisi*. Milan: Rizzoli, 1972.
Austin, John Langshaw. *How To Do Things With Words*. Cambridge: Harvard University Press, 1962.
Balduino, Armando. *Messaggi e problemi della letteratura contemporanea*. Venice: Marsilio, 1978.
Bàrberi Squarotti, Giorgio. *Poesia e narrativa del novecento*. 4th ed. Milan: Mursia, 1961.
———. *La cultura e la poesia italiana del dopoguerra*. Rocca San Casciano: Cappelli, 1966.
———. *Simboli e strutture della poesia del Pascoli*. Messina-Florence: G. D'Anna, 1966.
———. *Poesia e narrativa del secondo novecento*. 4th ed. Milan: Mursia, 1978.
Barthes, Roland. *Le degré zéro de l'écriture*. Paris: Seuil, 1953.
———. *Elements of Semiology*. Trans. Annette Lavers and Colin Smith. 1964. Repr. New York: Hill and Wang, 1968.
———. *Le plaisir du texte*. Paris: Seuil, 1973.
Benveniste, Émile. *Problèmes de linguistique générale*. Vol. I. Paris: Gallimard, 1966. Vol. II. 1974.
Bianchi, Lorenzo. *Versioni da Friedrich Hölderlin*. Bologna: Zanichelli, 1925.
Bigongiari, Piero. *La poesia come funzione simbolica del linguaggio*. Milan: Rizzoli, 1972.
Blanchot, Maurice. *La part du feu*. Paris: Gallimard, 1949.
Boarini-Bonfiglioli, Vittorio. *Avanguardia e restaurazione*. Bologna: Zanichelli, 1976.
Camon, Ferdinando. *Il mestiere di poeta*. Milan: Lerici, 1965.
Cicognani-Giordano. *Testi del '900 italiano*. Bologna: Zanichelli, 1972.
Conti Bertini, Lucia. *Andrea Zanzotto o la sacra menzogna*. Venice: Marsilio Editori, 1984.
Contini, Gianfranco. *La letteratura italiana: otto-novecento*. Vol. IV. Milan: Sansoni-Accademia, 1974.
———. *Schedario di scrittori italiani*. Florence: Sansoni, 1978.
David, Michel. *La psicoanalisi nella cultura italiana*. Milan: Mursia, 1967.
Derrida, Jacques. *La Dissemination*. Paris: Seuil, 1972.
———. *Of Grammatology*. Trans. Gayagri Chakravorty Spivak. Baltimore: Johns Hopkins University Press, 1976.
———. *Epérons: les styles de Nietzsche*. Preface by Stefano Agosti, "Coup sur coup." Paris: Flammarion, 1978.
De Sanctis, Francesco. *Storia della letteratura italiana*. Ed. Maria Teresa Lanza, with Introduction by Luigi Russo. Milan: Feltrinelli, 1967.
Ducrot, Oswald and Tzvetan Todorov. *Encyclopedic Dictionary of the Sciences of Language*, trans. Catherine Porter. Baltimore: Johns Hopkins University Press, 1979.

Elwert, W. Theodor. *Versificazione italiana dalle origini ai giorni nostri*. Florence: Felice Le Monnier, 1973.

Errante, Vincenzo. *La lirica di Helderlin. Vol. I: Saggio biografico critico: riduzione in versi italiani* and *Vol. II: Commento*. Florence: Sansoni, 1943.

Fages, Jean Baptiste. *Che cosa ha veramente detto Lacan?* Rome: Astrolabio-Ubaldini Editore, 1972.

Falchetta, Piero. *Oculus Pudens*. Abano Terme: Francisci Editore, 1983.

Felman, Shoshana. Ed. Special Issue *Yale French Studies* nos. 55/56 (1977).

Finzi, Gilberto. *Poesia in Italia*. Milan: Mursia, 1979.

Forti, Marco. *Le proposte della poesia e nuove proposte*. Milan: Mursia, 1963.

Fortini, Franco. *I poeti italiani del '900*. Bari: Laterza, 1977.

Frattini, Alberto. *La giovane poesia italiana*. Pisa: Nisi-Lischi, 1964.

Freud, Sigmund. *Beyond the Pleasure Principle*. Trans. James Strachey. New York: Norton, 1961.

———. "Das Unheimliche." In *Imago*, 5 (1919): Now as "The Uncanny." In Freud, *On Creativity and the Unconscious*, ed. Benjamin Nelson. New York: Harper and Row, 1958.

———. *The Ego and the Id*. Trans. Joan Riviere. New York: Norton, 1962.

———. *Jokes and Their Relation to the Unconscious*. Trans. James Strachey. New York: Norton, 1963.

———. *The Interpretation of Dreams*. Trans. James Strachey. New York: Avon Books, 1965.

———. *Psychopathology of Everyday Life*. Trans. A. A. Brill. 2d. ed. E. Benn, 1960.

Garelli, Jacques. *La gravitation poétique*. Paris: Mercure de France, 1966.

———. *Le réel et la dispersion: Essai sur le champ de lecture poétique*. Paris: Gallimard, 1978.

Guglielmi, Guido and Elio Pagliarano. *Manuale di poesia sperimentale*. Milan: Mondadori, 1966.

Guglielmino, Salvatore. *Guida al '900*. Milan: Principato, 1978.

Harrison, Thomas. Ed. *The Favorite Malice: Ontology and Reference in Contemporary Italian Poetry*. New York: Out of London Press, 1983.

Heidegger, Martin. *Poetry, Language, Thought*. Trans. Albert Hofstadter. New York: Harper & Row, 1971.

Heller, Thomas et. al. Eds. *Reconstructing Individualism: Autonomy, Individuality, and the Self in Western Thought*. Stanford: Stanford University Press, 1986.

Hölderlin, Friederich. *Oeuvres*. Paris: Pleiade, 1967.

———. *Poemes de la Folie*. Trans. Pierre Jean Jouve. Paris: Gallimard, 1930.

———. *Poems and Fragments*. Trans. Michael Hamburger. London: Routledge and Kegan Paul, 1966.

———. *Sämtliche gedichte; Studienausgabe, hrsg, und kommentiert von Detlev Luders*. Bad Homburg: Athenaum Verlag, 1970.

———. *Sämtliche Werke: Frankfurter Ausgabe*. Frankfurt: Verlag Roter Stern, 1975.

BIBLIOGRAPHY

———. *Sämtliche Werke*. Stuttgart: W. Kohlhammer Verlag, J G. Cottasche Buchhandlung Nachfolger, 1951.

Hytier, Jean. *The Poetics of Paul Valéry*. Trans. Richard Howard. New York: Anchor Books, Doubleday, 1966.

Jakobson, Roman. *Questions de poétique*. Paris: Seuil, 1973.

Lacan, Jacques. *Écrits I*. Paris: Seuil, 1966.

———. *Écrits II*. Paris: Seuil, 1971.

———. *Encore (Le Seminaire de Jacques Lacan, Livre XX, Encore, 1972–1973)*. Text established by Jacques-Alain Miller, trans. Alan Sheridan. New York: Norton, 1978.

———. *Écrits: A Selection*. Trans. Alan Sheridan. New York: Norton, 1977.

———. *Le Séminaire de Jacques Lacan. Livre XX. Encore. 1972–1973*. Text established by Jacques-Alain Miller. Paris: Seuil, 1975.

———. *The Four Fundamental Concepts of Psychoanalysis*. Ed. Jacques-Alain Miller, trans. Alan Sheridan. New York: Norton, 1978.

Laplanche, Jean and J. B. Pontalis. *The Language of Psychoanalysis*. Trans. Donald Nicholson-Smith. New York: Norton, 1973.

Leclaire, Serge. *On tue un enfant: un essai sur le narcissisme primaire et la pulsion de mort*. Paris: Seuil, 1975.

Leopardi, Giacomo. *Canti*. Ed. Niccolo Galli and Cesare Garboli. Turin: Einaudi, 1967.

———. *Operette morali*. In *Prose di Giacomo Leopardi*, ed. Giovanni Ferretti. 27–283. Turin: Unione Tipografico-Editrice Torinese, 1971.

———. *Zibaldone di pensieri*. Ed. Francesco Flora. Milan: Mondadori, 1973.

Lotman, Yury. *Analysis of the Poetic Text*. Ed. and trans. D. Barton Johnson. Ann Arbor: Ardis, 1976. Original title: *Analiz poeticheskogo teksta*.

———. *La struttura del testo poetico*. Ed. Eridano Bazzarelli. Trans. Eridano Bazzarelli, Erika Klein, Gabriella Schiaffino. Milan: Mursia, 1972. Original title: *Struktura knudozestivenogo teksta*. Moscow: Iskussttvo, 1970.

Machiedo, Mladen. *Letteratura italiana del dopoguerra*. Zagreb: Ed. filosowski fakultet, 1973.

Manacorda, Giuliano. *Storia della letteratura italiana contemporanea*. Rome: Editori Riuniti, 1967.

Marchetti-Portinari. *L'antologia-Il '900*. Turin: Marietti, 1976.

Marcona, Carlo. *Storia dei Papi*. Vol. I. Milan: Edizioni Librerie Italiane, 1961.

Majorino, Giorgio. *Poesia e realtà*. Rome: Savelli, 1977.

Mengaldo, Pier Vincenzo. *Poeti italiani del '900*. Milan: Mondadori, 1978.

Montale, Eugenio. *L'opera in versi*. Ed. Rosanna Bettarini and Gianfranco Contini. Turin: Einaudi, 1980.

Nuvoli, Giuliana. *Andrea Zanzotto*. Florence: La Nuova Italia, 1979.

Orelli, Giorgio. *Accertamenti verbali*. Milan: Bompiani, 1978.

Orlando, Francesco. *Lettura freudiana della "Phèdre."* Turin: Einaudi, 1971.

———. *Per una teoria freudiana della letteratura*. Turin: Einaudi, 1973.

Pagnini, Marcello. *Struttura letteraria e metodo critico*. Messina-Florence: G. D'Anna, 1967.

Pasolini, Pier Paolo. *Passione e ideologia.* Milan: Garzanti, 1960.
Pedulla, Walter. *La letteratura del benessere.* Naples: Libreria Scientifica Editrice, 1968.
———. *L'estrema funzione.* Venice: Marsilio, 1975.
Pento, Bortolo. *Letture di poesia contemporanea.* Milan: Marzorati, 1964.
Perella, Nicholas J. *Midday in Italian Literature: Variations on an Archetypal Theme.* Princeton: Princeton University Press, 1979.
Perrotta, Raffaele. Ed. *Italian Poetry Today: A Critical Anthology.* Also called *Altro Polo: A Volume of Italian Studies.* Sidney: Frederick May Foundation for Italian Studies, Univ. of Sydney, 1980.
Raboni, Giovanni. *Poesia degli anni Sessanta.* Rome: Editori Riuniti, 1978.
Ramat, Silvio. *Storia della poesia italiana del Novecento.* Milan: Mursia, 1976.
Searle, John. *Speech Acts: An Essay In The Philosophy of Language.* London: Cambridge University Press, 1969.
Sebeok, Thomas A. Ed. *Style in Language.* Cambridge: MIT Press, 1960.
Seminario d'Italiano (Freiburg, Switzerland). *Analisi testuale per l'insegnamento.* Padua: Liviana, 1975.
Siti, Walter. *Il realismo dell'avanguardia.* Turin: Einaudi, 1975.
Smith, Lawrence R. *The New Italian Poetry: 1945 to the Present.* Berkeley, Los Angeles, London: Univ. of California Press, 1981.
Spagnoletti, Giacinto. *Poesia italiana contemporanea, 1909–1959.* Bologna: Guanda, 1961.
———. *Profilo della letteratura italiana del '900.* Rome: Gremese, 1978.
Spitzer, Leo. *Linguistics and Literary History: Essays in Stylistics.* Princeton: Princeton University Press, 1948.
Spongano, Raffaele. *Nozioni ed esempi di metrica italiana.* Bologna: Casa Editrice Prof. Riccardo Patron, 1966.
U.E.R. des Sciences du Langage (Ed.). *Linguistique et Sémiotique: Travaux du Centre de Recherches Linguistiques et Sémiologiques de Lyon: L'Illocutoire.* Lyon: Imprimérie de L'Université Lyon II, April 1977.
Ungaretti, Giuseppe. *Vita d'un uomo: Tutte le poesie.* Milan: Mondadori, 1970.
———. *Vita d'un uomo: saggi e interventi.* Eds. Mario Diacono and Luciano Rebay. Milan: Mondadori, 1974.
Valesio, Paolo. *Strutture dell'allitterazione.* Bologna: n.p., 1967.
———. *Novantiqua: Rhetorics as a Contemporary Theory.* Bloomington: Indiana University Press, 1980.
Virgil. *The Aeneid, Eclogues and Georgics.* Trans. J. W. Mackail. New York: Random House Modern Library, 1950.
———. *Eclogues, Georgics, Aeneid 1–6.* Trans. H. R. Fairclough. Loeb Classical Library. Cambridge: Harvard University Press, 1974.
Welle, John P. *The Poetry of Andrea Zanzotto: A Critical Study of Il galateo in bosco.* Rome: Bulzoni Editore, 1987.

Index

Absence, 187
Adversative, 202–203, 228, 253
Aesthetic theory, 98–99
Agosti, Stefano, 100, 118, 275
Alienation, 186, 268 n. 33
Alterity, 44, 79, 86, 92, 101, 148
Anaphora, 48, 83, 84, 91, 97, 113, 174, 241
Anti-historicism, 34, 39, 116
Apollo, 86, 168, 242
Apposition, 48, 171
Aulic verses, 76
Austin, John L., 154, 183
Austria, 84
Authenticity, 127, 131, 167
Autumn, 186, 208

Baroque style, 31
Beginnings, 39, 44, 72, 263
Being, 212, 222, 232, 243, 254
La Belta (Zanzotto), 2–4
Bensmaia, J., 273 n. 52
Benveniste, E., 45, 143, 144, 154
Bergson, H., 33
Bianchi, L., 79
Biblical quotations, 153, 159
Birds, 46, 63, 66, 162, 205
Blindness, 233, 256
Body image, 94
Botticelli, S., 38

Cartoons, 258
Causality, 53, 129, 230
Cendrars, B., 41
Childhood, 246, 247
  landscapes of, 53, 59, 65
  memory of, 69, 72–73
  mirror stage of, 94–95
  mother and, 126, 189
Christ, 44, 250. *See also* Easter
Circularity, 193, 255
Constantine, 90
Copernicus, 213
Cubism, 266 n. 2

D'Annunzio, G., 66, 218
Dante, 26, 43, 76, 77, 85, 228, 229, 232
Daphne, 30, 231
Darwin, C., 35
David, M., 118, 271 n. 2
Dawn, 250
Death, 169, 203, 238
  Easter and, 39, 41–44, 105, 108
  landscape and, 54, 72, 239, 241
  memory and, 108, 129, 163
  otherness and, 115
  seasons and, 38–39, 106, 114
  subjectivity and, 191
  See also Temporality
Deity. *See* Gods
Descent, theme of, 72, 86
Desire, 73, 204
Diachrony, 102
Dialect, 17, 32, 63, 77, 126, 128
Dialogue, rhythms of, 193
Diana, 4, 5, 191, 255
Dietro il paesaggio (Zanzotto), 22–68, 245
  ascent and descent in, 46–50
  Easter in, 41–45
  landscapes of, 30–35, 53–57, 69
  regression in, 51, 75
  sun in, 57–61
  war and, 189
  See also *specific images, themes*
Dreams, 250
Ducrot, O., 154

Easter, 7–10, 39, 41–47, 93, 105, 108
IX Ecloghe (Zanzotto), 193–264
Elegia e altri versi (Zanzotto), 100, 104–106, 114–115
Elegy, 115, 116
Eliot, T. S., 31
Epiphany, 120, 122
Eroticism, 55, 57, 59, 63, 66, 74
Errante, V., 79
Ethos, 17
Eye(s), 203, 222
Eyeglasses, 63

293

INDEX

Faith, 166, 171, 172, 175, 183, 184, 252
Falsehood, 253
Father, 127, 251, 252
Feldman, R., 266 n. 6
Fellini, F., 72
Forests, 10–11
Formlessness, 252
Fosfeni (Zanzotto), 13–16
Freud, S., 33, 94, 95

Giacomini, A., 31, 100
Gli sguardi i fatti e senhal (Zanzotto), 4–6
Gods, 81–83, 85, 90, 122, 153
Grammar, history and, 99
Grammaticalismo, 118, 120, 141, 149, 154, 158, 160
Guglielminetti, M., 48

Hand, 200, 201
Happiness, 155, 157, 185
Heidegger, M., 194, 208
Hermetic poets, 6, 31, 71, 266 n. 9, 267 n. 21
History, 34, 39, 44, 99, 116
Hölderlin, F., 27, 48, 79, 81–83, 86, 90, 153, 251, 263
Homer, 209, 214, 223, 232
Homonymy, 96
Horace, 206
Horizons, 210
Hypotaxis, 48

Idioma (Zanzotto), 17–19
Il galateo in bosco (Zanzotto), 14
Illocution, 154, 155, 159
Imitation, 255
Insects, 93
Intertextuality, 28, 31, 32
Io, 51, 57, 69, 83, 193–263
  amore and, 122
  dreams and, 53
  eye and, 194
  illocution and, 192
  landscape and, 85, 93, 137
  poetry and, 220
  quotation and, 255
  rebirth of, 175
  sky and, 176
  unspecified, 95
  See also Subjectivity

Jakobson, R., 155
Janus, 88
Jargon, 195

La Beltà (Zanzotto), 2–4
Lacan, J., 2, 3, 7, 8, 10, 12, 34, 58, 92, 95, 271 n. 2
Lakes, 203
Landscapes, 26, 30, 54, 63, 71, 122, 152, 186
  disintegration of, 125, 179, 208
  eroticism and, 5, 55–59, 63, 66, 74
  forests, 10–11
  io and, 85, 93, 137
  metaphors and, 34, 200
  mountainous, 35, 47–50, 63, 79–81
  personified, 267 n. 20
  seasons and, 37, 138
  sky and, 160–161
  technology and, 208
Latin, 152, 153, 159, 195, 206
Lazarus, 203
Leopardi, G., 2, 26, 98, 229, 230, 245
Light, 58, 60, 63, 84, 91, 167, 239, 260. *See also* Sun
Linguistic theory. *See* specific concepts, theorists
Locution, 154
Loro, 79, 82, 83, 97
Love, 122, 184, 185, 229
Ludic imagery, 213, 216, 247
Lying, 253

Magianism, 269 n. 19
Mallarmé, S., 205
Materialism, 1
Maternity, 74, 126, 129, 130, 191, 192
Mathematical symbols, 261
Memory, 69, 73, 106, 111, 115
Metaphysics, 185
Metonymy, 26, 43, 47, 57, 168, 185
Milone, L., 75, 100, 116, 119
Mimetization, 171
Minimalization, 162, 165
Mirror images, 57, 59, 91
Mirror stage, 94–95
Montale, E., 6, 31, 32, 33, 266 n. 9
Moon, 48, 225, 255
Mortality. *See* Death
Mother. *See* Maternity
Mountains, 35, 47, 63, 81
Muteness, 128

Narration. *See Io*
Nestorian heresy, 33
Nino, 2, 17
Nominalism, 153
Nosferatu, 144

Objectivity, 99. *See also* Subjectivity
Obsession, 187

Odysseus, 211, 214, 218, 232
Orgasm, 139, 166
Oscar anthology, 118
Otherness, 44, 79, 86, 92, 95, 101, 115, 148

Paradox, 242
Parole, 2
Pasolini, Pier Paolo, 1
Pasque (Zanzotto), 7–10. *See also* Easter
Pastoral world, 197, 209
Pathos, 17
Pedagogy, 7, 243, 245, 249, 254
Perception, 228
Performatives, 154
Perlocution, 154
Perspective, 51
Petrarch, 26, 27, 34, 45, 52, 76, 77, 85, 111, 114, 115, 129, 228, 229, 231, 253, 270 n. 7
Phenomenology, 1
Photons, 13
Pieve di Soligo, 17, 22
Plato, 29
Polyphemus, 209, 214, 218, 232
Polysyndeton, 48
Popular songs, 195, 198, 278
Possibility, 262
Presence, 153
Psychoanalysis, 3, 33, 58, 95
Pygmalion, 63, 72

Reading, 26, 96, 155, 158
Referentiality, 48
Regression, 76
Renaissance poets, 195
Repetition, 148
Return, image of, 97
Rhythm, 24
Rilke, R. M., 177
River, 244, 245, 247, 252
Rocket, 194, 204, 206, 210, 223, 255

Satellite, 194, 210, 223, 255
Saussure, F., 33, 118
Science, 27, 195, 208, 213, 228
Searle, J., 154, 157
Seasons, 37, 38, 105, 111, 115
Self. See Io; Subjectivity
Self-reference, 159, 164
Semiotics, 10, 131. *See also* Signs
Sentimento del tempo (Ungaretti), 31
Serpents, 73
Shadows, 84, 86, 91
Signs
 arbitrariness of, 242, 259
 materiality of, 210

network of, 258
 signification, 33–34, 42, 48, 131
 subjectivity and, 17, 125, 144, 184, 198
 syllables and, 200
 value of, 260
Silence, 46, 105, 219, 276
Similarity, 113
Sky, 160–161, 171–175, 208, 218, 238
Sleep, 244
Slips, style of, 47
Snow, 3
Space, 99, 192
Speech, theory of, 92, 158
Spherical metaphors, 212, 214, 215, 222
Sphinx, 129
Spring, 175, 209, 215
Stars, 222
Stasis, 73
Strangeness, 95
Subjectivity, 14, 94, 106, 113, 118, 120, 238
 authenticity and, 184
 communication and, 2
 deictic, 153
 identity of, 126, 193
 illocution and, 155
 linguistic determination of, 17, 125–127, 139, 144, 184, 198, 258
 of love, 175
 materiality of, 188
 maternal origins, 131
 minimalized, 171
 movement of, 86
 objectivity and, 99, 104
 otherness and, 101
 silence and, 105, 133, 219, 276
 vocative and, 126
Summer, 192
Sun, 57, 59, 60, 61, 66, 86, 155, 166, 169, 173, 213, 238
Suspension of disbelief, 155
Swan, 205
Swann, Brian, 266 n. 6
Syllables, 200
Sylvester, St., 58, 89, 90, 120
Sylvia (Zanzotto), 230, 231
Symbols. *See* Signs; *specific images*
Synchrony, 102
Synethesia, 232

Technology, 27, 195, 202, 208, 218, 223, 228
Temporality, 38, 42, 126, 129, 141, 152, 242
Time. *See* Temporality
Todorov, T., 154
Trades, poems of, 17

295

INDEX

Translation, 28, 266 n. 6
Trees, 11
Trope, 157, 161, 255–257, 263
Tropics, 39

Uncanny, 94
Unconscious, 21, 262
Ungaretti, G., 6, 29, 31, 32, 33, 129, 266 n. 9
Universalization, 242
Urania, 221

Valesio, P., 1
Vampires, 144, 148, 149, 173, 250
Verticality, 165
Virgil, 195, 198, 232, 243, 256, 275
Vocativo (Zanzotto), 118–191
  "Colle di Giano," 167–171
  grammaticalism in, 118, 120, 141, 149, 154, 160
  illocution in, 155–159, 160–161
  landscape in, 137–139, 152, 160–161, 175, 179
  light in, 167–169, 173
  maternity in, 189–192
  second ending, 192–193

subjectivity in, 120–126, 130–139, 144–148
vampire motif, 148–149, 173

War, 89
Water, 59, 61, 64, 74, 105, 212
What was the point? (Zanzotto), 6–7
Winter, 105, 114
The Woodland Book of Manners (Zanzotto), 10–13

Yin-yang, 5
Youth, 124

Zanzotto, Andrea
  critical works of, 282–283
  in early fifties, 31
  identity of, 158
  mentors of, 195
  phonetic structures, 33, 65
  poetics of, 33–34, 159
  rhetorics of, 48–49
  titles of, 98–99
  translation of, 266 n. 6
  works in progress, 101–103
  See also *specific critics, themes, works*

Designer: Linda M. Robertson
Compositor: Prestige Typography
Text: 10/12 Palatino
Display: Futura Book
Printer: Braun-Brumfield, Inc.
Binder: Braun-Brumfield, Inc.